Christianity Made in Japan

Christianity Made in Japan

A Study of Indigenous Movements

MARK R. MULLINS

University of Hawai'i Press
HONOLULU

03   02   01   00   5   4   3   2

Library of Congress Cataloging-in-Publication Data
Mullins, Mark.
    Christianity made in Japan : a study of indigenous movements /
Mark. R. Mullins.
        p.   cm. — (Nanzan library of Asian religion and culture)
    Includes bibliographical references and index.
    ISBN 0–8248–2114–9 (alk. paper).
    ISBN 0–8248–2132–7 (pbk. : alk. paper)
    1.   Christian sects—Japan.   2.   Japan—Church history.
3.   Christianity and culture—Japan.   I.   Title.   II.   Series.
BR1307.M85   1998
275.2—dc21   98–35083
                                                        CIP

Camera-ready copy for this book was prepared by the Nanzan Institute
for Religion and Culture.

Contents

Preface

THERE IS IN JAPAN another Christianity than the familiar array of churches left behind by missionaries from the West, one virtually unknown abroad and as yet largely neglected by scholars of religion. It is the Christianity of indigenous movements established in a direct act of resistance to the failure of imported varieties of Christianity to reach deeply into the Japanese soul. This is a book about those movements: where they came from and how they developed.

Contrary to what one might at first expect, resources concerning Japan's indigenous Christian movements are plentiful, but since most of these groups publish their own materials and distribute them privately for use by the faithful, the literature rarely attracts the attention of those outside their own circles. From the time I began my visits to different movements, I was amazed—not to say in some cases dismayed by the work that lay in store—to discover that the collected works of individual founders alone typically ran to ten or twenty volumes, in addition to which most of the movements publish their own magazines and journals. As obscure and arcane as much of the material is, in sheer volume it is an embarrassment of riches.

Extensive contact with members of these movements, their leaders, and in some cases even their founders, has provided a healthy counterbalance to the written resources. My observation and interviews were by and large concentrated in the Kantō and Kansai areas of Japan's main island, where movement headquarters or larger churches tend to be located, but my fieldwork also took me on occasion to the islands of Shikoku, Kyūshū, and Okinawa, and to as far north as Sendai. Over the years I have participated in a wide range of religious services, from subdued memorial services for the dead to emotional revival meetings and charismatic healing services. I have sat with believers to study the Confucian classics following Sunday worship services, received training in meditation in summer seminars, and even celebrated a Friday evening sabbath meal with Japanese Christian Zionists singing in Hebrew in an isolated monastic retreat in the mountains outside of Kyoto. One particular group even made it their special mission to teach me how to speak in tongues. (To their collective disappointment, I turned out to be a slow learner.)

Needless to say, a project of this kind relies from start to finish on the cooperation of many people, and I count myself fortunate to have received so much kindness from so many. Religious leaders regularly opened their archives to my curious eyes and arranged for me to attend services and conduct interviews around the country. I cannot begin to record the names of all the individuals who welcomed me into their homes and churches, and who responded so patiently to my academic prying. The warm hospitality they showed through so many hours of conversation was a constant encouragement. At the same time, I suppose that not a few of those who thus shared in this study must be wondering about now what has happened to all the notes I was scribbling and all the experiences I had in their midst. I would like to say that this book is the answer, but the fact is, I have had to leave out far more than I have been able to put in in order to attempt a coherent interpretation of a dozen different movements. Each of them deserves an in-depth treatment of its own, and I trust that this labor lies in the near future of some other scholars. Meantime, I must content myself with scratching the surface of this unexplored world so as to focus on a broader perspective for placing these experiments in indigenous Christianity within the religious history of Japan.

The project has not been without its share of personal challenges. Like anyone who is a committed member of a church that has transplanted itself in Japan, the scholar's objectivity often proves thin armor against the sharp and often telling criticisms of Western Christianity put forward by leaders of indigenous movements. If my remarks ring defensive at times, I can only beg the reader to pass them over indulgently. My greater intention is to allow these Japanese Christians to speak their own minds in these pages.

In redirecting scholarly attention away from the study of Western missionary Christianity and its problems with self-inculturation to the indigenous and independent expressions of Christianity, I mean to do more than describe these minority movements as a socioreligious phenomenon peculiar to modern Japan. If it is not too wishful to think so, I would like this study to be seen as a small contribution to the shift from perceiving Christianity as a "Western" religion to imagining its unfulfilled possibilities as a truly "world" religion.

Many of the chapters of this book were presented in raw form to different audiences whose input has been invaluable. In particular, I would like to express appreciation to colleagues who responded to me at academic conferences: the Association for the Sociology of Religion (1988), the Canadian Society for the Study of Religion (1990), the Society for the Scientific Study of Religion (1990, 1991, 1992), the International Sociological Association (1994), and the Religious Research Association (1995, 1996). I was also privileged to make presentations of some of this material at the University of Calgary Institute for the Humanities Conference, "Global Culture: Pentecostal and Charismatic Movements

Worldwide" (1991), the St. Mary's College (London, England) Conference on "Japanese Culture: Christian Contributions" (September 1991), the Meiji Gakuin University's Institute for Christian Studies Conference on "Christianity in East Asia" (1993), the University of Stirling's Scottish Centre for Japanese Studies' Japan Seminar Series (1997), and the Centre for the Study of Christianity in the Non-Western World, New College, University of Edinburgh (1997). Here in Japan, Professor Yuki Hideo and Dr. Martin Repp were kind enough to offer me the opportunity of summarizing my findings to the 20th Annual Seminar on Japanese Religions sponsored by the NCC Center for the Study of Japanese Religions in Kyoto (September 1997). Although a number of these presentations were subsequently published as journal articles or as chapters in several books (for details of which, see the concluding Acknowledgments), everything has been thoroughly reworked for this volume.

The scholars and friends whose ideas have stimulated and shaped my research over the past decade are too many to mention, but I would like to single out for special thanks Araya Shigehiko (Seikei University), Shimazono Susumu (University of Tokyo), Ikegami Yoshimasa (Tsukuba University), Inoue Nobutaka (Kokugakuin University), Ian Reader (Scottish Centre for Japanese Studies, University of Stirling), Anthony Blasi (Tennessee State University), Thomas Hastings (Tokyo Union Theological Seminary), and Kayama Hisao, Richard Young, and Kuyama Michihiko (all colleagues at Meiji Gakuin University). Shortly after I returned to Japan in 1985, I had the good fortune of coming to know David Reid and David Swain, two veteran translators and editors (of the *Japanese Journal of Religious Studies* and the *Japan Christian Quarterly*, respectively). Their careful scholarship and scrupulous attention to detail left me with high standards for work in this field, and their friendship has given me encouragement on more occasions than I can count. During what often seemed an interminable project Joseph and Yuki Dunkle were a constant source of consolation and reinforcement, which I shall always remember as a special grace.

A sabbatical leave from Meiji Gakuin University from April 1996 to March 1997 enabled me to engage in several months of concentrated field research around Japan and to spend eight months as a visiting research fellow at the University of Edinburgh's Centre for the Study of Christianity in the Non-Western World in the Faculty of Divinity. I thank Professors Andrew Walls and David Kerr for arranging this enriching association. The Centre provided a stimulating environment for my work and I am grateful to the faculty and staff for their kind hospitality and for several opportunities to make presentations regarding my research.

Over the years, I have had a number of opportunities to work with the members of the Nanzan Institute for Religion and Culture on various projects. It is always reassuring to have such a capable team of editors, translators, and writers watching over your manuscript before publication. Without the help of Jim Heisig, Paul Swanson, Bob Kisala, Tom Kirchner, Ed Skrzypczak, and Clark Chilson, this would be a different book and probably still a long ways from seeing publication. I am proud to have my work listed as a title in the Nanzan Library of Asian Religion and Culture, and am grateful to Pat Crosby and the editors at the University of Hawai'i Press for their interest in the project.

Funding for research leading to this publication was provided by the Research Enablement Program, a grant program for mission scholarship supported by the Pew Charitable Trusts, Philadelphia, Pennsylvania, U.S.A., and administered by the Overseas Ministries Study Center, New Haven, Connecticut, U.S.A.

Like just about everything else I have written over the past two decades, a large share of the credit goes to my wife, Cindy. Ever a willing companion for my trips and a ready ear to my tales from the field, she is also a professional editor whose touch is everywhere in evidence to me. I dedicate these pages to her and to our two daughters, Sara Rachel and Megumi Catherine, with whom we make our life in Japan.

Tokyo, Japan
1 June 1998

CHAPTER ONE

Christianity as World Religion and Vernacular Movement

I N THIS BOOK I am concerned with what happens to a world religion when it is transplanted from one culture to another. By "world religion" I mean those missionizing religions of the world, such as Buddhism, Christianity, and Islam, that regard their religious teachings to be "truths" of ultimate significance for people of all times and places (truths, in other words, that transcend the boundaries of tribe, clan, and nation). For most of my adult life I have had a keen interest in the cross-cultural diffusion of these world religions. My interest is undoubtedly related to the fact that when I was still quite young my parents transplanted me—along with the gospel—to Japan. What was at one time no more than a vague, subconscious attempt to make sense of my cross-cultural childhood experiences and sense of marginality has evolved into my vocation.

It is no accident, therefore, that my studies in this field have focused on the two-way religious traffic between Japan and North America. Two decades ago I began by considering the transmission of Japanese Buddhism to North America, first through a study of Zen Buddhism and the counterculture movement of the 1960s and 1970s. This initial exploration prompted me to consider the transplantation of Pure Land Buddhism (Jōdo Shinshū), a tradition that accompanied Japanese immigrants to the United States and Canada during the past century. Since returning to Japan over a decade ago I have been studying various aspects of the transmission of Western Christianity and its encounter with Asian religion and culture. Just as the transplanters of Japanese Buddhist traditions have experienced considerable difficulty in adapting an essentially family-based religious tradition to the individualistic religious culture of North America, Christian missionaries to Japan have discovered that their message regarding faith and practice is difficult for most Japanese to accept or, perhaps, even to understand. Some of the "natives" in both cultures are currently engaged in the reinterpretation of these transplanted religious traditions. It is this process of appropriation—of making something foreign one's own—that I am concerned with in this study of Japanese Christianity.

Scholars have recently referred to these universalistic world religions as *global cultures*, drawing attention to the dialectic between the "universal" and "particular" in the process of cross-cultural transmission. Irving Hexham and Karla Poewe, for example, explain that

> a global culture is a tradition that travels the world and takes on local color. It has both a global, or metacultural, and a local, or situationally distinct, cultural dimension. As global cultures, the aim of universalistic world religions has been to spread a religious *metaculture* that was perfectly capable of remaining identifiable while being absorbed by local cultures.[1]

While it is often quite difficult to distinguish or disentangle the "metaculture" (universal elements) from the local variations or indigenous forms, these plural cultural expressions can be designated as part of a larger world religion because one can identify "striking continuities over time and space."[2] These "continuities," of course, are based on the fact that specific sacred texts (the Bible, Koran, or Tripitaka) record the central experiences and revelatory events that represent salvation for humankind. In the case of Christianity, Andrew Walls suggests that it is possible to identify such common features, as "continuity of thought about the final significance of Jesus, continuity of a certain consciousness about history, continuity in the use of Scriptures, of bread and wine, of water."[3] The fact that Christians often disagree about the significance and interpretation of these features need not concern us here.

While the category "world religion" is useful for referring to various religious traditions that share certain common features, it must be recognized that it only represents an ideal or abstraction. *Religion only exists in the vernacular,* or, to adapt a biblical phrase, the "treasure" only exists in "earthen vessels" (2 Corinthians 4:7). There is no such thing as a "pure" transcultural expression of Christianity or any other world religion—there are only particular cultural manifestations. Wendy James and Douglas Johnson accurately point out that

> Christian identity, as a confession of faith, does not bring with it or produce cultural and social uniformity; but because, as a personal experience, it inevitably goes with a characteristic sense of particular place or time, the theme of personal religious identity cannot be separated from that vernacular context. In this sense, *every Christian is a native.*[4]

Standing in the shadow of magnificent European cathedrals and churches, we find it easy to forget that Christianity was at one time a foreign religion on Western soil. Christianity began as a new religious movement, initially confined to the social world of Palestinian Judaism. Jesus of Nazareth was understood by his first followers in terms of the rather "particular" Jewish categories of rabbi and messiah. As this movement expanded out of Palestine into the larger Roman world, Gentile followers of "the way" came to confess this Jewish messiah as the divine Lord and Savior of humankind. The process of "de-Judaization" began as these new Christians were allowed to practice the faith without complete observance of traditional Jewish laws and customs. Greek and Latin vernacular expressions of the faith transformed the face of Christianity as it spread throughout Asia Minor and the Roman Empire over the course of the next several centuries. While de-Judaization characterized this first phase of cross-cultural transmission, the global development of Christianity over the past century has involved considerable efforts at "de-Westernization." In response to the modern missionary movement from Western Europe and North America, Asians and Africans have organized numerous independent churches and movements in an effort to disengage Christianity from its Eurocentric orientation and relativize the transplanted "vernacular" forms.

These expressions of Christianity cannot be understood as simple extensions of European and American mission churches, as they are often viewed in the West. Wilbert Shenk's frank observations regarding this tendency in Western scholarship are on the mark:

3

In the West, the history of the churches in Asia, Africa, and Latin America is generally assumed to be a subcategory of Western mission history. The development of the non-Western churches is indeed intertwined with the modern mission movement. However, the empirical reality of the Christian *ecumene* at the end of the twentieth century cannot be comprehended adequately through the category of mission history per se—it is considerably more than that.... We must move beyond the conventional framework, which is governed by the assumption that what happened in the course of Western Christendom is universally normative for Christian history.[5]

Wherever Western Christianity has been transplanted there have been those who have accepted what they regard as the "universal" significance of Jesus but have chosen, nevertheless, to develop their newfound faith outside of the mission churches. "Just as missionary orientation is fundamental to Buddhism and Christianity," James Heisig reminds us, "so is the *vernacular orientation* needed to loosen the hold that one particular time or culture or way of thinking has on teachings held sacred in order that they might enter other times and circumstances freely."[6] Although independent and indigenous forms of Christianity in Japan have not met with the success of similar movements in the African continent and Korea, for example, these movements nevertheless represent the "other side" of the Christian story in Japan. In order to accurately grasp the nature of world Christianity, we must give attention to the movements that fall outside standard mission histories.

SOCIOLOGICAL CONSIDERATIONS

Before focusing on these Japanese movements, it seems worthwhile to consider in more general terms some of the issues surrounding the transmission of religion from one culture to another. From a sociological perspective, the cross-cultural spread of religion is a complex process related to the interaction of several factors—ideological, environmental, and organizational. Ideology here is not used as a pejorative term. It refers to the beliefs, theology, or worldview of a social group, and more specifically to the "definition of mission" or understanding of the "world" embedded in the religious tradition. The manner in which groups define themselves and their relation to the surrounding environment has practical implications for the transplantation and development of an imported meaning-system. The nature or orientation of religious traditions varies considerably, from those that are ethnic and nationalistic to those that are missionary in orientation. This ideological factor largely determines the degree of effort that will be made in spreading the new meaning-system and the approach taken in proselytization. In particular the policies and allocation of resources for missionary activity is essentially shaped by this consideration. Robert Montgomery has recently drawn particular attention to Buddhism, Christianity, and Islam as three world religions that "have diffused most extensively," adding that "the cases of Judaism and Hinduism demonstrate that being a 'world religion' with universalistic doctrines apparently is a necessary, but not a sufficient, reason for a religion to diffuse widely by crossing many sociocultural boundaries."[7]

The environmental factor refers to the social, economic, and political conditions external to the "carriers" (i.e., immigrants, missionaries, religious organizations) of the transplanted meaning-system. It is therefore important to consider various aspects of the receiving society: the nature and role of the established or indigenous religion(s); the relationship between religion and the political order (i.e., are alternative religions permitted or tolerated?); the relative degree of social stability; and the potential for the existence of social groups outside of or excluded from the established religion or power structure. We are primarily concerned here with whether there exists a pool of likely or potential converts for an alternative meaning-system.

Finally, the organizational factor refers to the polity and social form of the carriers of the new meaning-system. This would include the relationship of a religious organization's headquarters to other levels or units of organization (congregations, temples, mission societies); the nature of religious authority; and the division of labor (this particularly concerns the relationship between the laity and religious professionals). Crucial to the transplantation process is the nature of the carriers of the new meaning-system. Is it carried by immigrants to another country as cultural baggage or is it brought by missionaries for the primary purpose of propagation? Does it accompany an ethnic community as a means of maintaining cultural identity or is it a part of a large missionary enterprise?

While these broad environmental factors help determine whether an alternative religion can be transplanted, the success of the transplantation process itself is significantly influenced by the degree to which forms of leadership, organizational structure, belief, and ritual are adapted to indigenous patterns and felt needs. As long as an imported religion retains its "foreign" character, it will more than likely have only a limited appeal to marginal individuals. For wider acceptance the imported religion must be rooted in the culture of the receiving society to the extent that it is no longer perceived as an alien or deviant phenomenon.

This indigenization process takes many years, of course, and is usually only achieved after considerable friction between the initial foreign carriers of the religion and the emergent indigenous leadership. The process whereby these "foreign" and previously irrelevant traditions become meaningful and rooted in local culture is referred to by such terms as indigenization, inculturation, contextualization, or syncretism. The choice of nomenclature is dependent on one's academic reference group or theological commitments. In the social sciences, for example, indigenization has been defined as the process whereby foreign-born religions are transformed through contact with native religion and culture.[8] In theological and missiological circles, the legitimate indigenization of Christianity is often referred to as the "inculturation" or "contextualization" of the Gospel. "Syncretism," a pejorative term, is reserved for illegitimate forms of religious synthesis. While the missionary "carriers" of a religious tradition certainly contribute to the process of cultural transformation through their translation efforts,[9] indigenization ultimately depends upon the creative efforts of those who belong to the local culture. Independent efforts to create vernacular Christian movements, in fact, are often resisted by the missionary carriers. This is not surprising, as F. F. Bruce explains:

> One important aspect of the fixing, or indeed petrifying, of tradition often appears when a community is transplanted from its former environment to a new and unfamiliar one. It may try to preserve its sense of identity and security by holding tenaciously to its traditions in the form which they had reached at the moment of transplantation. The Amish are perhaps the best known example of this—best known because their traditions comprise their total way of life. But on a less comprehensive scale the phenomenon is common enough....
>
> To many it seems safer and more comfortable to stay within familiar and old-established boundaries. The admission of more light may show up inadequacies in cherished traditions—inadequacies that would otherwise have remained hidden.[10]

This same tendency is certainly observable in many missionary situations. Representatives of established churches frequently regard adaptations of their traditions by the natives as "unauthorized religious production" and illegitimate syncretisms.[11]

THE JAPANESE CONTEXT

Japanese history provides rich data for the study of transplantation and indigenization with regard to several religious traditions in vastly different sociohistorical circumstances. The Buddhist tradition was introduced to Japan via China and Korea from the late sixth century, Roman Catholic Christianity was transplanted in the sixteenth century, and various Protestant denominations began missionary efforts from the latter half of the nineteenth century after Japan reopened its doors to the West. Although the focus of this study is on the Japanese reshaping of Christianity since the nineteenth century, we need to briefly consider the nature of Japanese religion and society prior to the arrival of Protestant missionaries.

Perhaps because of the vast, popular literature depicting the Japanese as a "homogeneous people," we tend to forget that in premodern Japan the population was highly divided by a variety of factors. Politically, Japanese were divided into 270 political domains (*bakuhan*) with their loyalty given to regional feudal lords. According to Maruyama Masao, it was not until the Meiji Restoration (1868) that national consciousness truly developed and led to "a sense of political solidarity and national unity." Describing the sociopolitical situation of the late Tokugawa period, Maruyama recalls the observations of Fukuzawa Yukichi, who commented that it was as if the "many millions of people throughout Japan were sealed up in many millions of separate boxes or separated by many millions of walls."[12]

Religious institutions also played their part in this divided nation. In the premodern period most Japanese were divided into particularistic village communities and united around local Shinto cults. Communal identities were reinforced through support of the local shrine and participation in various annual festivals. Shinto functioned essentially as the legitimizer of "subworlds," and was unable to integrate Japan under a "sacred canopy," to use Peter Berger's familiar phrase.[13] During the Tokugawa period (1600–1867), Buddhist temples received state patronage in exchange for administering the *danka seido*, a system in which all the residents of a given area were required to register their household with a local temple and notify it of births, marriages, and deaths. As a part of this system, priests issued certificates (*tera-uke*) to individuals each year attesting that the person in question was not a member of the proscribed religion (Christianity). Thus Buddhist priests were used by the Tokugawa regime to monitor and control the entire population. The system was localized, however, and did not provide a means of unifying the nation—for the most part it served to firmly link Buddhist temples with individual households or extended families (*ie*).

In this way, Japanese religiosity evolved in the premodern period into a syncretistic system of "layered obligations."[14] Living in rather isolated village communities, most Japanese naturally participated in the annual festivals and rituals of the local Shinto shrine and Buddhist temple. Participation in religious events and rituals was primarily motivated by the sense of duty and obligation that accompanied membership in a household and community, not by clearly defined beliefs or exclusive creeds. Over time, Shinto came to dominate rituals associated with this-worldly concerns of birth and fertility, and Buddhism the rituals associated with other-worldly concerns and care for the dead. In fact, the dominant role of Buddhism in the care of the dead has earned it the popular designation "funeral Buddhism."[15] By the time Japan embarked on its push to modernization most Japanese were integrated into this system of household (Buddhist) and communal (Shinto) religious obligations. This is the religious and cultural context within which we must try to understand the transplantation and indigenization of Christianity over the past century.

APPROACHING INDIGENOUS CHRISTIAN MOVEMENTS

Although the study of new religious movements represents one of the main concerns of sociologists and religious studies scholars in Japan, generally speaking those movements with origins in the Christian tradition have not received serious attention. The main reason for this comparative neglect is probably the fact that such movements are rather modest in size, with memberships ranging from several hundred to more than twenty thousand. With half a dozen New Religions each claiming memberships equal to or several times larger than the total number of Protestants and Catholics in Japan, and with scores of other movements claiming to have memberships numbering in the hundreds of thousands, it is not surprising that these smaller Christian movements have yet to claim the attention and time of scholars. It is only natural to focus attention on the most prominent or successful groups.[16]

For the most part, scholarship within Christian circles has also ignored the "unauthorized religious production" represented by these independent religious traditions, though the *Christian Yearbook* usually provides a brief paragraph on each movement. While the issue of the indigenization of the Gospel has been a serious topic for theological discussion on and off for decades, the conversation has been largely confined to transplanted mission churches and those Japanese denominations ecumenically related to the churches in the West. Even Jan Swyngedouw, a veteran observer of the religious scene in contemporary Japan, is puzzled by the general neglect and indifference toward these indigenous movements:

Japan is known as a fertile ground for new forms of religion. The Christian tradition is no exception, and there exist in fact many indigenous groups that claim a Christian label. It is, however, somewhat surprising that these groups, even when their numerical growth or some other factor gains public attention, are seldom viewed by mainline Christian bodies in terms of orthodoxy versus heterodoxy. *It is as though the new groups hardly merit any notice.*[17]

In fact, it is these groups—independent of the Western churches and their concerns for theological and ritual conformity—that have been able to deal more directly and freely with the issues related to indigenization that so often remain latent or suppressed in many of the "mainline" and transplanted Christian denominations.[18]

Because of its relatively recent arrival in Japan, Christianity is often regarded as a "foreign" and "Western" religion. This study will show that for some smaller religious subcultures in Japan this is no longer the case. Simply because Christianity lacks a long history and is sometimes in tension with other Japanese traditions does not mean it cannot be "authentically" Japanese. "In seeking to parse the tradition and culture of any people," Robert J. Smith reminds us, "it behooves the outsider always to remember that authenticity is not a function of antiquity and that recency is not evidence of triviality."[19] Cultures are made and remade from old and new elements. As noted above, Buddhism and Confucianism were initially "foreign" (Chinese) elements, but over the course of many centuries were adapted and reinterpreted so that they became part of the native cultural tradition.[20] Through the process of indigenization, Japanese have similarly transformed Christianity into a religion of their own. For the members of indigenous movements, Christianity is now perceived as a Japanese religion.

In this volume I have attempted to document forms of Christianity that have fallen outside the scope of traditional studies. Although scores of independent evangelical sects or churches are scattered throughout Japan, I have restricted my study to a dozen representative indigenous Christian movements, each established by a charismatic founder and made up of an association of groups or translocal congregations.

My primary concern has been to understand what Japanese Christians have done with Christianity, independent of the authority and control of the mission churches. In order to explain the development of these movements it is first necessary to understand them, which means becoming familiar with the language, symbols, and practices of those involved and discovering the significance accorded this involvement by the participants themselves. Field research, participant observation, and interviews, therefore, have been as important as documentary and archival research in this study.

In this book I draw on various sociological perspectives, typologies, and concepts, but my concern has not been to develop a general theory of indigenous Christian movements. Rather, I attempt to answer some basic questions about their emergence, character, and development. Why did some Japanese accept Christianity but reject the missionary carriers and their traditions? What role did charismatic leaders play in this process? What new social forms were developed by Japanese Christians? How do these Japanese Christians understand their faith and its relation to the "pre-Christian" religious traditions? What new rituals have been institutionalized in the development of indigenous Christianity?

Since this book is written from a sociological standpoint, it necessarily bears the limitations inherent to such a perspective. As an initial effort in interpretive understanding and descriptive analysis, it does not address important theological questions or attempt to evaluate these Japanese expressions of Christianity. While these are certainly legitimate areas of inquiry, they are beyond the scope of this study. Nevertheless, I hope that people from churches in the West can gain a deeper self-understanding through careful attention to these Japanese responses to transplanted mission traditions.

In order to enhance the readability of this volume, I have relegated much detail and reference information to the endnotes and appendix (Bibliographical Guide to Indigenous Christian Movements). Those wishing to pursue some of the issues raised in the body of this work will find that I have left a sufficient bibliographical trail to follow.

CHAPTER TWO

The Social Sources of Christianity in Japan

C HRISTIANITY IN contemporary Japan consists of diverse subcultures. It includes the many church traditions transplanted by Western missionaries, numerous indigenous movements (churches or sects organizationally independent of Western churches), as well as the personal belief systems of Japanese influenced by Christianity but unaffiliated with any of its organizational forms. It may sound rather strange—especially to those from countries where many "mainline" or established churches have dominated the religious landscape for centuries—to refer to Christian subcultures in this way, given that less than one percent of the Japanese population are affiliated with a Christian church of any kind. Nevertheless, cultural diversity is one of the undeniable features of Christianity in Japan, although the size of most denominations or groups, admittedly, reminds one of the miniature bonsai plants or small gardens that Japanese have cultivated so remarkably for centuries.

11

This chapter briefly introduces the two primary sources of Christianity in Japan: first, the transplanted churches and denominations from the West, and second, the independent Christian movements founded by Japanese leaders.[1] Although this book is primarily concerned with the new indigenous Christian traditions, it is impossible to understand them in isolation from the imported traditions introduced by foreign missionaries.

FROM ROMAN CATHOLIC TO PROTESTANT MISSION CHURCHES

Although there is some evidence that Nestorian Christianity may have reached Japan as early as the thirteenth century,[2] the first historically verifiable encounter between Christianity and Japanese culture began in the mid-sixteenth century with the Roman Catholic mission to Japan. Accompanying the colonial expansion of the Portuguese and Spanish into Asia, Jesuit missionaries arrived in the archipelago in 1549. These missionaries met with considerable success, so much so that this period has been referred to as "the Christian century in Japan,"[3] with the ratio of Christians to non-Christians probably several times higher than what it is today.

In light of the macropolitical situation at the time, it is hardly surprising that many Japanese authorities came to regard Christianity as the deviant religion of incursive foreign powers with designs on Japan, and as a serious threat to the nation's internal stability and national security. This first encounter between Christianity and Japan "officially" ended by the mid-seventeenth century with government decrees prohibiting Christianity, ordering the expulsion of European missionaries, and mandating the systematic persecution of Japanese converts. Although the Christian success story was thereby brought to an abrupt end, the encounter with Christianity continued "unofficially" for the next two centuries as the "hidden Christians" (*kakure kirishitan*) sought to survive in the hostile environment and secretly carry on the faith they had received.[4]

The second phase of mission to Japan began in 1859 (only six years after Commodore Perry persuaded Japan to open its doors to the West) with the arrival of the first Protestant missionaries and the return of the Roman Catholics. This was a time of widespread confusion and chaos. The feudal order was disintegrating rapidly by the end of the Tokugawa period (1600–1868), and the new Meiji government had not yet begun to build the new social order. It was during this difficult transition period that missionaries arrived in Japan. It is important to recall that they did not begin their work with a "clean slate." Christianity continued to be popularly understood as a heretical and evil religion (*jakyō*).

Since the mid-nineteenth century over two hundred mission societies, representing scores of churches and denominations as well as numerous national cultures, have been transplanted to Japanese soil (see table 1 on pages 14–15). The missionary impulse has been especially strong in North America, with the United States and Canada being the home base for approximately one-third of all missionary societies that have been active in Japan.

FROM TRANSDENOMINATIONAL COOPERATION TO DENOMINATIONAL MISSION CHURCHES

Although Christianity in Japan today consists of a bewildering array of transplanted denominations and sects, the earliest Protestant missionaries initially made serious efforts to cooperate in providing a more united witness to the Christian faith. The first Protestant church in Japan was organized along non-denominational (or transdenominational) lines in 1872 under the leadership of Samuel Robert Brown (Dutch Reformed), James Curtis Hepburn, and James Ballagh (both Presbyterian). Avoiding Western denominational labels, this church was called the Church of Christ in Japan (日本基督公会 Nihon Kirisuto Kōkai). Missionaries from Reformed, Presbyterian, and Congregational church traditions met that same year for the first Protestant Missionary Conference to discuss how cooperative missionary activities could be carried out and schismatic Western-style denominationalism averted in Japan. In order to create a united "body of Christ in Japan," it was decided that denominational names would be avoided and missionaries from various traditions would all use the name "Church of Christ" when organizing new congregations. The form of church government adopted (i.e., whether presbyterian or congregational polity) would be determined on a congregation-by-congregation basis, taking into account the missionary leadership and consensus of the local members.[5]

This was the general orientation of the Protestant missionaries until 1873, when the notices proscribing Christianity were finally removed. With the change in political climate to one of relative freedom came a rather sudden reversion to the old denominational orientation on the part of many missionaries. The concern for a united witness through cooperative mission was soon replaced by a focus on establishing Western denominational churches. Although some missionaries continued to stress collaborative efforts and had by 1875 organized Church of Christ congregations in fifty locations in the Kantō and Kansai areas, it was only a matter of time until the denominationalism of the other missionaries won the day. Missionaries found that they could no longer work

Table 1. Start of Work by Christian
Mission Organizations in Japan, 1859–1992

Year	Organization	Country of Origin	Year	Organization	Country of Origin
1859	Presbyterian Church in the U.S.	U.S.A.	1907	Societas Verbi Divini	Germany
1859	Protestant Episcopal Church	U.S.A.	1908	Missionskongregation	Holland
1859	Reformed Church in America (Dutch)	U.S.A.	1908	Societas Jesu	France
1859	Société des Missions Etrangères	France	1908	Societas Sacratissimi Cordis Jesu	France
1860	American Baptist Churches	U.S.A.	1910	Apostolatus Orationis	France
1860	American Seamen's Friend Society	U.S.A.	1913	Missionary Band of the World	U.S.A.
1860	Southern Baptist Convention	U.S.A.	1915	Society of Saint-Vincent de Paul	France
1861	Holy Orthodox Church in Japan	Russia	1917	Church of Christ, Scientist	U.S.A.
1869	American Board of Commissioners		1918	American Wesleyan Mission	U.S.A.
	for Foreign Missions	U.S.A.	1920	Community of the Epiphany	England
1869	Congregational Church	U.S.A.	1920	Kongregation der Franziskanerinnen	Germany
1869	Church Missionary Society	England	1921	Sœurs de la Charité	France
1871	Wesleyan Methodist Church	Canada	1923	American Friends Service Committee	U.S.A.
1872	L'Institut des Sœurs de l'Enfant	France	1925	Congregacion de Religiosas	Philippines
1872	Methodist Episcopal Church	U.S.A.	1925	Franciscan Sisters of Annunciation	Canada
1873	Methodist Church of Canada	Canada	1926	Maryknoll Sisters of St. Dominic	U.S.A.
1873	Finnish Missionary Society	Finland	1926	Pia Societas sancti Francisci Salesii	Italy
1873	Methodist Church of Canada	Canada	1926	Les Sœurs Missionnaires	Canada
1873	Methodist Women's Missionary Society	Canada	1927	Liebenzeller Mission	Germany
1873	Society for the Propagation of the		1927	Ordo Sancti Benedicti	Italy
	Gospel in Foreign Parts	England	1927	Watch-Tower (Jehovah's Witnesses)	U.S.A.
1874	Edinburgh Medical Mission	Scotland	1928	Congregacion de Adoratrices	Spain
1874	United Presbyterian Church	Scotland	1928	Opus Dei	Spain
1875	National Bible Society of Scotland	Scotland	1929	Instituto delle Figlie di Maria	Italy
1876	British and Foreign Bible Society	England	1929	Student Christian Movement	England
1876	Evangelical Church of North America	U.S.A.	1930	Ordo Fratrum Minorum	Italy
1877	Congrégation des Sœurs de l'Enfant	France	1930	St. Benedict's Priory	U.S.A.
1877	Cumberland Presbyterian Church	U.S.A.	1931	Congrégation Romaine de Dominique	Italy
1878	Baptist Missionary Society	England	1931	Les Sœurs des Saints Noms	Canada
1879	Reformed Church in U.S. (German)	U.S.A.	1932	Congrégation de Notre Dame	Canada
1880	Methodist Protestant Church	U.S.A.	1932	Fratres Scholarum Christianarum	France
1880	Young Men's Christian Association	England	1933	Maryknoll Missioners	U.S.A.
1883	Christian Church (Disciples of Christ)	U.S.A.	1933	Society of St. John the Evangelist	U.S.A.
1885	Evangelical Protestant Missionsverein	Germany	1933	Sœurs Missionnaires du Christ-Roi	Canada
1885	Religious Society of Friends (Quakers)	U.S.A.	1934	Ancillae Sacratissimi Cordis Jesu	Spain
1885	Presbyterian Church in the U.S. (South)	U.S.A.	1934	Pia Societas Sancti Pauli Apostoli	Italy
1885	Wesleyan Missionary Society	England	1934	Les Sœurs de l'Assomption	Canada
1886	Methodist Episcopal Church (South)	U.S.A.	1934	Sœurs de Sainte Anne	Canada
1887	America Christian Convention	U.S.A.	1935	Christian Evangelistic Church	U.S.A.
1887	La Société de Marie	France	1935	Congrégation de Notre Dame	France
1887	Unitarian Association	U.S.A.	1936	Ordre de Ste. Ursule	Canada
1888	Christian and Missionary Alliance	U.S.A.	1938	Orthodox Presbyterian Church	U.S.A.
1888	Plymouth Brethren	England	1946	Missionsbenediktinerinnen	Germany
1890	Church of Christ	U.S.A.	1947	Congregatio Immaculati Cordis Mariae	Belgium
1890	Missionary Society of the Church		1947	Ordo Saecularis Carmelitarum	Spain
	of England	Canada	1947	Conservative Baptist Mission	U.S.A.
1890	Universalist General Convention	U.S.A.	1948	Clerics of St. Viator	Canada
1892	Evangelical Lutheran Church (South)	U.S.A.	1948	Congregatio Missionariorum	France
1892	Women's Auxiliary, Church of England	Canada	1948	Far East Gospel Crusade	U.S.A.
1895	United Brethren in Christ	U.S.A.	1948	Franciscan Friars of the Atonement	U.S.A.
1895	Free Methodist Church of North America	U.S.A.	1948	Missionsgesellschaft Bethlehem	Switzerland
1895	Salvation Army	England	1948	Scarboro Foreign Missionary Society	Canada
1896	Trappist Order (men)	France	1948	Baptist General Conference	U.S.A.
1896	Seventh-day Adventists	U.S.A.	1948	Societas Sancti Columbani	Ireland
1898	Franciscaines Missionnaires de Marie	India	1949	Congregatio Missionis	France
1898	Trappist Order (women)	France	1949	Evangelical Lutheran Church	U.S.A.
1901	Latter-day Saints (Mormons)	U.S.A.	1949	Gideons International	U.S.A.
1901	Young Women's Christian Association	England	1949	Misioneras Eucaristicas	Mexico
1905	Church of the Nazarene	U.S.A.	1949	Mennonite Central Committee	U.S.A.
1907	Ordo Fratrum Minorum	Italy	1949	Sweden Mission	Sweden

Year	Organization	Country of Origin	Year	Organization	Country of Origin
1949	Evangelical Free Church Mission	U.S.A.	1953	Sœurs de la Charité de Québec	Canada
1950	Church of the Foursquare Gospel	U.S.A.	1954	Free Will Baptists	U.S.A.
1950	Free Christian Mission	Norway,	1954	Ordre de Moniales Cisterciennes	Belgium
		Denmark	1954	Fraternité des Petites Sœurs de Jésus	France
1950	Ordo Scholarum Piarum	Spain	1955	Catholic Mission Sisters	U.S.A.
1950	Philadelphia Church Mission	U.S.A.	1955	Religiosas de Maria Immaculada	Cuba
1950	Societas Missionariorum	France	1956	Congregation of Sisters of St. Joseph	U.S.A.
1950	St. Benedict's Priory	U.S.A.	1956	Instituto de Santa Maria de Guadalupe	Mexico
1950	Suore Pie Discepole	Italy	1956	Our Lady's Missionaries	Canada
1950	Swedish Holiness Union	Sweden	1956	Petits Frères de Jésus	France
1951	Apostolic Christian Church	U.S.A.	1957	Franciscan Sisters of the Atonement	U.S.A.
1951	Christian Reformed Church	U.S.A.	1957	Religiose della Passione	Italy
1951	Deutscher Diakonissenerband	Germany	1958	Association des Prêtres du Prado	France
1951	Evangelical Orient Mission	Norway	1958	Institutum Saeculare Missionariarum	Italy
1951	Figlie della Carità Canossiane	Italy	1959	Ordinis Societatis Mariae	France
1951	Filiae Iesu	Spain	1959	Società Missionarie di Maria	Italy
1951	Frères de l'Instruction Chrétienne	France	1959	Unification Church	Korea
1951	Grey Sisters	Canada	1961	Gospel Fellowship Mission	U.S.A.
1951	Hospitaller Brothers	Spain	1970	Fratres Caritatis	Belgium
1951	Institut des Sœurs des Missions	France	1972	The Family	U.S.A.
1951	Ordo Carmelitarum (men)	Italy	1975	Evangelical Baptist Churches	Canada
1951	Les Petites Filles de St. Joseph	Canada	1975	Rex Hubbard World Outreach	U.S.A.
1952	Congregatio Passionis Jesu Christi	Italy	1976	Full Gospel Church Mission	Korea
1952	Religious of the Assumption	Philippines	1977	Verbum Dei Apostolic Institute	Spain
1952	United Pentecostal Church	U.S.A.	1979	Petites Sœurs de l'Évangile	France
1953	Ancillae Divini Cordis	Spain	1980	P.T.L. Club	U.S.A.
1953	Apostolic Faith Mission	U.S.A.	1984	Jimmy Swaggart Ministry	U.S.A.
1953	Brethren in Christ Missions	U.S.A.	1992	Baptist Church of Denmark	Denmark
1953	Church of God	U.S.A.	1992	Japan Free Evangelical Mission	Norway
1953	Religiosas Concepcionistas	Spain	1992	Volunteer Youth Ministry	U.S.A.

This is an adaptation of data from Noriyoshi Tamaru and David Reid, eds., *Religion in Japanese Culture: Where Living Traditions Meet a Changing World* (Tokyo: Kodansha International, 1996), 185–86, used here with the permission of the publisher and author. In preparing this table, I have only included those organizations that define themselves as "Christian" (though several are not always recognized as such by the older established churches and denominations); drawing on a more complete listing of evangelical mission organizations active in Japan, I have also added some religious organizations that were not listed in the earlier table.

together on the basis of a common confession in Jesus Christ and the Bible as the standard of faith. Unable to reconcile the various church polities within the Church of Christ congregations, missionaries resorted to establishing denominational churches, each with its distinctive form of government and confession of faith. By this time the presence of the Methodist Episcopal Church had contributed another alternative polity to add to the confusion.

It should be noted that this conflict and subsequent denominationalism was not entirely the result of missionary opinion and leadership. After ten years of study in the United States, Niijima Jō returned to Japan in 1874 and made a strong appeal to the Church of Christ congregations in the Kansai area to adopt the congregational polity in order to create a free and independent church in Japan. No new Church of Christ congregations were established after 1877, and all existing congregations eventually became part of either the Presbyterian, Congregational, or Methodist Episcopal denominations.[6]

A case could be made that the cooperative outlook of the earliest missionaries was shaped in part by their fewness in number and their need for mutual support in the difficult environment they found themselves in. For over a decade Protestant missionaries had to cope with the fact that their faith and missionary activity were illegal. The number of missionaries from various Protestant traditions increased significantly after the notices proscribing Christianity were removed in 1873. With increasing numbers, each church had enough missionaries to create distinct communities of support without relying on missionaries from other denominations. Likewise, missionaries felt increasing pressure from the organizations that were supporting them financially to report on the number of "their" churches that had been established in Japan.

CHRISTIANITY AS A LAY MOVEMENT:
THE SAPPORO AND KUMAMOTO BANDS

Studies of Protestantism in Japan often refer to the three "bands," or initial groups of Christians, that formed in the locations of Kumamoto, Yokohama, and Sapporo.[7] While the influence of ordained Presbyterian and Dutch Reformed clergy was dominant in the Yokohama Band, it is particularly significant that in Kumamoto and Sapporo Christianity was spread by lay Christian educators who had been invited by the Japanese to serve as teachers in newly established institutions. Their interpretion of the Christian faith provided an alternative to that of the church-related missionaries who seemed preoccupied with ecclesiastical matters and the preservation of denominational distinctiveness.

In 1871 Captain Leroy Lansing Janes arrived in Kumamoto to teach English in the School of Western Learning (Yōgakkō) established by Lord Hosokawa. Janes also taught his students the Bible in his home, and from 1875 a number of these students converted to the Christian faith. Even though Janes was only a lay person, he nevertheless baptized these early converts and led them in the celebration of the Lord's Supper. Janes transmitted his Christian faith and understanding of the Bible without the theological confessions and church-related political concerns that characterized many of the ordained missionaries. In 1876 some thirty individuals from the Kumamoto school moved to Kyoto and entered Dōshisha English School, which had been established the year before.

This became the center for the development of Congregational churches in Japan under the strong leadership of Niijima Jō.

Another lay Christian, William S. Clark, arrived in Hokkaidō in 1876 to assist the Japanese government in the establishment of Sapporo Agricultural College. In addition to providing instruction in agricultural studies, Clark taught his students the Bible and introduced them to the Christian faith. In 1877 he organized the Covenant of Believers in Jesus with several of his students. This "Covenant" involved a commitment to read the Bible and live an ethical life, but did not require baptism and made no reference to the church or to theological confessions and creeds. Although Clark was only in Sapporo for a short period of eight months, his evangelistic efforts had a lasting influence. The year after Clark returned to the United States, Uchimura Kanzō entered the college and converted to Christianity under pressure from the "Covenant" group Clark left behind. This tradition of "lay Christianity" is an important background for understanding the subsequent development of indigenous Christian movements that had an "experiential" orientation and little sympathy for the "theological" and "ecclesiastical" concerns of the mission churches.[8]

THE DEVELOPMENT AND GROWTH OF THE MISSION CHURCHES

Christian missionary efforts in Japan finally began to meet with some success after the Japanese government rescinded the edict prohibiting Christianity in 1873. After two long decades of anti-Christian sentiment and resistance, Japan entered a brief period of *seiyōsūhai,* or "worship of the West." The persistent efforts of Protestant missionaries suddenly began to pay off in this new social climate of openness. Even missionaries were overwhelmed by the positive response and rapid growth of mission churches and institutions in the 1880s. In addition to church-planting efforts, by 1882 Protestant missions had established 9 schools for boys, 15 for girls, 39 coeducational institutions, and 7 theological seminaries.[9]

According to the statistics compiled by the Christian Yearbook,[10] there were only 59 Japanese Protestant Christians in 1873. Less than two decades later, by 1891, Protestant church membership had grown to 31,361. The rapid growth of Protestant churches during this period has been attributed to a series of revivals that occurred between 1882 and 1885 and to the "craze for everything Western" from 1885 to 1890. This brief honeymoon period was so encouraging that at the second Conference of Protestant Missionaries of Japan held in 1883 it was almost taken for granted that Japan would become a Christian nation in the near future. As Otis Cary observed in his history of this early period, "Some went so far as to say that, if the call sent out by the Conference asking for reenforcements was heeded by the churches at home, the work of evangelising Japan could be accomplished within ten years, or at least before the close of the century."[11] Even some non-Christian Japanese leaders and politicians were advocating that Christianity be adopted as the state religion of Japan. This was understood as an effective strategy for making Japan a recognized member of the international community as quickly as possible. By the end of the "glorious" 1880s, Protestant missions were successfully organizing churches, recording baptisms, and watching their enrollments increase in over one hundred mission schools.[12]

The Roman Catholic Church, recovering some members from among those who had remained "hidden" during the Tokugawa period (1600–1868), also grew during this decade, and by 1890 had a membership of 44,505. More remarkable during this same period was the development of the Russian Orthodox Church under the leadership of Bishop Nikolai. By 1900 the church had trained "376 Japanese clergy (compared to 196 for the Congregationalists, Anglicans, Presbyterians, and Roman Catholics combined) and 25,698 members, only slightly less than the Congregationalists, Anglicans, and Presbyterians combined."[13]

This initial period of growth for Christian churches ended as the Meiji government stabilized and began to recast a national identity based upon State Shinto and the emperor system. The leaders of the Meiji government established an alternative ideology to control the process of Japan's modernization: Western technology and learning would be adopted without Christianity. The Constitution of 1889 and the Imperial Rescript on Education of 1890 symbolized the national polity being cultivated by the Meiji authorities. From this point on there was a negative reaction to Westernization which, combined with the emergence nationalistic sentiments, served to put a damper on the growth of Christianity for at least a decade. As the strong arm of the state took control of Japan's modernization, the role of Christian institutions was quickly overshadowed.[14]

The strong anti-Western sentiments of the 1890s subsided and Christian mission activity began to experience a greater responsiveness from the Japanese from the early 1900s until around 1930. By this time, Japan was well into its industrial revolution and experiencing the many problems associated with a rapidly changing economy. Individuals most responsive to the Protestant missionary efforts were found among the rapidly growing white-collar class concentrated in urban areas, and the membership of the Protestant denominations grew from 50,785 in 1901 to 193,937 in 1930.[15] The Roman Catholic Church similarly grew from a membership of 56,321 in 1901 to one of 92,798 in 1930. While Christian denominations continued to record growth on into the 1930s, by the end of that decade the growing nationalism supported by State Shinto brought the growth of the churches to a virtual halt.

TRANSPLANTED CHURCHES UNDER JAPANESE CIVIL RELIGION

Although the Meiji Constitution guaranteed religious freedom, by the late 1930s the government became increasingly totalitarian, requiring members of every religious group to participate in civil religious rituals and conform to the state-defined orthodoxy. The national religion created by the government bureaucrats was largely an "invention of tradition"[16] projected back on Japanese history; though nominally Shinto, it differed considerably from the previous forms of Shinto belief and practice. It was used, nevertheless, to unify and integrate the heterogeneous population and mobilize the people for nation-building, modernization, and military expansion.

The authorities defined Shinto as a "nonreligious" institution of the state, and participation in its rituals came to be viewed as the "patriotic" duty of all Japanese regardless of personal religious convictions. These civil religious demands coalesced with traditional religious obligations in the wartime period to create an almost unbearable tension for Christian churches. Christians who did not comply with the government directive to worship at the shrines of State Shinto—the duty of all loyal citizens—faced not only persecution but constant suspicion concerning their identity as Japanese.

In order to deal with religious deviants and bring all groups into conformity with the state-defined orthodoxy, the Diet passed the Religious Organizations Law *(shūkyō-dantai hō)* in 1939. This empowered the state to disband any religious organization whose teachings were in conflict with the Imperial Way *(kōdō)*. In addition, the Peace Preservation Law *(chian'iji hō)* was revised in 1941 in order to address the subversive potential of various religious groups. Designed initially in 1925 to control radical socialists and the communist movement, this law prohibited the organization of any association or group that denied the right to private property or sought to overthrow the national polity *(kokutai)*. The revised version, however, was extended to suppress a wide variety of dangerous ideas *(kiken shisō)* that showed disrespect toward the imperial household and its shrines or were in conflict with the national polity (by this time interpreted to mean Japan as a divine country under the absolute rule of one manifest deity—*arahitogami*—the emperor).

Given the legal measures and intense government pressures noted above, it is not surprising that most transplanted churches and Christian institutions gradually accommodated themselves to the nationalistic environment. After varying degrees of resistance to the claims of the state, the Roman Catholic Church and most Protestant denominations eventually instructed their members to participate in the rituals of civil religion. By the late 1930s most churches had also created some form of theological rhetoric to legitimize the Imperial Way, including support for Japanese military expansionism. According to these indigenous theologies, the rule and kingdom of the emperor were none other than the kingdom of God, and the Japanese people were a chosen race with a destiny to establish this kingdom of peace and prosperity throughout Asia.[17]

The formation and subsequent activities and policies of the United Church of Christ in Japan (Nippon Kirisuto Kyōdan, hereafter referred to as the Kyōdan) provides one of the clearest illustrations of this dominant pattern of accommodation and collaboration.[18] While a number of church leaders had worked for a united Christian witness for many years, it was not until the Japanese government forced the creation of this union that the diverse Protestant religious bodies actually came together. In accordance with the 1939 Religious Organizations Law, Christian churches were required to comply with conditions set by the Ministry of Education in order to receive official recognition or legal status. Indicating that it would only recognize one Protestant denomination, the Ministry directed the various churches to form one organization. Denominational representatives met for serious discussion in August 1940, and on October 17 passed a resolution to unite their various churches. In 1941, as a government-directed union of thirty-four denominations, the Kyōdan absorbed all transplanted Protestant mission churches (with the exception of a section of the Anglican Church, the Seventh-day Adventists, and a few small evangelical churches who refused to cooperate).[19] Needless to say, for many of the participating churches this was a less than happy union that resembled a forced or arranged marriage.

From the beginning, as David Reid points out, the "Kyōdan rested on an uneasy combination of 'sacred' and 'secular' motivation."[20] At least for its first four years of existence, the 'secular' demands of the state proved to be the most dominating influence. Writing in the midst of this difficult period, D. C. Holtom suggested that the overall weakness of Christianity made this pattern of response almost inevitable:

The Christian movement in Japan today is still too weak, in numbers as well as influence, to take more than a subordinate position when powerful forces in the state set about turning all the resources of the national life into directions that cut across those along which the Christian church has traveled. Under the circumstances the church has only two roads open to it: persecution and martyrdom or compromise and accommodation. The Japanese Christian church has chosen the latter.[21]

Until the end of the war, the Kyōdan was largely guided and controlled by numerous government demands. On 11 January 1942, for example, representatives of the Kyōdan went to Ise Jingū (the major Imperial Shinto shrine) to report to the national gods the founding of the Kyōdan, to pray for its development, and to pledge contributions to the nation. Before the end of 1942 (10 December) the head office of the Kyōdan instructed all churches to precede each worship service with *kokumin girei* (citizen rituals), which involved bowing in the direction of the imperial palace, singing the *Kimigayo* (hymn to the emperor), and silently praying for those who had died in service to the emperor. All aspects of church life came under the increasing scrutiny and control of the authorities. Hymnbooks were edited and shortened to about one hundred selected entries; songs with references to peace or God as creator and judge were excised. In order to show that it was fully behind the government's war effort, the Kyōdan even began a fund-raising campaign for the military in November 1943 for a warplane named *Nippon Kirisuto Kyōdan*. By 1944, the government went so far as to issue themes for sermon topics to all the churches through the Kyōdan office. The General Secretary of the Kyōdan even instructed the churches to choose another date to celebrate Christmas, since 25 December was to be observed as a national holiday honoring the late Emperor Taishō's birth. While the Kyōdan during wartime may be regarded as a "Japanized" expression of Christianity, it can hardly be regarded as a spontaneous development and example of what I understand as an indigenous Christian movement.

THE POSTWAR PERIOD

The development of Christianity in postwar Japan has been framed by the fundamental changes in the political and legal system that resulted from Japan's defeat on 15 August 1945 and the arrival of the Occupation Forces. Within several months the Supreme Commander for the Allied Powers (SCAP) issued the Directive for the Disestablishment of State Shinto (15 December 1945) and set in motion policies that effectively reduced Shinto to the status of a voluntary organization without special legal authority or financial support from the state. In accord with the Directive, the wartime laws regulating religion were abolished and all religious organizations, including Shinto groups, were required to register as "religious juridical persons" *(shūkyō hōjin)* and placed on equal legal footing. Articles 20 and 89 of the postwar Constitution of Japan (1947) clearly articulated the principle of religious freedom and separation of religion and state, thus fulfilling the constitutional reform objectives of the Occupation authorities. The disestablishment directive accomplished the "secularization" of State Shinto in record time, but it also created a free-market religious economy that allowed diverse religious groups to compete on a relatively level playing field for the first time in Japanese history.

Another major factor shaping postwar religious trends was the population shift that accompanied the rebuilding of Japan following the wartime devastation. Japan's economic recovery required an extensive pool of laborers to work in the developing industries located primarily in the urban areas, necessitating a major population shift from rural regions to the cities. Abandoning agricultural communities in search of a better livelihood, workers poured into urban areas in the 1950s and 1960s to meet the demands of the recovering and expanding industrial economy. An urban population of 37.5 percent in 1950 had increased to 76.1 percent by 1980.

The demographic changes related to postwar industrialization helped to create a more favorable environment for Christian missionary activities, since Christian organizations were largely concentrated in metropolitan areas (unlike Shinto shrines and Buddhist temples). In addition to these political and demographic changes, a large-scale crisis of meaning had been created by the wartime devastation and the shock of defeat. The ideology that had united and propelled Japan as a nation since the 1930s disintegrated with Japan's surrender. Christianity and various new religions that emerged from the war's aftermath provided one means of coping with this crisis.

With the establishment of religious freedom by the Occupation Forces in 1946, many groups left the Kyōdan to reestablish their prewar denominational identities. The most significant departures were the Anglican Episcopal Church, the Lutheran Church, plus numerous Baptist and smaller Evangelical and Holiness churches. In addition to these reestablished prewar denominations, numerous other evangelical churches from North America and Europe responded to General MacArthur's call for missionary reinforcements to join in building a new Japan. Between 1949 and 1953 over fifteen hundred new missionaries arrived in Japan, and the churches began to show signs of recovery.

During this early postwar period Christian churches made considerable progress, particularly among members of the educated middle class. The Roman Catholic Church, whose membership had dropped to around 100,000 during the war, grew to a membership of 323,599 by 1960. Protestant churches experienced a similar expansion, from a low of about 190,000 in 1942 to over 400,000 in 1960. The annual growth rate, however, began to decline gradually for both Protestants and Catholics alike in the early 1950s. David Barrett notes that the Roman Catholic Church's relatively high annual growth rate of 10.4 percent in 1951 fell to 7.9 percent in 1953, initiating a trend that by 1971 had skidded to only 0.34 percent.[22] A similar pattern can be seen in the Protestant churches. While churches have continued to report membership increases, annual statistics have indicated for decades that no more than one percent of the Japanese are church members. The hard reality is that the rate of defections and the increase in the Japanese population have kept Christian churches from gaining a larger share of the market in Japan's religious economy. Indigenous new religious movements, on the other hand, have capitalized on the new demographic profile and deregulated religious economy and, according to the most reliable Japanese scholarship, have memberships totaling between 10 and 20 percent of the population.

As this brief review has shown, many of the transplanted mission churches have experienced significant periods of growth over the past century. In spite of the numerous challenges and difficulties, the missionary impact on Japan has been significant. In addition to the transplantation of many denominations and churches, the missionary movement contributed to the development of modern Japan through its efforts in the fields of education and social welfare. While acknowledging this widespread influence, it must be said that the evangelistic efforts of the mission churches have not found a very receptive audience. When one considers the number of missionaries and financial resources invested by both Roman Catholic and Protestant mission societies, it is hardly a picture of success. As noted above, institutionally affiliated Christians still only amount to approximately one percent of the population. In a word, the dominant response to Western missionary efforts has been one of rejection. Over a decade ago, the NHK Survey on Japanese Religious Consciousness (1984) provided a slightly more optimistic picture, finding that two percent of the Japanese identify themselves as Christian and 12 percent feel a certain empathy toward Christianity.[23] Nevertheless, even accepting the more generous assessment provided by survey research that suggests there may be some *kakure kirishitan* in contemporary Japan, the efforts to transplant Christianity in Japan have not been too successful.

Also hidden within these meager statistics are the numerous indigenous Christian movements that developed in reaction to the transplanted mission churches over the past century, the story that we now consider.

FROM TRANSPLANTED CHURCHES TO INDIGENOUS MOVEMENTS

As latecomers to Japan's religious scene, both Catholic and Protestant churches have experienced considerable difficulty in shedding their reputation as "foreign religions." While at times the "Westernness" of Christianity has contributed to its appeal among Japanese, for the most part it has been viewed as a problem. Many early Japanese converts to Christianity felt that this was largely the fault of the foreign missionaries. Christianity was unnecessarily bound to Western organizational forms, denominational politics, and missionary control. Although the statistics indicate that most Japanese have rejected the evangelistic appeals and demands of Western missionaries, the development of indigenous and independent Christian movements suggests the possibility of a more nuanced yet critical response to transplanted Christianity. This distinctive approach was expressed as early as 1890 in rather strong terms by Nitobe Inazō, a close friend of Uchimura Kanzō from their days together at Sapporo Agricultural College in Hokkaidō:

> The sectarian bigots revive on a heathen land their own petty jealousies, for which their forefathers fought and burned one another. Nothing is more ugly and repugnant to Japanese eyes than these sectarian quarrels and jealousies; worse than that, the Japanese seekers find themselves puzzled by a maze of conflicting teachings of different Christian bodies.[24]

Nitobe goes on to say that "the divine religion of Christ, divested of all human wrappage—of sacramentalism, sacerdotalism, sectarianism—alone is welcome." If human wrappings are necessary, he concludes, they should be "a homemade garment."[25] Religion without "human wrappings," of course, is not really an option. The choice is only between imported or indigenous forms. The development of indigenous forms usually takes many years and is only achieved after struggles between the initial foreign "carriers" of the religion and the emergent native leadership. The nativistic reactions of Japanese to mission churches and their creative appropriations of Christianity have led to the development of numerous "homemade garments," providing alternative interpretations and sociocultural expressions of this foreign-born religion. As may be seen in table 2, a wide variety of indigenous groups have been organized over the past century.

Table 2. Indigenous Christian Movements in Japan

INDIGENOUS MOVEMENTS	FOUNDER	YEAR ORGANIZED
Nonchurch movement 無教会	Uchimura Kanzō	1901
The Way 道会	Matsumura Kaiseki	1907
Christ Heart Church 基督心宗教団	Kawai Shinsui	1927
Glorious Gospel Christian Church 栄光の福音キリスト教	Sugita Kōtarō	1936
Living Christ One Ear of Wheat Church 活けるキリスト一麦教会	Matsubara Kazuhito	1939
Christian Canaan Church 基督カーナン教団	Taniguchi Toku	1940
Japan Ecclesia of Christ 日本キリスト召団	Koike Tatsuo	1940
Spirit of Jesus Church イエス之御霊教会	Murai Jun	1941
Holy Ecclesia of Jesus 聖イエス会	Ōtsuki Takeji	1946
Sanctifying Christ Church 聖成基督教団	Konmoto Kaoru	1948
Original Gospel (Tabernacle) 原始福音(幕屋)	Teshima Ikurō	1948
Life-Giving Christ 活かすキリスト	Imahashi Atsushi	1966
Okinawa Christian Gospel 沖縄キリスト教福音	Nakahara Masao	1977

With the exception of the Nonchurch movement founded by Uchimura Kanzō, our knowledge regarding most of these indigenous movements has been limited to a brief paragraph provided each year in the *Christian Yearbook*. The current membership of these groups varies widely, ranging from several hundred to over twenty thousand. Together, therefore, they constitute a significant development of the Christian tradition in Japan. (Consult the Appendix for basic information and resources on each movement.)

25

Self-Definition (Claims to Legitimacy)	Degree of Change	
	Indigenous ←——————→ Nonindigenous Self-support, self-control, self-propagation	
	Native-Oriented	Foreign-Oriented
Monopolistic (Sectarian)	Spirit of Jesus Church	Mormons Jehovah's Witnesses Baptist International Mission
Pluralistic (Denominational)	Nonchurch movement Christ Heart Church The Way Original Gospel	United Church of Christ Roman Catholic Church Anglican Church Lutheran Church* Baptist Church* Presbyterian Church* Reformed Church*

* There are a number of Lutheran, Baptist, Reformed, and Presbyterian churches in Japan that represent various European (German, Norwegian, Finnish) and North American traditions.

Figure 1. Typology of Indigenization

CHURCH-SECT THEORY AND THE STUDY OF INDIGENIZATION

Japanese scholars refer to many of these movements as Christian-related New Religions, and several such groups were included in the massive reference work on New Religions published in 1990.[26] These groups, however, do not fit easily into typologies of Japanese New Religions because of their indebtedness to the established Christian traditions. For this reason, in fact, several years ago Shimazono Susumu, one of the leading scholars in the study of new religious movements in Japan, suggested that a separate typology was needed to adequately deal with Christian-related New Religions in Japan.[27]

Adapting church-sect theory, figure 1 provides a comparative typological framework for understanding Christian religious organizations in Japan according to three criteria: *basic orientation, self-definition,* and *degree of indigenization.* This framework is hardly intended to be a definitive statement, but it should serve as a typological "bridge" to carry readers from the familiar world of

Western Christianity to the relatively unmapped territory of Japanese indigenous Christianity and, hopefully, clarify in a new way the complex relationship
between imported and indigenous traditions.[28] This typology is based on an
interpretative sociology of religion rather than on theological criteria, and priority is given to the actors' definition of the situation. As Peter Berger and
Hansfried Kellner explain, sociological concepts "must relate to the typifications
that are already operative in the situation being studied."[29] While some groups
included in figure 1 might be regarded as heretical and non-Christian by certain
established churches, I have included them in this typology because the actors
involved define themselves and their organizations in Christian terms or in continuity with the Christian tradition.

First of all, it is necessary to distinguish indigenous movements from the
imported denominations and independent evangelical churches in terms of
their basic orientation or dominant reference group. Christian religious bodies
in Japan tend to be either "foreign-oriented" or "native-oriented." Transplanted
religious organizations, including the Anglican Church, the Roman Catholic
Church, the Lutheran denominations, and the United Church of Christ (the
largest Protestant religious body in Japan, which incorporated Methodist, Reformed,
Presbyterian, and Congregational churches) are still "foreign-oriented" in many
respects and therefore located at the nonindigenous end of the continuum.
These denominations still receive foreign missionaries, and their understanding
of theology and models for church polity and organization are taken primarily
from Western churches. This tendency is so strong that it is not uncommon to
hear it referred to in terms of the "German captivity" of the churches. Noting
how Troeltsch, Barth, or Brunner inevitably emerge from the pages of the Bible
when it is opened in many Japanese churches, one Japanese sociologist rather
cynically remarked that "one cannot help but wonder to whom these churches
are trying to communicate their message."[30]

Readers should keep in mind that this framework is based on a continuum
and understand that I am not arguing that indigenization has not occurred in
these foreign-oriented religious bodies, only that the process has proceeded
more slowly than in indigenous movements founded by Japanese. Similarly,
there are scores of independent evangelical groups in Japan whose dominant
reference group tends to be American evangelicalism. While these independent
groups are indigenous in terms of the standard criteria of self-government, self-
support, and self-propagation, their "foreign-orientation" is still apparent in
their literature, tracts, and theology, which is largely "translated" material from
North America. Indigenous movements, on the other hand, are "native-oriented"

and do not measure their perception of religious truth by the standards of ortho-doxy defined by Western theology or ancient church councils. Whether sectar-ian or denominational, the important point is that all of these movements are indigenous in terms of the standard criteria of self-control, self-support, and self-propagation. All are self-governing and have adopted their own style of leader-ship and organization. None receive financial support from foreign churches and all are self-propagating (in fact, some even send their own missionaries abroad).

According to most indigenous movements, God's self-revelation did not end with the canon of the Christian Scriptures. God continues to reveal deeper truths to those who are open to the ongoing work of the Holy Spirit. While some of these movements operate with the closed canon (the Nonchurch movement, for example), many share a common belief that God continues to reveal new truths hidden from or as yet ungrasped by Western churches. Most of these groups produce their own literature, including monthly or quarterly magazines, editions of the Bible (sometimes specially edited versions), and collections of the founder's writings and lectures. If not revealing radically new truths, indigenous movements at least share in common the conviction that God is calling them to develop Japanese cultural expressions of the Christian faith that are at least as legitimate as the national churches and denominational forms that have emerged over the centuries in Europe and North America.

Although indigenous movements share many common features, they can be distinguished in terms of their self-understanding and claims to legitimacy. Religious organizations can be distinguished according to whether they claim to be "uniquely legitimate," thus denying the legitimacy claims of other groups, or "collegially legitimate," thus accepting the claims of other groups. This distinc-tion has been incorporated in the typology and is regarded as the basic feature that distinguishes a "sect" from a "denomination."[31]

The mission churches have a checkered history in this regard. Although often making efforts in cooperative Christian work, the competition and conflict between various "denominational" mission churches led many Japanese to regard them as sectarian groups, each claiming to be uniquely legitimate. In this typology, however, I have placed most transplanted mission churches in the denominational category, since this has usually been their self-understanding (even though not consistently practiced).[32]

Most indigenous movements are placed in the denominational category (for want of a better term) because they make only modest claims for them-selves.[33] The Nonchurch movement, The Way, Christ Heart Church, the

Original Gospel, and the Holy Ecclesia of Jesus, for example, only claim to be Japanese expressions of Christianity, not exclusive paths to salvation. In other words, they usually regard themselves as legitimate expressions of a Christianity for Japan, not as exclusive "vessels" of truth. Uchimura Kanzō, the founder of the Nonchurch movement, clearly articulated this point of view as follows:

> To us it makes no difference whether that man becomes a Roman Catholic, or a Greek Catholic, or a Baptist, or a Presbyterian, or a member of any one of the six-hundred and more of the Christian sects and churches, which, we hear, exist in Christendom. We are thankful, yea, we rejoice, when a man is saved from his sins to a pure, humble life in Jesus Christ. But missionaries seem not to rejoice and be thankful unless a heathen is converted and *he joins their own respective churches.*[34]

The central affirmations of most indigenous movements indicate that they understand their particular expression of Christianity to be a part of a larger Christian tradition. Nevertheless, some of these groups appear rather separatistic or sectarian at times because they usually do not emphasize ecumenical or cooperative relations with other Christian bodies and often criticize each other on various points of theology or practice. Many leaders in the Nonchurch movement, for example, have condemned the Original Gospel (Tabernacle) as a heretical movement because of its Pentecostal distinctives.

The Spirit of Jesus Church is the only group in the category of indigenous sects because of its tendency to emphasize exclusive truth claims. The Spirit of Jesus Church is consistently sectarian and regards all other Western and Japanese expressions of Christianity as apostate. Murai Jun, the founder of the movement, was extremely critical of conservative evangelical churches for their rejection of his pentecostal emphasis on speaking in tongues and healing. According to Murai, these groups had "blasphemed the Holy Spirit" and were unpardonable. He was equally harsh in his assessment of the indigenous Nonchurch movement for its rejection of spirit and water baptism, going so far as to say that "Mukyōkai cannot last very long since it is not something from heaven."[35]

With all due respect to Nitobe, it is only fair to note that Western churches are not fully responsible for the "sectarianism" and conflicting interpretations of Christianity in Japan. A study of indigenous Christian movements reminds us that there are numerous "homegrown" sources of conflict and diversity. The rather idealistic image of a "harmonious" Japan prior to the impact of the West is highly misleading. The Japanese population has always been more heterogeneous than such popular characterizations would suggest. It is probably safe to say that the myth of the homogeneous Japanese is largely a creation of the Meiji, Taishō, and Shōwa eras. Prior to the Meiji Restoration and unification of the population under the emperor system and State Shinto, Japan lacked a strong national identity. Too often, in fact, we forget that premodern Japan was characterized by its diversity, and that there were politicized Buddhist sects, protest groups comprised of peasants and small landowners, and various groups distinguished by loyalties to different lords and clans. D. C. Holtom, writing during the Second World War, explained that the unification of Japan under Shinto nationalism was extremely difficult because of this social, political, and religious diversity:

> Modern Japan has had to struggle for the unification and coordination of her national life in the face of strongly diversifying, not to say disintegrating, tendencies. There has been much internal heterogeneity to overcome. The particularism of a feudal regime that was split into rival clans and pocketed behind mountain barriers and secluded on separate islands has not even yet been fully transcended. *Religious diversity has revealed itself in a tendency toward separatism that seems to reflect what amounts almost to a national genius for sect-making and for breaking up into small esoteric groups.*[36]

Holtom goes on to point out that in Japan this diversity has usually been under the control of a ruling class or small elite from above.

The typological framework introduced in this chapter is only intended to provide an initial orientation to the study of indigenous movements by delineating their basic characteristics and clarifying their relationship to imported religious bodies. While self-government, self-support, and self-propagation are understood as the minimum requirements for an indigenous church, indigenization involves much more than mere organizational independence. It also refers to the process whereby foreign-born religions are transformed through contact with native religion and culture. This transformation may involve new organizational forms, new styles of leadership, and adaptations in beliefs, rituals, and liturgies. In the following chapter I will sketch the social background of these indigenous movements and consider the role of charismatic minor founders in the development of these new cultural forms.

CHAPTER THREE

Charisma, Minor Founders, and Indigenous Movements

T HOSE OF US familiar only with the world of established churches, denominational bureaucracies, and large Christian institutions tend to forget
that Christianity began as a new religious movement with a leader who
was known as a healer and exorcist. In *Jesus: A New Vision*, Marcus J. Borg draws
attention to the charismatic nature of the early Jesus movement and maintains
that it is necessary for us to give serious attention to the "world of Spirit" in order
to accurately understand the place of Jesus in the Judeo-Christian tradition. The
world of Spirit, he explains, refers to

> another dimension or layer or level of reality in addition to the visible world of
> our ordinary experience. This notion of "another world," understood as actual
> even though nonmaterial, is quite alien to the modern way of thinking. The

modern worldview or "picture of reality" sees reality as having essentially one dimension, the visible and material realm.... But the notion of another reality, a world of Spirit, was the common property of virtually every culture before ours, constituting what has been called the "primordial tradition."

According to Borg's analysis, Jesus belonged to the charismatic stream of Judaism that took this worldview for granted, and he served as a mediator between the world of everyday reality and the world of spirit.[1]

It is widely recognized that early Christianity continued to develop as a part of this charismatic stream. The Acts of the Apostles and various New Testament letters indicate that the disciples of Jesus and many leaders in the early Christian church were also deeply rooted in the world of Spirit.[2] Prophetic messages from God, speaking in tongues, healing, and exorcism were important features of Christianity as it spread through the Roman empire.[3] In time, however, charismatic gifts declined, and the rituals of healing and exorcism were institutionalized in the priesthood and became incorporated into the sacramental system of the Roman Catholic Church. The renewed interest in the Scriptures that characterized the Protestant Reformation, we should note, did not extend to the New Testament materials on charismatic gifts and healing. It has only been in the last century that these "spiritual gifts" have again become a prominent feature of Christianity in various regions of the world.

The reappearance of charismatic Christianity is due in part to the indigenous responses to transplanted Protestant mission churches from Europe and North America. Over the course of the past century scores of Protestant mission organizations have established churches throughout Asia and Africa. For the most part these missionary efforts have been by churches that no longer recognize the use of charismatic gifts or healing rituals. One particularly interesting and persistent pattern of response to this missionary movement has been the development of independent and indigenous Christian movements in various regions of the non-Western world. These movements are generally founded by charismatic individuals who accept the Christian faith but reject the missionary carriers and their "Western" and "doctrinal" understanding of religion. In many cases the size of these indigenous movements has surpassed that of the mission churches (whose sponsoring denominations in North America and Europe are struggling with serious declines in membership). A decade ago, according to D. B. Barrett, there were already some 332 million Pentecostal-charismatic Christians worldwide. Most of these individuals belonged to one of the 11,000 Pentecostal or 3,000 independent charismatic denominations, though some were involved in the charismatic renewal movement within one of the old established churches. Barrett emphasizes that the growth of Pentecostal-charismatic forms of Christianity is truly multicultural, with members "found in 8,000 ethnolinguistic cultures and speaking 7,000 languages."[4] Christianity in Japan certainly reflects this global pattern of development (though the growth figures are on a much smaller scale than in South Korea and various African countries).

In approaching the study of Christianity in Japan, it is important to recognize that in some respects it is a "New Religion" in this context and cannot be viewed as an established religion, as in many Western countries. In referring to Christianity as a New Religion, I am not simply drawing attention to the fact that it is a foreign-born tradition that only arrived in Japan relatively recently. Rather, "newness" is related primarily to the fact that the indigenous Christian movements broke away from the mission churches and share many features not only with other Japanese New Religions but also with the early Christian movement. The prominent role of charismatic leaders and the manifestation of various charismatic phenomena are important features of indigenous Christian movements that distinguish them from most transplanted mission churches. One cannot explain the break with the mission churches nor account for the various innovations in Christian belief, practice, and social organization apart from these charismatic founders. In this sense, therefore, it is necessary to analyze these Christian-related movements as New Religions in the Japanese context. Hence Byron Earhart's proposal that we give attention to *precipitating factors*, *enabling factors*, and *personal-innovative factors* in the rise of New Religions has influenced the shape of the following discussion.[5]

THE SOCIAL BACKGROUND OF THE INDIGENOUS MOVEMENTS

As noted in the previous chapter, the development of numerous indigenous and independent expressions of Christianity represents a nuanced response to the missionary initiatives: an acceptance of Christianity, but a rejection of the missionary carriers. For the most part, these movements began by breaking away from the Protestant mission churches rather than from the Roman Catholic, Anglican, or Russian Orthodox traditions. This poses some interesting questions for Protestant missionary theology and practice. What is it about the Protestant approach to Christianity that these Japanese Christians were unwilling to accept?

Although the Japanese founders of indigenous Christian traditions were indebted to the Protestant missionary movement in many respects, tensions and conflicts emerged over time as a result of fundamental differences in their understanding of the relationship between the Gospel and Japanese culture.

"Christ against culture," to borrow H. Richard Niebuhr's familiar expression, was the perspective that shaped the attitudes of most missionaries. This was true for the earliest pioneer missionaries of the late nineteenth century as well as for the wave of evangelical Protestant missionaries that arrived in Japan during the postwar period. Most came with a great zeal for evangelizing Japan, but their theological training had provided them with very few resources for understanding other cultures and religious traditions. Without denying that Protestant missionaries have also been "transformers of culture" through their activities in the fields of education (particularly for women) and social welfare, the fact remains that their understanding of the relationship between the Gospel and Japanese culture has been fundamentally negative.

Missionary theology and practice have tended to emphasize a total discontinuity between the Christian faith and Japanese religious traditions and practices. Indigenous traditions needed to be "displaced" or removed to make room for the Gospel and authentic Christian faith. The missionaries had the "truth of the Gospel," and the Japanese were totally lost in sin. Cyril Powles sums it up succinctly:

> American Protestantism challenged the Japanese tradition. Theologically, it regarded the latter as pagan and corrupt. Culturally, it believed it to be archaic and outmoded. The American missionary therefore looked for the conversion of Japan to Christianity, which implied the destruction of the old cults.[6]

While there were certainly some exceptions to this perspective,[7] the dominant missionary model viewed Christianity as antithetical to Japanese religious culture (see figure 2).

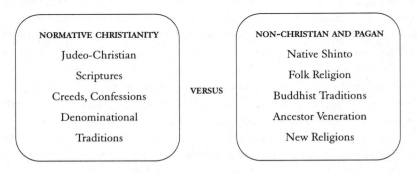

NORMATIVE CHRISTIANITY		NON-CHRISTIAN AND PAGAN
Judeo-Christian		Native Shinto
Scriptures		Folk Religion
Creeds, Confessions	VERSUS	Buddhist Traditions
Denominational		Ancestor Veneration
Traditions		New Religions

Figure 2. Dominant 19th–early 20th-c. Protestant Missionary Model

Although the missionaries were capable of distinguishing the Christian faith from Japanese culture, they often lacked such critical reflection when it came to their own cultures. It has been noted in many different contexts that foreign missionaries often fail to distinguish their national culture from the religious faith they seek to transplant. Many Protestant missionaries operated as though their transplanted churches and traditions were the normative expression of the Judeo-Christian Scriptures. Transplanted missionary cultures, which included creeds, confessions, polity, and the missionary way of doing things, were the authentic expression of Christian faith. Protestant missionaries to Japan have been no exception, as Joseph Kitagawa explains:

> More often than not, European and American missionaries attempted to Westernize as well as Christianize the Japanese people and culture. Japanese converts were made to feel, consciously or unconsciously, that to decide for Christ also implied the total surrender of their souls to the missionaries. The task of evangelism was interpreted by most missionaries as transplanting *in toto* the church in the West on Japanese soil, including the ugly features of denominationalism—an unhappy assumption, indeed.[8]

There was an initial attempt to establish a nondenominational church in Yokohama, as we noted earlier, but it was a short-lived experiment. As the number of missionaries and denominations increased each felt it must recreate its own denominational tradition on Japanese soil. Hence Presbyterians felt that an authentic church in Japan must adopt the Westminster Confession and organize churches with elders, sessions, presbyteries, and synods. Methodists, of course, needed a Bishop. Baptists and Congregationalists, on the other hand, wanted no authority above the local church, pastor, or missionary. Despite the fact that these various traditions and interpretations of Christianity had developed in very different cultural-national-political contexts over many centuries, missionaries assumed that their tradition was the "authentic" or "normative" one. The "plurality of cultures" within the Protestant missionary movement was not overlooked by the native Christians. Uchimura Kanzō expressed his pessimism regarding the prospects of transplanted Western Christianity as early as 1886 with the following words:

> Which of the *nineteen* different Christian denominations which are now engaged in evangelizing Japan is to gain the strongest foothold there? In our view—and let us express this view with the most hearty sympathy toward the earnest endeavors of the missionaries of all the denominations—none of them. One reason is that mere transplanting of anything exotic is never known on

35

Japanese soil. Be it a political, scientific, or social matter, before it can be acclimatized in Japan, it must pass through great modifications in the hands of the Japanese.[9]

Early on in missionary circles there were certainly discussions on developing indigenous churches, but this was understood primarily in terms of the "three selfs": self-support, self-control, and self-propagation. The idea that Japanese Christians might have their own insights and ways of organizing and practicing the faith was generally not entertained. Transmission of the missionary culture—without corruption or addition—was the primary concern. It is not surprising that Japanese found this displacement theology rather abrasive and hard to swallow. In a culture that had found a place for Buddhist, Shinto, and various folk beliefs and practices, the stress by Christian missionaries on exclusive belief and practice required too great a reorientation. Even many Japanese who made a commitment to the Christian faith struggled with lingering doubts about the "absoluteness" of missionary versions of Christianity.

After Japanese converts were introduced to the Scriptures and went on to serious theological studies, many realized that it was possible to distinguish the Christian faith and biblical tradition from the theology, church polity, and cultural values of the American and European missionaries. As native leaders gained a more critical understanding of the Christian tradition and saw the significant differences between the mission churches, they began to assert themselves more confidently as equals of their missionary teachers. The fact that numerous denominations were competing for converts on Japanese soil (each with its own doctrinal peculiarities and forms of government) indicated to many leaders that there might be room for Japanese interpretations and cultural expressions of Christianity.

For the founders of independent Christian movements, the transplanted missionary traditions, though a valuable resource to draw upon, were hardly the absolute truth. As the Japanese struggled to make sense of the Christian faith for themselves, they found it necessary to criticize missionary versions of Christianity on a number of grounds. Many Japanese leaders sought to distinguish between the religion of Jesus recorded in the Scriptures and the interpretation, and cultural expression, of Christianity that had been transplanted by mission churches. A recurring phrase in the Japanese Christian literature is that transplanted Christianity is *batā-kusai* (literally, "reeking of butter"). In other words, Japanese recognized that missionaries were bringing too much unnecessary (and "smelly") cultural baggage with them as they sought to transmit the

Gospel. This was essentially a critique of the missionary imposition of Western denominational forms. Writing in 1926, Uchimura Kanzō reflected on his struggle with missionaries over this issue:

> I am blamed by missionaries for upholding Japanese Christianity. They say that Christianity is a universal religion, and to uphold Japanese Christianity is to make a universal religion a national religion. Very true. But do not these very missionaries uphold sectional or denominational forms of Christianity which are not very different from national Christianity?... Is not Episcopalianism essentially an English Christianity, Presbyterianism a Scotch Christianity, Lutheranism a German Christianity, and so forth? Why, for instance, call a universal religion "Cumberland Presbyterianism"? If it is not wrong to apply the name of a district in the state of Kentucky to Christianity, why is it wrong for me to apply the name of my country to the same? I think I have as much right to call my Christianity Japanese as thousands of Christians in the Cumberland Valley have the right to call their Christianity by the name of the valley they live in.[10]

Uchimura's observations effectively relativized the absolutist claims of many mission churches and cleared the way for other Japanese to move ahead with the creation of Japanese cultural expressions of this universal faith.

Teshima Ikurō, the founder of the Original Gospel movement, a Pentecostal expression of Nonchurch Christianity, elaborated upon Uchimura's view with his distinction between a religion's external forms and its inner reality or truth.[11] He argued that missionaries had brought the external forms of Western Christianity (music, architecture, doctrine, and rituals, for example) and given them to Japanese to wear like uniforms. The heart of religion, however, is spiritual and hidden from the eye. In worrying so much about transplanting the proper "shell" of Christianity, Teshima concluded that missionaries had failed to effectively communicate the heart of the faith. In a word, missionaries should have been more concerned with communicating a spiritual message and allowed the Japanese to develop their own cultural expression of the faith.

Another common criticism of the mission churches had to do with their doctrinal rigidity and intellectualism and their failure to give adequate attention to the experiential dimension of faith. Dissatisfaction with this overly cerebral version of Christianity appears in the writings of all the founders of indigenous movements. Some refer to it disparagingly as "conceptual Christianity," while others suggest it is a lifeless, hardened, or frozen form of Christianity. This hardened doctrinal understanding of Christianity, these critics maintained, prevented missionaries from seeing the experiential dimension of faith so central to the New Testament as well as the truth and goodness outside of their narrow denominational traditions.

While these theological differences were the source of considerable conflict, what the Japanese leaders found most unbearable was the condescending attitude of missionaries. Many missionaries, it seems, were unwilling to receive instruction from their Japanese disciples. Uchimura Kanzō severely criticized this characteristic as he argued for an indigenous church:

> Missionaries come to us to patronize us, to exercise lordship over us, in a word, to "convert" us; *not* to become our equals and friends, certainly *not* to become our servants and wash our feet.... We believe that the Gospel of Christ is the power of God unto salvation to every one that believeth; but unless through God's grace we save ourselves, we shall not be saved—certainly *not* by foreign churches and missionaries.[12]

An incident recorded in the biography of Matsumura Kaiseki (1859–1939), an early convert of Dutch Reformed missionary James Ballagh and a member of the Yokohama Band, illustrates the tensions that existed between missionary teachers and their students. Matsumura, who had returned to Ballagh's school to assist with the teaching and supervision of students, recalls that on one occasion he explained to Ballagh that all of their missionary teaching and preaching would be of no avail if they continued to treat Japanese as no more than cooks or helper boys. Coming to her husband's defense, Mrs. Ballagh accused Matsumura of being possessed by the devil. He was promptly dismissed from his school responsibilities. After a varied career as a pastor, newspaper editor, and teacher, he eventually went on to organize an independent church, The Way.[13]

The founder of Christ Heart Church, Kawai Shinsui, who also began his Christian training and ministry at a mission-related theological institution, departed because of conflict with the missionaries, and eventually went on to establish an independent church.[14] Following theological studies at Tōhoku Gakuin College, an institution in Sendai related to the German Reformed Church, Kawai was assigned to a struggling mission church in the town of Tsuruoka in Yamagata Prefecture in 1901. Upon receiving word that his father was extremely ill, he left Tsuruoka to check on his condition without prior permission from the mission office in Sendai. His father's illness was so serious that he had his wife stay and care for him and requested a new assignment nearer his father's home. The mission board responded that it could neither give him another assignment nor approve of husband and wife living separately. Kawai, concluding that the missionary leadership was unreasonable and that his

Christian conscience demanded he fulfill his filial duties, terminated his association with the mission. Following a brief term as editor of the *Hakodate Daily Newspaper* and several years as principal of Kyōai Girls' School in Maebashi City, Gumma Prefecture, Kawai was appointed as head of the education department of the Gunze Silk Manufacturing Company in 1909. In 1927 Kawai established the independent Christ Heart Church within the grounds of Gunze.

However, the development of indigenous Christian movements was not merely the result of personality conflicts and power struggles with foreign missionaries. These disagreements, we must remember, did not occur in a placid environment. By the late Meiji period the social climate, following an earlier phase of worshipping everything Occidental, had become decidedly anti-Western and nationalistic. In his study of attitudes toward modernization in Japan, Marius Jansen notes that "the responses of representative and leading Japanese were necessarily conditioned by the climate of opinion within which they moved."[15] This statement is equally valid with respect to Japanese Christian leaders active during this period. The establishment of State Shinto and the revival of Confucianism were thus accompanied by parallel developments among Japanese Christians.[16] In the increasingly nationalistic environment the identification of Christianity with the West had become a stumbling block to propagation, and many leaders became convinced that "Japanization" or "de-Westernization" was the only way forward.[17] Independent indigenous movements were the most obvious expression of this process. While nationalism and conflict with missionaries were important precipitating factors that clarify the timing of these movements, we must consider other factors to explain their content.

THE ENABLING FACTOR: IMPORTED AND NATIVE ELEMENTS

In referring to indigenous Christian movements as New Religions, I do not intend to suggest that they were created *ex nihilo*. New religions do not appear out of thin air, as Byron Earhart points out, but draw on "vital elements of the religious heritage."[18] Consequently, we must give attention to this "enabling factor" in the development of New Religions.

In the Japanese context, New Religions draw from a vast reservoir of beliefs and practices related to ancestors, the spirit world, Buddhism, Shinto, and Confucianism. In his book *Salvation Religions in Contemporary Society*, for example, Shimazono Susumu, one of the leading scholars of Japanese New Religions, identifies syncretic folk religion, lay associations of the Nichiren Buddhist tradition, and Confucianistic moral cultivation movements as the three primary sources that founders have drawn on in the development of new religious movements during the past two centuries.[19]

Similarly, although the charismatic founders of Christian movements may have unusual insights and creative insights, they do not start from scratch when organizing a new church or movement. Rather, they draw on the imported teachings, rituals, and organizational forms of the mission churches as well as on various indigenous religious traditions. Notwithstanding the popular myth of the homogeneous Japanese, it is necessary for us to recognize the cultural diversity of this receiving society in order to understand these new indigenous forms of Christianity. Religious diversity (folk religion, Shinto, Buddhist sects, Confucianism) and competing group loyalties (rival clans, social classes, and regions) provided the complex matrix for Japan's encounter with Christianity. This is a significant point when we consider the reception, understanding, and reinterpretation of Christianity by indigenous movements in Japan. In our study of indigenization it is necessary to distinguish between the beliefs and practices of the various social strata that constitute the native culture to which Christianity has been forced to adapt. At the very least, we must distinguish between what might be called "elite religiosity" and "mass religiosity," the former being associated with the educated ruling class of samurai (and their successors) and the latter with the "ruled" majority of Japanese.

The Confucian ethos has certainly been a dominant element of the "elite" strata, while folk religion has provided the basic orientation for the masses. In terms of the movements under consideration in this study, those organized in the first three decades of this century largely represent an indigenous Christian expression of "elite religiosity," while those organized since the 1940s have closer connections with the folk religious traditions.[20]

In spite of the fact that indigenous movements share a number of features in common, each represents a distinct Christian subculture and must be understood as such. The founders of Japanese movements have maintained that truth and goodness are found not only in the Bible and Christian tradition but also in the religions of Asia, and that new insights could be drawn from spiritual experience or additional revelation from God. This inclusivistic approach to understanding Christianity is illustrated in figure 3. The religious experiences of indigenous leaders and their unique combination of foreign and native elements have given rise to the development of new Christian traditions in Japan. According to most indigenous movements, religious truth is not limited by the standards of orthodoxy as defined by Western theology and ancient church councils.[21] Their newly crafted theology interprets the Bible in the light of native culture without

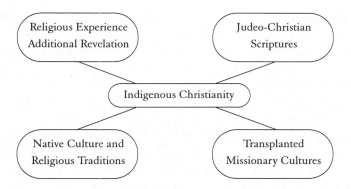

Figure 3. Religious and Cultural Sources of Indigenous Christianity

the authoritative guidance of the ecumenical creeds. As one might expect, most missionary interpreters of Christianity maintained that the "orthodox" faith was to be based solely on the Scriptures (as defined and understood by the missionary's denominational tradition) and regarded religious experiences and additional sources of truth as unreliable or completely out of bounds.[22]

It is no easy task to unravel the various transplanted and indigenous elements that have been adapted and incorporated into Japanese Christian subcultures. The Judeo-Christian Scriptures add to the complexity of the situation, since many of the movements under consideration have attempted to recover "apostolic Christianity" by reading the Bible unmediated by church tradition and interpretation. This strategy is hardly new, and has been attempted repeatedly throughout the history of Christianity. The attempt to "return to the origins," however, inevitably results in the creation of new cultural forms. It has certainly led the Japanese in many different directions. This should hardly surprise us since the New Testament canon itself has preserved a "pluralism" of Christian traditions. In a widely known study, James D. G. Dunn identifies Jewish Christianity, Hellenistic Christianity, Apocalyptic Christianity, and Early Catholicism as the primary traditions contained in the New Testament, noting:

> *There was no single normative form of Christianity in the first century.* When we ask about the Christianity of the NT we are not asking about any one entity; rather we encounter different types of Christianity, each of which viewed others as too extreme in one respect or other—too conservatively Jewish or too influenced by antinomian or gnostic thought and practice, too enthusiastic or tending towards too much institutionalization.[23]

41

The differences between the various indigenous movements are related in part to those strands or traditions of the New Testament that they emphasize or neglect. Just like churches in the West, indigenous movements invariably operate with a "canon within the canon."

Table 3 highlights the dominant foreign and native influences on selected minor founders, whom we shall take up in more detail shortly. The religious experiences of minor founders and their unique combination of exogenous and indigenous elements have provided the basis for new formulations of Christian beliefs and doctrine, new rituals and forms of religious practice, new forms of social organization, and in some cases an enlarged canon of sacred texts. In the following chapters we will explore in more detail how different streams of foreign influence (reformed theology, pentecostalism, dispensationalism, Unitarianism) have been mixed in unique ways with indigenous elements to produce these alternative Japanese Christian traditions.

Table 3. Selected Minor Founders and Indigenous Movements

MINOR FOUNDER	MOVEMENT	DOMINANT WESTERN INFLUENCES	DOMINANT NATIVE INFLUENCES
Uchimura Kanzō (1861–1930)	Nonchurch Movement (1901)	William S. Clark, Professor and lay Christian, Sapporo Agricultural College, Amherst	Confucianism *Bushidō*
Matsumura Kaiseki (1859–1939)	Church of Japan (1907) The Way (1907)	James Ballagh, Dutch Reformed Church, Yokohama Band, New Theology, Darwinism	Neo-Confucianism (Yōmeigaku), Shinto
Kawai Shinsui (1867–1962)	Christ Heart Church (1927)	Tōhoku Gakuin College (German Reformed Church)	Confucianism, Buddhism, mountain asceticism, Kyōkenjutsu
Murai Jun (1897–1970)	Spirit of Jesus Church (1941)	Aoyama Gakuin College (Methodism), True Jesus Church, Taiwan, Unitarian Pentecostalism	Folk religious traditions and the ancestor cult
Ōtsuki Takeji (1906–)	Holy Ecclesia of Jesus (1946)	Dispensationalism, Holiness tradition, revivalism, Roman Catholic spirituality, Jewish traditions, Zionism	*Nembutsu*, ancestor cult
Teshima Ikurō (1910–1973)	Original Gospel or Tabernacle (1948)	Zionism, Jewish traditions	Uchimura Kanzō and Nonchurch movement, folk religious traditions, mountain asceticism
Nakahara Masao (1948–)	Okinawa Christian Gospel (1977)	Plymouth Brethren Missionary influence, Dispensationalism	Okinawan shamanism

MINOR FOUNDERS, INNOVATION, AND CHARISMATIC AUTHORITY

As we have seen, the anti-Western social climate, growing nationalism, and dissatisfaction with Western missionaries were important precipitating factors in the development of indigenous Christian movements. However, they still do not provide a complete explanation of the birth of these movements. Like other Japanese New Religions, indigenous Christian movements represent much more than reactions to social crises and imported Christianity. The break with Western mission churches and the creation of viable alternative forms required strong charismatic leaders. "The innovative decision of the founder," Byron Earhart points out, "cannot be completely subsumed by either social factors or the influence of prior religious factors."[24]

Drawing attention to this "personal-innovative factor" in the study of religion is hardly new, but it is a factor worth reemphasizing in relation to the study of indigenous movements. Writing years ago, Joachim Wach also emphasized the need to consider the central experiences of the founders in order to understand the development of religions:

> A sociological study of the personalities of the great founders of religion involves a difficulty which must be clearly recognized. The sociologist, though not called upon to deny or confirm religious claims, cannot ignore them. In estimating the effects of the initiative of the founders, their own theological claims must be taken into account, because the sociological effectiveness of their work is dependent on the significance which they attach to themselves and to their message.[25]

How are we to understand the charismatic leaders who play such a key role in the development of indigenous movements? Max Weber made no distinction between charismatic individuals who renewed an old religion and those who founded new religions, but subsumed both under the category of prophet.[26] Werner Stark, however, drew attention to the need for another concept to deal with innovations within a religious tradition:

> In order to describe Paul of Tarsus correctly, we need some such concept as that of a minor founder. In Paul, we behold an archetype which was to be reincarnated many times in the history of the Church. Behind him, there appear such figures as Benedict, Francis, Dominic, Bernard, Ignatius, Alphonso, and many others. They were all minor founders, revolutionaries and reformers and even reactionaries (goers back to the original) rolled into one, and certainly not routinizers in the sense of Kipling and Weber.[27]

43

Although Stark's comments are limited to the role of minor founders in the history of European or Western Christianity, this category seems equally relevant to understanding the development of Christianity in non-Western contexts.

More recently, Anthony Blasi has drawn attention to the category of "minor founder" in his study of early Christianity, *Making Charisma: The Social Construction of Paul's Public Image*. Arguing that Paul was much more than a "routinizer" of the charisma of Jesus, Blasi characterizes him as

> a "minor founder," a founder who resembles major founders in so far as he was an agent of change but who was more conservative than they insofar as he maintained a basic continuity with what had come before him. Paul did something new, but he did it within an already recognizable Christian subculture.[28]

Similarly, the charismatic leaders of indigenous Christian movements also create something new, but in recognizable continuity with an existing religious tradition. Minor founders in Japan departed from the religious traditions imported by foreign missionaries in significant ways, but at the same time passed the Christian heritage on to people in this new cultural context. Perhaps we could summarize by saying that a "minor founder" is a charismatic individual who gives birth to a new religious movement in an effort to address the needs of a new type of member, while at the same time conceiving of the movement as an extension, elaboration, or fulfillment of an existing religious tradition.

Although the indigenization of Christianity in Japan is the focus of this study, it is interesting to consider suggestive hints and parallels from the history of Buddhism in Japan. A number of Japanese scholars have noted the important role played by charismatic native leaders in the development of Japanese forms of Buddhism during the Kamakura period (1192–1336). Innovative Buddhist leaders such as Hōnen (1133–1212), Shinran (1173–1263), and Nichiren (1222–1282) did much more than copy or translate Chinese Buddhist traditions. "New sects of 'Japanese' Buddhism," Fujii Masao explains, "were established through recording the founder's particular religious experience and particular doctrines."[29] Similarly, Hoshino Eiki points out that these "founding figures in Japanese Buddhism appear, not only as eminently creative figures that initiated new doctrinal systems and methods of practice, but as beings that transcend time and place and have secured a kind of eternity in their charisma." In short, the indigenization and popularization of Buddhism in Japan had a great deal to do with these charismatic and innovative leaders.[30]

Interesting parallels have also been noted in the study of other Japanese New Religions. Shimazono Susumu, for example, makes a similar distinction between those founders who are regarded as the "carriers" of ultimate truth and the embodiment of salvation and those who are seen as reformers or revitalizers of an existing religious tradition. In the latter case, the "founder-like leader" is essentially trying to recover the "original teaching" or rearticulate an existing religious tradition under new circumstances. The founders of Risshō Kōsei Kai and Sōka Gakkai, for example, are regarded as revitalizers of the Nichiren Buddhist tradition rather than creators of entirely new religious traditions. Shimazono refers to this process as the placing of a particular religious movement within an existing tradition. This is precisely what has occurred in the development of indigenous Christian movements in Japan.[31]

From a sociological perspective, "charisma" and "charismatic authority" can only be understood in terms of the social relationship between leader and followers. An individual may claim to have had direct contact with God and to have received new revelations, but a movement will not be born unless the new message meets the needs and aspirations of a significant audience. The message must have some appeal, and potential followers must be convinced that the messenger has a special connection with the sacred.[32] The break with existing tradition—in this case with imported mission churches—requires a powerful figure whose personhood authenticates the inevitable rupture. While founders vary in the degree to which they reject existing traditions and introduce new elements, at the very least they claim to have direct access to the sacred and an independent basis of religious authority. In Weberian terms, therefore, the appearance of minor founders in Japanese Christianity represents a shift from institutional "charisma" (i.e., the authority of the mission churches, creeds, clergy, and traditions) to the "personal charisma" of Japanese leaders.

Thus the charismatic authority of minor founders is based not only on their charismatic personalities but also on the persuasiveness of their claims to direct contact with the sacred and, occasionally, to additional revelations. Kawai Shinsui, the founder of Christ Heart Church, for example, argued that direct religious experience—*satori*—is what is required for real confidence, unmoving faith, and authority in religious matters. In his lectures on the New Testament letter to the Galatians, Kawai finds parallels between Paul's relationship with the church in Jerusalem and his own relationship with the mission churches.[33] According to Kawai's reading of Galatians, Paul taught that the core of the faith is direct experience of and relationship to God. Although Paul was criticized for not being a direct disciple of Jesus and had to face challenges to his authority, he maintained that his personal encounter with the living Christ on the road to Damascus legitimized his ministry. The legitimacy of Kawai's own ministry—

a ministry independent of the mission churches—was likewise grounded in profound religious experiences, in Kawai's case gained through intense training in remote mountain areas. Kawai elaborates this experiential foundation in his autobiography as follows: "As Jehovah appeared to Moses in thunder on Mt. Sinai, and Christ called to Paul in lightning in the neighborhood of Damascus God renewed all things in me through sacred Mt. Fuji."[34]

All of the other minor founders likewise emphasize the importance of direct encounter with God through the Scriptures or religious experience—that is, through ways unmediated by Western theology or tradition. In addition to religious experience, miraculous healings have been important support for religious authority with most founders in the early stages of these movements. Thus Matsumura, Kawai, Murai, Teshima, Ōtsuki, and Nakahara—six of the seven founders included in table 3 above—each claimed to have either experienced personal healing or been used by God to heal others.

During subsequent phases of the institutionalization process the charismatic authority of these minor founders is reconfirmed and routinized. In some cases the teachings and writings of the founder come to be viewed as of equal or similar authority to the Bible. Even if religious groups distinguish in principle between the canon (Bible) and the founder's writings, in practice the latter tend to function with similar authority in the community. Religious services normally include numerous references to the founder's teachings, actions, or writings. Just as Christians normally view the Hebrew Bible and Jesus' interpretations of these ancient texts as "sacred," members of indigenous Christian movements tend to merge the Scriptures and their founder's interpretation.[35]

These minor founders sometimes even become the object of veneration. Kawai Shinsui, for example, is paid ritual respect, with bows to his photograph at the beginning and end of each service. His writings are also quoted as frequently as the Judeo-Christian scriptures. On a number of occasions I have even heard the deceased founder addressed in prayer ("Chichinaru Kamisama, Iesu Kirisuto, mata Kawai Shinsui Sensei" ["Father God, Jesus Christ, and Kawai Shinsui..."]), expressing the conviction that he is now in the immediate company of the heavenly hosts.

This tendency to venerate minor founders has a long history, as Nakamura Hajime explains with reference to Japanese Buddhism:

> One result of this absolute devotion to a specific person is that the faithful of the various Japanese sects are extreme in the veneration with which they acknowledge the founder of the sect and perform religious ceremonies around him as the nucleus. *One has absolute faith in the master as well as in the Buddha, with-*

out feeling that there is the slightest contradiction. It is not that one pays less attention to the Buddha, but the idea is perhaps that a profound faith in the master
and devotion to the Buddha have the same significance.[36]

In much the same way, members of Christ Heart Church appear to experience
no cognitive conflict in "believing in Jesus Christ" and venerating the founder,
Kawai Shinsui, who made the salvific significance of Christ real to them
through his teaching and example.[37]

What distinguishes indigenous Christian movements from other New
Religions is the fact that minor founders link their new insights to the existing
religious tradition. This can take the form of "fulfillment" or "restorationist"
explanations. In fulfillment explanations the teaching of these founders is
understood as the additional truth Jesus promised his disciples ("when the Spirit
comes he will guide you into all truth," John 16:13). This new insight fulfills or
even supersedes the understanding of Christianity found in the Western
churches. In restorationist explanations Western churches are viewed as degen-
erate, and indigenous movements assert that they are only recovering or restoring important truths once held by the early church. No matter how severely
these movements are assessed or criticized by mission churches or the dominant
orthodoxy, in one form or another each regards itself as a continuation of the
Christian religion or, at the very least, as a fuller expression of the teachings and
intention of Jesus.

THE REAPPEARANCE OF CHARISMATIC CHRISTIANITY

All of the indigenous movements established in Japan had charismatic beginnings and emphasized direct religious experience. The break with the mission
churches required the strong leadership of charismatic individuals who had self-
authenticating religious insight and authority. Japanese Christianity, as
Uchimura Kanzō put it, "is Christianity received by Japanese directly from God
without any foreign intermediary; no more, no less."[38] For Uchimura this direct
encounter with God came about through reading the Scriptures with one's own
eyes and heart. This required that one ignore the denominational traditions and
creeds and "return to the original Scriptures." Uchimura's Sunday services
became, therefore, Bible lectures that explored the original Greek and Hebrew.[39]

Without denying the importance of Uchimura's movement in the development of Christianity in Japan, it must be recognized that the Nonchurch movement represents only one type of indigenous Christianity. The attention given to

Uchimura Kanzō by both Japanese and Western scholars and the productivity of many biblical scholars associated with the Nonchurch movement have contributed to a one-sided and somewhat distorted understanding of indigenous Christianity. Uchimura clearly served as an inspiration to many other Japanese Christians, but his interpretation of Christianity, and the Nonchurch movement itself, subsequently became the target of criticism because of their intellectual and Confucian orientation.

While the charismatic nature (in Weberian or sociological terms) of Uchimura and other founders is important, in what remains of this chapter I would like to consider the broader manifestation of the "world of Spirit" in indigenous Christian movements. As may be seen in table 4, the development of most indigenous movements has been accompanied by a wide range of charismatic or Pentecostal phenomena. In many respects these indigenous expressions of Christianity represent a revitalization of the primordial spiritualistic worldview referred to above. In spite of Uchimura's personal charisma, the Nonchurch movement has lacked the charismatic phenomena associated with Christianity in the New Testament and reemphasized by most indigenous movements in Japan. Perhaps it would be more accurate to say that charismatic expressions of Nonchurch Christianity have been forced to develop as separate movements—both the Original Gospel movement and the Japan Ecclesia of Christ were founded by teachers who began as members of the Nonchurch movement.[40] Thus the charismatic features that characterize most indigenous movements deserve fuller treatment.

Continuing Revelation and Modified Canon

The traditional Protestant understanding of revelation has been that God spoke through the prophets, Jesus, and the apostles, and that this process of revelation ended with the canonization of the Old and New Testament Scriptures. Most Protestant denominations maintain that the charismatic gifts also ended with the early church, since their primary purpose was to confirm the truth of the Gospel for the first Christian communities. Indigenous movements, for the most part, maintain that God's self-revelation did not end with the canon of the Christian Scriptures, and that God continues to reveal deeper truths to those who are open to the ongoing work of the Holy Spirit. While most of these movements operate with the closed canon, many share a common belief that God continues to reveal new truths hidden from or as yet ungrasped by Western churches.

Table 4. Charismatic Features of Indigenous Christianity

INDIGENOUS MOVEMENT	YEAR ORGANIZED	CONTINUING REVELATION	SPIRIT BAPTISM	SPEAKING IN TONGUES	HEALING AND/ OR EXORCISM	SPIRIT WORLD INTERACTION	EXTENDED OR MODIFIED CANON
Nonchurch movement 無教会	1901	▓					
The Way 道会	1907	▓	▓		▲ ▓		
Christ Heart Church 基督心宗教団	1927	▓	▓		● ▓	▓	▓
Glorious Gospel Christian Church 栄光の福音キリスト教団	1936		▓		▓		▓
Living Christ One Ear of Wheat Church 活けるキリスト一麦教会	1939		▓	■	▓	▓	
Christian Canaan Church 基督カーナン教団	1940		▓		▓		
Japan Ecclesia of Christ 日本キリスト召団	1940		▓		▓		
Spirit of Jesus Church イエス之御霊教会	1941		▓	▓	▓	▓	
Holy Ecclesia of Jesus 聖イエス会	1946		▓		▓		
The Sanctifying Christ Church 聖成基督教団	1948		▓		▓		
Original Gospel (Tabernacle) 原始福音 (幕屋)	1948		▓	▓	▓	▓	
Life-Giving Christ 活かすキリスト	1966				▓		
Okinawa Christian Gospel 沖縄キリスト教福音	1977				▓	▓	

Shaded cells indicate the presence of related phenomena either in the earlier stages of development or in contemporary religious practice.

▲ The founder, Matsumura Kaiseki, experienced personal healing, but this did not become a part of the movement.

● The founder, Kawai Shinsui, performed healing rituals on occasion, but this is no longer part of the religious practice in Christ Heart Church.

■ Speaking in tongues is practiced in private by some members but is not a part of public worship.

Matsumura Kaiseki and Kawai Shinsui, the founders of two of the older movements, The Way and Christ Heart Church, both believed that revelation from God not only continues today but is also to be found outside of the Judeo-Christian Scriptures. In their various writings they record a number of revelations from God that were important for shaping their religious consciousness. While many Protestant missionaries interpreted commitment to Jesus Christ as requiring a rejection and devaluation of all other religious traditions, both Matsumura and Kawai argued that the scriptures of various Asian religions were likewise vehicles of revelation. Kawai pointed out repeatedly that Jesus came to "fulfill" rather than "destroy" what had come before him (Mt. 5:17). For Kawai this included not only the Old Testament but also the wisdom, ideals, and aspirations of the religious traditions of Asia. In fact, Kawai referred to these traditions and their writings as the "Old Testament for Japanese Christians."

Kawai claimed that saints like Buddha and Confucius, like Jesus Christ and the Old Testament prophets before him, were sent to their respective countries according to the grace and providence of God. Through the discipline of meditation he likewise realized that "the mind of Christ and the spirit of Confucius were indeed similar manifestations," so much so that he revered Confucius "as a forerunner to Christ." The reason why there is truth and goodness in these Asian traditions worthy of our study and inclusion, Kawai explains, is that both Buddha and Confucius had encountered the spirit of Christ.[41]

Prophecies, visions, and special messages from God have also been important for the Christian Canaan Church, the Holy Ecclesia of Jesus, and the Spirit of Jesus Church. In 1938, for example, the founder of the Holy Ecclesia of Jesus received special revelations regarding Israel and the Second Coming of Christ—revelations that have come to be central to the life and mission of this church today. Followers believe that the founder, Father Ōtsuki, continues to receive special guidance from God. Examples of continuing revelation also abound in the Spirit of Jesus Church. In 1941 the founder's wife, Murai Suwa, received a direct revelation from God that the official name of the church was to be *Iesu no mitama Kyōkai*. The indigenous hymnbook used by this church is likewise based on revelatory experiences. *Rei sanka* (Spirit hymns) is a collection of 166 hymns all said to have been received from heaven by Tsuruhara Tama, a woman who was active in the early years of this church. The preface to this hymnbook states that no changes in the contents are permitted since the hymns were given in a direct revelation from God.

While all of these movements recognize the validity of continuing revelation, only The Way and the Christ Heart Church have redefined the Christian canon according to their new understanding of the faith. As early as 1908, Matsumura Kaiseki stated that The Way would add to its canon of Scriptures as it deemed appropriate.[42] In 1928, The Way published a selection of passages from the writings of the Neo-Confucian Ō Yōmei (Chin., Wang Yang-Ming 王 陽明) and others, with comments and explanations by Matsumura.[43] All these materials were regarded as valuable for self-cultivation and spiritual develop-ment. As it turned out, Matsumura also considered it appropriate to eliminate portions of the traditional Christian canon. In 1928 Matsumura published his own edition of the Bible, which consisted of various selections from the New Testament.[44] The influence of higher criticism is apparent in Matsumura's selec-tion. He includes passages from the synoptic gospels, but omits the Gospel of John as something that moves beyond the actual life and teachings of Jesus. He viewed the birth narratives in Matthew and Luke as later additions, so his selec-tions begin with the appearance of John the Baptist and the baptism of Jesus. Matsumura also omits 2 John and 3 John, Jude, and the Book of Revelation. He writes that this last book contains prophetic materials and riddles, but not really anything worth serious study—the apocalyptic vision of the New Testament is apparently irrelevant to The Way's interpretation of Christianity. In the postwar period, Matsumura's adopted son and successor, Matsumura Kichisuke, wrote a commentary on an important Neo-Confucian text, and this commentary is now read as "scripture" (seiku, 聖句) for one service each month.[45]

The Christian canon was also modified by Christ Heart Church under the influence of Kawai Shinsui. As noted above, Kawai felt that many of the sacred writings of the East represented a form of "Old Testament" for the Japanese. Next to the Bible, for example, he recommended that his followers read the Analects of Confucius. Although Kawai expressed high regard for these other scriptures, he did not designate them officially as a part of the canon. Several of his own writings, however, have been designated as such and have a central place in the teaching and liturgy of the church today. These include the Seven Great Vows (七大誓願 Shichi daiseigan), the Creed (信条 Shinjō), the Eulogy on Jesus Christ (耶蘇基督讃 Iesu Kirisuto san, a poem on the life of Christ), and Perfect Faith (完全の信仰 Kanzen no shinkō).

Spirit Baptism, Tongues, and Healing

The recovery of apostolic Christianity has been regarded as the primary aim of many indigenous movements. Teshima Ikurō, the founder of the Original Gospel, explained that for this to occur Japanese would have to encounter the same heavenly light that transformed "Saul" into "Paul." The Old Testament prophets, the apostles, and all of the early Christians after Pentecost had this transformative encounter with the Holy Spirit and the light from above. According to Teshima, two things are essential for authentic religion: the encounter with light and the baptism of the Spirit. Belief in Christian teachings alone is clearly inadequate. We need an experience that converts us and brings us new life.[46]

While the baptism of the Holy Spirit is regarded as indispensable by many of these movements, their interpretation of this experience tends to differ somewhat, following two basic patterns. The Glorious Gospel Christian Church, Living Christ One Ear of Wheat Church, the Sanctifying Christ Church, and the Holy Ecclesia of Jesus all resemble the Holiness tradition, emphasizing baptism by the Holy Spirit and the miraculous gift of healing. These groups do not regard speaking in tongues as a necessary "sign" of this baptism, nor do they regard tongues as significant for church life today. The Christian Canaan Church, Spirit of Jesus Church, Original Gospel movement, Life-Giving Christ, Japan Ecclesia of Christ, and the Okinawa Christian Gospel maintain that the signs, miracles of healing, exorcism, and tongues that accompanied the coming of the Holy Spirit in the New Testament (Acts 2, 5, 19) are still present and will be until the end of the church age.[47] Most groups follow the New Testament example of anointing with olive oil to cure sickness (James 5:14). In fact, oil is kept in a small container on the front altar of many churches for regular use in healing rituals (this is especially true in the Spirit of Jesus Church and Holy Ecclesia of Jesus).

In order to experience the baptism of the Holy Spirit, a number of different approaches are advocated. When the Spirit of Jesus Church presents the Gospel to newcomers they call individuals to accept Jesus and encourage them to be baptized in the spirit and water immediately, chanting "receive the Holy Spirit, receive water baptism." To bring on the experience of spirit baptism and speaking in tongues, individuals are encouraged to repeat the phrase "hallelujah" over and over again. Teshima Ikurō often held all-night prayer meetings to provide the time necessary and create the atmosphere conducive to this emotional religious experience. Other movements introduce this teaching more gradually and usually with less pressure. While these groups may differ in their interpretation of baptism and in the significance they place on speaking in tongues, all of them agree that Christianity today is to be a religion of "signs and wonders" just as in New Testament times (see Mark 16).

Spirit World Interaction

Most of the movements covered in this study share what might be referred to as a "spiritualistic worldview." This worldview consists of a belief in the reality and interdependence of "this world" and another "spirit world" (i.e., the world of the ancestors). Transplanted missionary Christianity, for the most part, advocated a complete severing of relations with the spirit world. Many indigenous Christian movements, on the other hand, articulate the meaning of the Christian faith in terms of an ongoing interaction between these two worlds. This is a particularly important dimension of indigenous movements, one that we will consider in some detail in chapter seven.

CHAPTER FOUR

The Fountainhead of
Japanese Christianity Revisited

WHILE ONE OF the aims of this book is to give attention to a number of relatively unknown indigenous movements, the numerous references to the Nonchurch movement and quotations from Uchimura's writings thus far show how impossible it is to entirely ignore this earliest expression of Japanese Christianity. Uchimura's writings contained numerous strands of thought that were subsequently elaborated (and sometimes rejected) by other leaders and movements. In short, the Nonchurch movement is significant not only as an independent expression of Christianity but also for what it has given birth to throughout its history. Without a central authority or bureaucracy, it has functioned as the fountainhead of indigenous Christianity in Japan and given rise to many other movements.

Many Japanese critics of transplanted mission churches expressed a longing for the "pure" or "spiritual" religion of Jesus without Western institutions, rites, and dogmas. The God of Christianity "is spirit and truth," Uchimura wrote, "and they that worship Him are commanded to worship in spirit and truth—i.e., *without forms, or with a minimum of forms.*"[1] Nitobe Inazō, however, recognized that ultimately a religion without forms or "human wrappage" [sic] was impossible and pleaded for the development of "homemade garments." The fact that a number of Japanese accepted Christianity but rejected missionary traditions implied there were alternative interpretations of the Christian faith with their accompanying cultural forms and institutions. Charismatic minor founders were not only responsible for the break with transplanted mission churches and traditions but subsequently became the creative force in the development of new Christian traditions. As F. F. Bruce has perceptively observed, "It is noteworthy how often the renunciation of an old tradition is followed by the speedy development of a new one, held at least as tenaciously as ever the old one was."[2] Although these words were written in a very different context, they accurately capture the process of "tradition-making" in Japanese Christianity.

UCHIMURA KANZŌ AND THE NONCHURCH MOVEMENT

The Nonchurch movement is undoubtedly the most widely known and respected expression of Japanese Christianity. This is due largely to the fact that Uchimura was a prolific writer respected by many individuals both within and outside Christian circles. The complete works of Uchimura consists of some 50 volumes: 17 primarily biblical and exegetical studies, 25 volumes of theological and topical works, and 8 volumes of diaries and correspondence. Many of his disciples have likewise been well-known intellectual figures, authors, and university presidents. In light of Uchimura's prominent place in Japanese intellectual history and in the development of Christianity in Japan, it is understandable why he and his movement have been the focus of so much attention. The literature produced by or about this movement is now so immense that a 1990 bibliography of materials related to Uchimura and the Nonchurch movement exceeded 100 pages.[3] Each year since then new materials have continued to roll off the press.

Another reason Uchimura and the Nonchurch movement are widely recognized, at least in church circles, is due in part to the work of Emil Brunner, the Swiss theologian, who became fascinated with this movement during his stay in Japan from 1953 to 1955. Brunner was quite sympathetic with the aims of the Nonchurch movement as a lay reform movement within Christianity. He subsequently played a major role in introducing this form of Christianity to the Western world through his writings in German and English. Many observers have recognized that Brunner was an important "bridge" between this independent movement and the established churches while in Japan.[4]

Uchimura Kanzō, on a walk near Tōzansō, 1917 (age 57).

In his otherwise illuminating monograph, Carlo Caldarola mistakenly defined his study of the Nonchurch movement as an analysis of an indigenous form of Christianity "totally independent of Western influence."[5] While the Nonchurch movement and other indigenous movements have clearly been independent of Western "control," they have hardly been independent of Western influence. In stark contrast to Caldarola's view, Ohta maintains that "Uchimura was a man nurtured by Western culture for the whole of his life," and as evidence points to the library Uchimura bequeathed to Hokkaidō University: 746 titles were books in European languages (mostly English) and only 109 titles in Japanese and Chinese.[6] What obviously needs to be clarified is how Uchimura and leaders of other movements have critically appropriated imported traditions and reshaped them in light of Japanese concerns and native religious and cultural traditions.

WESTERN TRADITIONS AND THE BIBLE IN UCHIMURA'S CHRISTIANITY

For all his stress on "independence" and the need for a Japanese Christianity, Uchimura's version of the faith is clearly indebted to various Western traditions. His first serious encounter with Christianity occurred as a young man at Sapporo Agricultural College. Prior to Uchimura's arrival, William S. Clark had spent the year assisting the Japanese government in the establishment of this

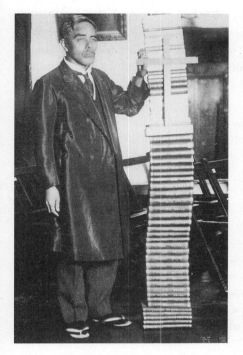

Uchimura Kanzō, standing beside a stack of his biblical writings, 1925 (age 65).

college. While his primary role was to teach agriculture, Clark was a committed lay Christian who introduced his students to the Christian faith through a Bible class (see chapter two). All of his students converted and signed the "Covenant of Believers in Jesus," committing themselves to continue studying the Bible and to do their best to live ethical lives. Clark returned to the United States after less than one year, but Uchimura felt his influence through the small Covenant group that was left behind. Under considerable pressure from his *sempai* (the upper classmen), Uchimura signed the Covenant during his first year at the college at the age of sixteen and went on to receive baptism from a Methodist missionary in 1878.[7] Dissatisfaction with the mission church, however, led Uchimura and his Japanese cohorts to establish an independent church in Sapporo, an experiment that was a precursor to the Nonchurch movement. Through Clark's teaching and example, this small band of Japanese Christians understood that it was possible to practice or live an authentic life of faith without dependence on an institution or clergy. This became the central affirmation of Uchimura's Christianity.

This evangelical faith was nurtured over a four-year period (1884–1888) in the United States. Uchimura departed for the United States following a brief and unhappy first marriage. He was first befriended by Mr. and Mrs. Wister Morris, a committed Quaker couple, who helped him find employment shortly after his arrival in Pennsylvania. The faith and pacifism of these Quakers made a lasting impression upon Uchimura. Following eight months of stressful work in a mental hospital, Uchimura resigned and traveled through New England, entering Amherst College in September 1885. Julius Hawley Seelye, the president of Amherst College, became his spiritual mentor and guided him into a deeper understanding of the Christian faith.

It was while a student at Amherst College that Uchimura had a profound religious experience that gave him an inward confirmation of his faith. Settling into his dormitory room at Amherst, he vowed "never to move from the place till the Almighty should show Himself unto me." The 8 March 1886 entry to his diary records the revelatory experience as follows:

> Very important day in my life. Never was the atoning power of Christ more clearly revealed to me than it is today. In the crucifixion of the Son of God lies the solution of all the difficulties that buffeted my mind thus far. Christ paying all my debts, can bring me back to the purity and innocence of the first man before the Fall. Now I am God's child, and my duty is to believe Jesus. For *His* sake, God will give me all I want. He will use me for His glory, and will save me in Heaven at last.[8]

This religious experience, combined with studies with Dr. Seelye and others at Amherst, had a lasting influence. Writing many years later in his magazine, *The Christian Intelligencer*, Uchimura still spoke highly of this man: "The great president opened my eyes to the evangelical truth in Christianity. He is my father. For forty years, since then, I preached the faith taught me by that venerable teacher."[9] Reflecting on his spiritual pilgrimage thus far, Uchimura explains that he became aware of his condition as a "sinner" through his participation in the Covenant of Believers in Sapporo, but for years had tried to achieve personal holiness by his own efforts. It was not until the "revelatory" experience at Amherst that he truly realized the evangelical gospel that his righteousness was in the crucified Christ and not something achieved by his own effort.

With Seelye's encouragement, Uchimura went on to Hartford Theological Seminary in the fall of 1887, after graduation from Amherst. He only studied at the seminary for one year, returning to Japan in 1888. While Uchimura had a great deal of respect for some clergymen and theologians, he wanted no part of the ordained ministry. Uchimura explains that his samurai background was the basis for rejecting ordination, because "priests live by charity, and we believed the sword to be a more honorable means of existence than charity." In Japan the Christian ministry, furthermore, implied subservience to a foreign power:

> To be a priest is bad enough; but to be a Christian priest I considered to be the end of my doom. In a heathen country like mine, Christian ministers are supported either directly or indirectly by foreigners, and are to place themselves under the jurisdiction of foreign bishops of one kind or another.[10]

Uchimura returned to Japan in 1888 at the age of twenty-seven with an evangelical Protestant faith deeply rooted in the Bible and New England

Puritanism. These were the formative Christian traditions behind Uchimura's independent expression of Japanese Christianity. Even today, insiders define the Nonchurch movement as an expression of Christianity whose "father" is Puritanism and whose "mother" is Quakerism, born in Japan according to the direct revelation of God.[11] In essence, Uchimura gratefully received the Bible and its message of salvation from the missionaries, but found he had no use for Western ecclesiastical traditions. In fact, Uchimura conceived of the Nonchurch movement as an effort to complete the Protestant Reformation, which had ended prematurely as "an arrested movement." According to Uchimura:

> Protestantism institutionalized was a return back to the discarded Roman Catholicism. We need another Reformation to bring Protestantism to its logical conclusion. The new Protestantism must be perfectly free without a trace of ecclesiasticism in it—a fellowship, not an institution—free communion of souls, not a system or an organization. Practically, it will be a churchless Christianity, calling no man bishop or pastor, save Jesus Christ, the Son of God. (April 1928)[12]

As a continuation of the Protestant movement, Uchimura stressed the "priesthood of all believers" and rejected an ordained clergy or priesthood that stood as an intermediary between the individual and God. Likewise, Uchimura continued to stress the characteristic Protestant doctrine of salvation by faith, and for that reason rejected the sacraments of baptism and the Lord's Supper (Eucharist). These were understood as the two remaining ritual obligations associated with Christianity that the Protestant Reformation in Europe had failed to eliminate. Requiring observance of these rituals, Uchimura reasoned, obscured the Biblical teaching of salvation by faith and cultivated a dependence on a separate priestly class. In an effort to complete the Reformation, therefore, Uchimura rejected the sacraments and an ordained clergy set apart for their proper observance. These theological emphases in Uchimura's faith are hardly "unique" Japanese interpretations of the Biblical tradition, but resemble other movements that developed in the West. As Paul Peachey explains:

> Phenomenologically, the movement Uchimura initiated would fall somewhere between Quakerism and Anabaptism. Like the Quakers, though not for the same reasons, *Mukyōkai-shugi* [Nonchurch ideology] rejects clergy, hierarchy, and sacraments. Like the Anabaptists, *Mukyōkai-shugi* is Bible-centered rather than dependent on the "inner light."[13]

Uchimura's faith continued to evolve over the course of his life. Two particular emphases that emerge later on are pacifism and a strong faith in the Second Coming of Christ. Within a few years of his return to Japan, Uchimura backed the Japanese government in the Sino-Japanese War. He regarded Japan's involvement in Korea as a "holy war," necessary to protect this small struggling nation from China. Following the end of the war in 1895, however, he came to regret his earlier support, since Japan did not honor the provisions of the peace treaty. A decade later Uchimura took a stand against the Japanese government in the Russo-Japanese War (1904–1905). Over against his earlier support of the use of the sword to bring about justice, Uchimura had become an outspoken critic of Japan's military involvements and a convert to the pacifism of his Quaker friends.[14] Some years later Uchimura reached the conclusion that peace could ultimately be realized only by God's direct intervention in human affairs. It was this rather late discovery of faith in the Second Coming of Christ that gave Uchimura hope for the future.[15] He declared his belief in the Second Coming of Christ in 1918 and became actively involved in promoting this doctrine among Christians throughout Japan. Uchimura felt that this issue was so important that he participated in a speaking tour with the Holiness Church leader Nakada Jūji and Congregationalist Pastor Kimura Seimatsu, traveling to Osaka, Kyoto, Kōbe, Hokkaidō, Fukushima, Miyagi, Okayama, and Yamagata. During the course of one year Uchimura gave sixty lectures dealing with the Second Coming, reaching close to twenty thousand with his message. Uchimura came under considerable criticism for his advocacy of this "apocalyptic" version of Christianity.[16]

CHRISTIANITY AS A JAPANESE RELIGION

With so much in common with Western interpretations of Christianity, one may wonder what could be "indigenous" about Uchimura's version of the faith. While Uchimura was clearly indebted to certain aspects of Western Christianity, he rejected the denominationalism and displacement theology of the mission churches, arguing that native traditions provided a positive foundation for Christianity in Japan. In order to create authentic faith in Japan, Uchimura reasoned, Japanese Christians must build on this foundation independent of Western church control and finances. Uchimura's first job upon returning from the United States was as principal of Hokuetsu Gakkan, a boys' school in Niigata. Uchimura quickly ran into trouble with missionaries associated with the school when he sought to introduce lectures on Confucianism and Buddhism into the curriculum. Fundamental differences with these missionaries over educational policy led Uchimura to resign from this post in less than a year after his appointment.

While missionaries could only see discontinuity between the Gospel and Japanese culture, Uchimura found many positive connections. One significant pattern in the new indigenous traditions of Christian thought may be referred to as the "Christianization of the pre-Christian past."[17] As Japanese struggled to make sense of the Christian faith for themselves, it was only natural that they sought to find common ground and points of continuity with native traditions and religious experience. Japanese Christians felt the need to redeem the past and consider how God had been at work in Japanese history and culture before the arrival of Western missionaries. Again, Uchimura Kanzō led the way in articulating this more inclusive conception of truth over against the dominant missionary perspective. Writing in his English magazine, the *Christian Intelligencer*, Uchimura argued:

> The fault-finder can never be Christian. He is bound to be a truth-hunter in everybody and in everything. Those representatives of the Christian Religion who take delight in finding darkness in other religions other than their own are very poor representatives of their religion. The Christian is glad when he meets goodness in Buddhism, Confucianism, Taoism, anywhere. His eyes are sharpened to detect light, and he is loathe to look at darkness. Therefore, when Christianity shines with its genuine light, it is the discoverer of what is best in the world.[18]

In his April 1926 editorial, Uchimura went on to express the inclusive orientation of his faith in a short piece on the relationship between Buddha and Christ.

BUDDHA AND CHRIST

Buddha is the Moon; Christ is the Sun.
Buddha is the Mother; Christ is the Father.
Buddha is Mercy; Christ is Righteousness.

> ...I love the moon and I love the night; but as the night is far spent and the day is at hand, I now love the Sun more than I love the Moon; and *I know that the love of the Moon is included in the love of the Sun, and that he who loves the Sun loves the Moon also.*[19]

Uchimura spent most of his life in serious Bible study and teaching and never went on to elaborate this perspective in a detailed study of Asian religions, but his fundamental outlook was shared by other founders of indigenous Christian movements. Truth and goodness were to be found outside of the narrowly defined missionary traditions.

Uchimura's interpretation of Christianity reveals an indebtedness to the ethical traditions associated with the samurai or warrior class. Born into a samurai family, Uchimura was shaped by the values and traditions summed up by the word *bushidō*, the way of the samurai. According to Uchimura's account, his father was a "good Confucian scholar" who passed on to him the precepts of the Chinese sages. "Loyalty to my feudal lords, and fidelity and respects [sic] to my parents and teachers, were the central themes of the Chinese ethics."[20] Uchimura's Confucian version of Christianity is related to the fact that his primary concern was to graft Christianity on to *bushidō*.

> *Bushidō* is the finest product of Japan. But *bushidō* by itself cannot save Japan. Christianity grafted upon Bushidō will be the finest product of the world. *It* will save, not only Japan, but the whole world.... There was a meaning in the history of Japan. For twenty centuries God has been perfecting *bushidō* with this very moment in view. Christianity grafted upon *bushidō* will yet save the world. (January 1916)[21]

"Independent, money-hating, loyal"—these were the values and virtues that made even the Apostle Paul "a true samurai, the very embodiment of the spirit of *bushidō*."[22]

In addition to the ethical values of loyalty, duty, and filial piety, Uchimura looked to the Confucian educational model based on a personal relationship between teacher and disciple as the appropriate pattern for the development of Christianity in Japan.[23] After his return from the United States, he reached the conclusion that the Western denominational forms were ill-suited to Japan and decided to organize along the lines of a school or *juku*. Instead of worship services in church buildings, Uchimura held lectures in rented halls and homes. Although Uchimura rejected Western denominationalism, he could not entirely resist the need for some kind of organization.

During Uchimura's lifetime, the Nonchurch movement took various organizational forms. His direct disciples were essentially paying members of his private school. As subscribers to his magazine grew, supporters outside of Tokyo sought some ongoing relationship with other Nonchurch members. Uchimura organized the Kyōyūkai in 1905, with 14 branches and 119 members. The purpose of this association was defined in the following profession of faith:

> We who believe in God and His Only Son whom he sent (into the world), uniting together, form the Kyōyūkai. With the help of God the Father we shall help our comrades and live lives that are in harmony with His sovereign Will.

Membership was restricted to individuals who had "endeavored to live the Christian life for at least a year." The guidelines for this early association included a commitment to meet monthly, to spend Sunday nurturing faith and morals, and to abstain from tobacco and liquor. Another group called the Kashiwagi Brotherhood formed around Uchimura in 1918 to support his adventist lecture meetings around the country. This group was dissolved after two years.[24]

Uchimura was surrounded by various informal groups of supporters throughout the remainder of his life and continued his Sunday Bible lectures. After his death the group that had formed around his weekly Bible lectures was disbanded and his publication, *Seisho no kenkyū* (Bible studies) was terminated. Following Uchimura's example, the Nonchurch movement continued as a lay movement guided by a number of charismatic teachers and evangelists. As a lay Christian movement, members were expected to evangelize in and through their secular occupations. The religious authority of Nonchurch movement leaders continues to be based on personal charisma, since there is no central organization or institution for the training and ordination of religious specialists. In clear contrast to the understanding and practice of leadership and authority in established churches, where leaders are educated, tested, and ordained, successive leaders in the Nonchurch movement embark on an independent ministry on the basis of their individual charismatic authority without fulfilling formal requirements.[25] New groups are formed when an individual is confident of his own understanding of the Bible and senses a personal call to form an independent meeting. Following Uchimura's example, most teachers publish their own monthly Bible study magazines. These publications and special lectures are regarded as the primary means of evangelism.

The financial base of the Nonchurch movement also differs from that of the mission churches. Admission fees to Bible lectures and magazine subscriptions have replaced the church finances based on offerings or tithe. In other words, the Nonchurch movement leaders "earn" their own way rather than receiving a salary. Although Uchimura rejected Western institutions and the ordained clergy, one could make the case that the teachers or *sensei* in the Nonchurch movement have a special status in spite of their rhetoric about being equal participants in a lay movement. While the Nonchurch movement's organizational structure is quite fluid, with Bible study groups dissolving and reforming, charismatic teachers exercise considerable religious authority over their followers. As Ohara Shin points out:

> Each *sensei* functions as a minor 'shaman' who has charisma. He is not only the teacher for the religious subject concerned, but also an advisor in the personal affairs of his disciples—as in arranging marriages and choosing occupations.[26]

In spite of Uchimura's numerous references to the *bushidō* foundation of his faith, in many respects the ethos and practice of the Nonchurch movement resembles the expression of Christianity he encountered during his time of study in the United States. Some would argue that it is much more than simple "resemblance." Tosh Arai, for example, maintains that the Nonchurch movement is as indebted to New England Puritan Christianity as the transplanted mission churches. His observations are worth quoting at length:

> Both the Mukyōkai and church Christians in Japan are twin babies of New England Puritanism. After I had discovered that nineteenth-century American Protestantism was the prototype for Japanese Protestant institutions, I spent two years in New England comparing the two. To my surprise, the Mukyōkai Christians, who have claimed to be the most nationalistic and indigenous Japanese Protestants, can be shown to have deep roots in American Christianity. The distinctive spirit of American Christianity over the last two hundred years has been one of independence and self-support. I checked through the records of missionary conferences in Japan during the 1880s, and I found a strong emphasis on establishing "self-supporting churches." The long Bible-centered sermons, the simple anti-liturgical services, the attacks on church symbolism, and the teetotaler moralism were all there. We even adopted a style of church buildings at the time when American churches were at their ugliest. In fact, New England church buildings were called "meeting houses," and the Mukyōkai people translated this into Japanese, *kōgisho*.[27]

Impossible as it is to determine whether "native" elements or "foreign" elements were most influential in shaping the stark and simple style of the movement, the subservient place of women in the movement is clearly indebted to Uchimura's Confucian heritage. The Confucian orientation of this movement, especially during the first and second generations, has been widely recognized. Uchimura was far more conservative than many missionaries and Japanese church leaders when it came to the status and role of women. Unlike more progressive leaders, such as Uemura Masahisa and Ebina Danjō, Uchimura continued to hold the old-fashioned view that women should walk behind men. Even at his Bible lectures, men and women were expected to sit on different sides of the hall.[28] Carlo Caldarola's study discovered that the Nonchurch movement prides itself on being a "manly expression of Christianity." This is reflected not only in the dominance of male leadership, but also in the fact that over sixty percent of the membership is male. Today there are feminist groups within the Nonchurch movement who are critical of this Confucian heritage and who actively advocate change, but the Confucian orientation still predominates.

Closing ceremony of Uchimura's Kashiwagi Bible Seminar.

For Uchimura, the Confucian-oriented *bushidō* tradition provided the foundation for Japanese Christianity; at the same time, the Gospel was understood as a fulfillment of the religious aspirations of Japanese Buddhists. A common distinction in Japanese Buddhism is often made between the two paths of self-power (*jiriki* 自力) and dependence on Other-Power (*tariki* 他力). Carlo Caldarola referred to the Nonchurch movement as a "Zenlike Christianity," because Uchimura and his followers reported a *satori*-type experience of forgiveness and salvation.[29] I find this designation misleading, however, since Zen is associated primarily with the path of *jiriki*, whereas Uchimura placed a primary emphasis on a *tariki*-like salvation by faith. Furthermore, Biblical teaching and lectures, rather than meditation, form the core of the Nonchurch movement religious life. Uchimura, in fact, points to close parallels between Christianity and the Pure Land Buddhist faith in Amida, or "other power."

> Salvation by faith is a higher and deeper faith than salvation by works. If Buddhists should know upon what firm ethical bases the Christian justification by faith is grounded, they would transfer their allegiance to Christianity, without repudiating their allegiance to their old faith. The simple fact that Amida

65

was a mythical personage while Jesus Christ was a historical person ought to be enough to induce all thinking people to seek the rest to their minds and souls in the latter rather than in the former. I speak this without any spirit of prose-lytism, which I hate with all my heart. The time when the Japanese evangelical Buddhists find the true foundation of their faith in "Him who was crucified for the sins of the world," will be the time when the world will witness the greatest revival that has ever happened.... May such a time come soon; and come it will, if Christianity is presented to them not as a foreign religion by foreign mis-sionaries, but as a Japanese religion by Japanese messengers.(June 1926)[30]

For almost a century Uchimura and his successors have presented Christianity as an authentic "Japanese religion." The mass conversion of Japanese Buddhists, nevertheless, seems as remote a possibility today as it did when these words were first written.

CONCLUSION

Uchimura's Japanese interpretation of Christianity, although highly influential among intellectuals, never became the foundation for a mass movement. It did, however, contain potent ideas that were developed by other indigenous leaders. Over against the ecclesiasticism and extrabiblical traditions of the transplanted mission churches, Uchimura and his followers claimed to have a Bible-centered faith rooted in the apostolic message of the cross, resurrection, and second com-ing of Christ. Even though Uchimura identified the *bushidō* tradition as a posi-tive indigenous foundation, the Bible is regarded as central to Nonchurch Christianity. The lectures, magazine articles, and scholarly studies of the origi-nal Hebrew and Greek Bible are clear enough evidence of this. But while it is undeniable that Uchimura drew heavily on the Biblical tradition, at the same time it must be recognized that he was selective and clearly operated with a "canon within the canon."

In general terms, one could say that Uchimura was enamored of the "prophetic" tradition over against the "priestly" tradition in the Hebrew-Christian Scriptures. His writings clearly echo the prophetic critique of ceremo-nialism and hypocrisy in religious practice. His closest disciples certainly regarded him as a modern prophet, placing him in the company of Amos, Isaiah, and Jeremiah.[31] Although the Hebrew Bible also accords an important place and legitimacy to the Levitical priesthood in the religious life of Israel, this form of religion is clearly inferior for Uchimura and irrelevant to his concerns. Likewise, the earliest "Jewish" version of the Jesus movement, which included traditional Jewish laws, observances, and customs, is also largely ignored. In terms of the New Testament traditions identified by James Dunn, Uchimura's Christianity was based primarily on the Hellenistic tradition. The Apostle Paul, missionary to the Gentiles, was in many respects Uchimura's ideal. Independent of the Jerusalem church, Paul worked as a tent-maker to support himself as he spread the Gospel throughout the Roman Empire. Although Uchimura did discover the New Testament's Apocalyptic tradition rather late in life, he never recognized (or rejected) what scholars regard as the "early Catholic" tradition in the New Testament, writings that show the early "routinization of charisma" and concern with church structures, religious authority, and leadership (i.e., bishops, presbyters, and deacons).[32] These neglected traditions were to become important for several indigenous Christian movements that developed in the postwar period as new efforts to recover "apostolic" Christianity.

CHAPTER FIVE

Christianity as a Path of Self-Cultivation

S WE HAVE SEEN, Uchimura Kanzō was the first Japanese leader to articulate a clear alternative to transplanted Christian churches. His call for
the development of an independent and indigenous expression of the
faith resonated with the deep aspirations of numerous other Japanese
Christians. Many shared Uchimura's independent spirit and sympathized with
his break from mission churches, but some were not entirely satisfied with the
alternative version of Christianity he created. Carlo Caldarola has referred to
Uchimura's Nonchurch movement as "Christianity the Japanese *Way*," imply-
ing that it was the only authentic Japanese expression of Christianity. The successive appearance of indigenous movements over the past century, however,
suggests that there are other *ways* to be both Japanese and Christian.

This chapter considers the reinterpretation of Christianity by two other
important figures involved in the earliest phase of indigenization: Matsumura

Kaiseki, who founded The Way in 1907, and Kawai Shinsui, who founded Christ Heart Church in 1927. These two groups represent important Japanese alternatives to both the mission churches and Uchimura's Nonchurch movement. In some respects the early faith of both these founders closely resembled Uchimura's evangelical Christianity, despite the fact that their introduction to the faith came by way of missionaries of the Presbyterian and Reformed traditions with strong ecclesiastical concerns that contrast with those of W. S. Clark, the lay educator who had a formative influence on the Sapporo Band that nurtured Uchimura's early faith. In their autobiographies, Matsumura and Kawai refer to their early understanding of Christianity, a reliance on Other-Power. Eventually they came to the conclusion that this is only the beginning of the Christian life, and that authentic faith also requires the exercise of self-power. It seemed to them that Uchimura, like the Western missionaries, put too much stress on Other-Power to the neglect of self-cultivation and self-exertion. One of Kawai's disciples went so far as to claim that the founder had "graduated" from the intellectualism of Uchimura and laid the experiential foundation for Japanese Christianity.

Matsumura and Kawai also conceived of Christianity more as a "path" or "way" than as a narrowly defined set of doctrines. Kawai, for example, referred to his version of Christianity as the "heavenly way"; and the name that Matsumura chose for his movement, *Dōkai*, means literally "Association of the Way." Despite their shared conviction of the excessively doctrinal leanings of Western Christianity, their own Japanese reinterpretations of the faith were not without distinctive creeds and the contours of a basic theology. Moreover, although Matsumura and Kawai show a similar stress on the importance of self-cultivation in the religious life, their interpretations of Christianity differ markedly. A comparison of the two founders and the movements they initiated further illustrates the complex interaction of various religious traditions that goes into the process of indigenization. The following treatment does not by any means aim to be exhaustive, but it will attempt to identify the major religious and cultural elements that have been incorporated into these distinct interpretations of the teaching and practice of Christianity.

MATSUMURA KAISEKI AND THE WAY

Matsumura Kaiseki (1859–1939) is relatively unknown today, but in the world of Japanese Christianity during the late-Meiji, Taishō, and early Shōwa periods he was a leading intellectual figure In fact, it was not uncommon for him to be referred to as one of the "three muras" along with Uchimura and Uemura Masahisa.[1] While the latter have been given a central place in most historical accounts, Matsumura has largely dropped out of the picture, even though he played a similarly important role in the Japanese church of his time. Matsumura was not only an important intellectual figure within Japanese Protestantism but also a widely respected leader in the field of moral education. Like Uchimura, Matsumura was a prolific writer and popular speaker. The bibliography of his published works runs to over fifty pages and includes more than forty books and pamphlets devoted to religion.[2] Through his lectures and writings he also had an influence on the founders of other new religious movements.[3]

In spite of Matsumura's importance, it is not hard to understand why his name has fallen into obscurity. The movement he initially intended as an authentic Japanese expression of Christianity soon evolved into a new religion that denied the traditional doctrines of the incarnation and atonement. Consequently, Matsumura was labeled as an apostate[4] and ignored by the wider Christian community in Japan. His movement had to struggle for survival in the postwar period and in the end all but disappeared, leaving today no more than three hundred members nationwide. Notwithstanding the ambiguous status of The Way as a "Christian" movement, I have included it in this study because at various stages in its historical development the founder and followers understood themselves as an indigenous expression of Christianity.

Matsumura's Conversion and Religious Development

Matsumura was born in Akashi, a town just southwest of Kobe, in 1859—the very year the first Protestant missionaries arrived in Japan. Like Uchimura, Matsumura was from a samurai family and received his early education in the Chinese Confucian classics from his father. Following the Meiji Restoration and the new government's 1873 promulgation of a new law of military conscription for all, many a young man born into the several hundred thousands of samurai families of Japan found himself without land or stipend, and was forced to find another means of livelihood. With the encouragement of his father, Matsumura decided to pursue an academic career. At the age of twelve he was sent to Tokyo to continue Confucian studies in the *juku* of Yasui Sokken (1799–1876). Many leaders in the early Meiji period recognized the importance of Western learning for Japan's modernization, with the result that scores of young men from samurai families were prompted to continue their education in one of the schools of Western Learning that were being set up in various locations around the country. In 1874, at the age of sixteen, Matsumura began his study of English at the Osaka School of Foreign Languages. Later that year he moved to Kōbe and continued his English studies with the missionary John Atkinson. This was Matsumura's first direct encounter with Christianity and the Bible. Two years later he returned to Tokyo to pursue his studies and in 1876 entered the Hepburn School in Yokohama, then under the direction of John Ballagh, an American missionary of the Dutch Reformed Church.

Besides his study of English, Matsumura wrestled with the doctrines of Christianity that were being taught by missionaries associated with the Hepburn School and the Yokohama Band. According to his spiritual autobiography, *Fifty Years in the Faith*, one night in December 1876 he had a divine revelation that the God of Christianity was none other than *Tentei* 天帝, the God of Confucianism. As a result of this experience he made a profession of faith and was baptized in 1877 in the Sumiyoshi-chō Church. The following year he returned home for a brief visit to evangelize members of his own family. For a short while he supported himself on a meager income by assisting missionaries with translation and evangelistic activities and by working as an elementary school teacher. Unable to cope with the pressures of his new responsibilities, Matsumura had a nervous breakdown diagnosed as neurasthenia, apparently triggered by overwork and an erratic diet. James Ballagh made arrangements for him to recuperate in the village of Yamanaka in the Hakone region. During his convalescence, while at prayer one evening in the mountains, Matsumura had another decisive revelatory experience, which persuaded him that he was being called by God to serve in Christian ministry as an evangelist.

To prepare for the ministry Matsumura returned to Tokyo in 1880 and enrolled in Union Theological School, an institution established by a number of Presbyterian and Dutch Reformed missionaries associated with the Yokohama Band. After only two months Matsumura felt obliged to withdraw from the program. By his own account, he was disappointed with the quality of the teachers and students. He was also unable to accept the strict missionary interpretation of the Sabbath and the prescription against smoking and drinking, which led to conflicts with various missionary instructors, including James Ballagh and the President James Amerman. The final straw was the refusal of the school authorities to observe a school holiday commemorating the anniversary of the death of Emperor Jinmu. The missionaries argued that this festival was simply a form of idol worship and as such should not be honored with a school holiday. Matsumura maintained that the missionaries were ignorant of Japanese history and the national character of the Japanese people, and that the school should cancel classes out of respect for tradition. The missionaries went on with business as usual, but a number of the students sided with Matsumura and absented themselves. After being called in and reprimanded for the negative influence he was having on his classmates, Matsumura had no choice but to leave the seminary.[5]

Following this abrupt departure in 1881, Matsumura moved to the Kansai area for a period of six years. After being employed briefly by a newspaper in Osaka, he served as pastor of the Takahashi Church in Okayama for three years and then returned to Osaka as a writer for the Christian newspaper *Fukuin shimpō* (Gospel news). This was a formative period in Matsumura's intellectual development as he encountered many new ideas and came in contact with a much larger circle of missionaries and Japanese Christian leaders. His first year in Osaka, for example, he read Darwin's *Origin of the Species*, which shook the foundations of his traditional Christian faith. While he was able to recover his "faith in God" after several days of deep doubt and distress, he found he was no longer able fully to accept the "orthodox" doctrines of traditional Christianity.[6]

During this time he also came to the realization that the Reformed-Presbyterian tradition of the Yokohama Band was only "one among many" versions of Christianity. Some European missionaries and denominations, in fact, were advocating a more rational interpretation of Christianity and, in stark contrast to Matsumura's American missionary teachers, were far more relaxed in their attitudes toward alcohol, tobacco, and the Sabbath. In particular, the leaders associated with the Congregational and Unitarian churches exposed him to new ideas that were to radically reshape his interpretation of the Christian tradition. Two persons deserve mention in this connection.

Kanamori Michitomo (1857–1945), who was trained at Dōshisha and ordained for ministry in the Congregational Church by Niijima Jō, befriended Matsumura when he moved to the Kansai area and helped position him in his first pastorate. Niijima also introduced Matsumura to the new theology and the higher biblical criticism that had recently been imported from Europe. Several years later Kanamori was to make a name for himself as the leading exponent of the new theology. In 1892, his free translation of Otto Pfleiderer's *Religionsphilosophie auf geschichtlichter Grundlage* (1878) appeared in Japanese, and along with his own book, *The Present and Future of Christianity in Japan* (1891), played a major role in introducing the new theology to Japan.[7]

It was also during his stay in Osaka that Matsumura was introduced to the Neo-Confucian philosophy of Ō Yōmei by another Japanese pastor, Yoshioka Kōki (1847–1932). Matsumura's encounter with Yoshioka not only rekindled his interest in the Confucian classics, which had formed the core of his early childhood education, but also provided him with a new philosophical perspective from which to integrate the spiritual wisdom of East and West. From that point on, Matsumura began thinking seriously about forging a Confucian Christianity that could be integrated with the new theology from Europe.

After a brief stint as editor of the *Kirisutokyō shimbun* (Christian newspaper) in Tokyo, Matsumura spent a time in educational work. He served as the head teacher of the Yamagata English School for approximately six months and then moved to Niigata, where he succeeded Uchimura Kanzō at the Hokuetsu Gakkan in 1887. Like Uchimura, Matsumura's educational philosophy was to excite serious criticism from the missionaries associated with the school, leading to his resignation in 1891. His next appointment was as lecturer at the Kanda Kirisutokyō Seinen Kaikan, which lasted for approximately five years. Through his lectures and writings his influence spread. By the end of his term his Saturday lectures were attended by four or five hundred people. Despite his popularity, the board of directors were less than pleased with his theological views, and he was asked to resign in 1897.

Withdrawing from public life, Matsumura spent the next few years in Kamakura engaged in serious study and writing, publishing such works as *A History of the Rise and Fall of Nations* (1902), *Modern European History* (1903), and *Saint Socrates* (1903). This was a time of harsh religious discipline for Matsumura and of deep reflection on his life and future. Although he had been planning to return to the field of education, another "direct revelation" from God instructed him to devote the rest of his life to religious work. In 1905, at the age of forty-seven, Matsumura resolved to begin an independent church and to commit his remaining years to teaching "pure religion" with the aim of bringing about a new, reformed Christianity for Japan.[8]

From Church of Japan to New Religion

During the first several years of its development Matsumura's independent expression of Christianity evolved rapidly.[9] He initially called his movement the One Heart Association, but in 1907 renamed it the Church of Japan and rented quarters to hold regular meetings. The following year he launched the magazine *The Way*, which became the primary carrier of his new Confucian version of Christianity. In one of the early issues Matsumura laid out the purposes of the magazine as to express independent religious views, to explore psychic phenomena, to apply higher criticism to Christianity, and to integrate the culture and ideas of East and West.[10]

Matsumura Kaiseki, founder of The Way.

Matsumura initially organized the Church of Japan, as we mentioned, to create a new and reformed Japanese Christianity independent of Western control. As his religious beliefs and convictions gradually came to be systematized, it became increasingly apparent that it was misleading to refer to his movement as a "Church." Ironically, it was his most sympathetic Japanese colleagues from the Unitarian Church who forced him to recognize that he had clearly departed from the Christian faith.[11] To reflect his new orientation, Matsumura renamed the movement The Way in 1912, referring to it as a "new religion" of the "eternal way." Some years later Matsumura explained that he started the Church of Japan in an effort to reform the traditional version of Christianity, to rid it of its many superstitions, and to ground faith and religious beliefs on scientific thought. What began as a reform ended up as a revolution that could only be called a "new religion."[12] Although Matsumura's new position took shape over a number of years in the pages of The Way, it was the publication of his 1925 book, New Religion, that was the final turning point.

Matsumura understood his new religion as an effort to get back to the essentials of authentic religion. He maintained that all religions had been corrupted by unnecessary accretions that were only a source of competition and conflict. In this sense, The Way represented an attempt at purification and simplification. It was also an effort to reconcile religious belief and practice with the results of higher criticism and modern science. This emphasis is particularly clear in his 1929 book, A Critique of Religions. Matsumura admits that he had once believed in the traditional Christianity of the missionaries and worked to spread this version of the faith. But critical scholarship had convinced him that the central beliefs of orthodox Christianity were no longer tenable. In fact, he went so far as to claim that the doctrines of the infallibility of the Bible, the virgin birth of Jesus, and the theory of atonement are nothing more than lies.

Traditionalist churches have no future, he concluded, because they continue to proclaim these falsehoods, ignoring the advance of knowledge and scholarship.[13] Critics argued that a Christianity without Christ as Savior would not stand, but Matsumura stood his ground and maintained that the Fatherhood of God and the Brotherhood of Man were the only essential teachings of Jesus.[14]

The Teachings of The Way

In addition to the claim that he was establishing a New Religion, Matsumura argued that he was elaborating the basic truths shared by all the ancient religions of the world. His teaching was based on claims to personal experiences of revelation as well as on an appreciation of the truths contained in the sacred writings of Christianity, Buddhism, and Confucianism.[15] His approach is condensed in a small booklet, *The Summit Moon*, which was based on a radio talk he gave on 7 February 1926.[16] In it he summarizes in simple terms the basic beliefs and intent of The Way. The title is drawn from the line of the well-known *waka* poem:

分けのぼる麓の途は	Many are the roads
多けれど同じ高嶺の	ascending from the foot of the mountain,
月を見るかな	but the same summit moon is visible to all.

Gautama the Buddha looked at the moon from India, Confucius from China, and Jesus from Palestine, but each was affirming the same basic reality. Established religions have obscured this common religious experience and faith through corruption and the secondary trappings of scriptures and doctrinal elaborations. All doctrinal debates between religions and between denominations within Christianity are ultimately irrelevant and fruitless. (He mentions by name the conflict between James and Paul in the New Testament, between Luther and Zwingli within the Reformed tradition, and between Catholics and Protestants.) What ultimately matters is spirit, sincerity, and character—not theory. The Way is based on the conviction that it is possible to reduce the central truths of all major religions to the following four basic teachings, which he calls the 四綱領 *shi kōryō* :

1. Belief in God (信神 *shinjin*)

The most basic shared belief is faith and worship of the Lord of the universe (天地主宰の神 *Tenchi shusai no kami*). In Christianity this is spoken of as faith in the Creator who is God the Father; Buddhism speaks of True Suchness or ultimate reality; and in Shinto the focus of this faith is referred to as *Ōmoto no Kami*

(大元の神) or *Ame no minakanushi* (天の御中主). Whether faith be monotheistic, polytheistic, or pantheistic, each religion is founded on belief in the same ultimate reality—the same summit moon. Faith in ultimate reality or God is central, but not in the sense of an absolute Other-Power. Human character can never be improved without discipline and self-exertion.[17] Indeed, Matsumura notes, many religions have deteriorated precisely because they focused exclusively on belief in God without teaching that individuals are responsible for their own development.

2. Cultivation of Moral Character (修徳 *shūtoku*)

Authentic religion is not concerned with "this-worldly benefits" but focuses on the cultivation of virtue and requires strenuous effort to follow the Way. In one fashion or another, all religions instruct us to cultivate virtue and harmonize our lives with the Way. In Shinto this is referred to as *rokkon shōjō* (六根清浄), the purification of the self through detachment from the senses; in Christianity it is explained as ridding oneself of sin; Buddhism exhorts followers to avoid evil (諸悪莫作 *shoaku makusa*) and to do good (衆善奉行 *shūzenbugyō*); finally, Confucianism teaches individuals to rectify the heart (心を正す *kokoro o tadasu*) and master the body (身を修める *mi o osameru*). In short, true religion requires discipline and ascetic practice. It is worth dwelling briefly on this point, which is central to the faith of The Way.

Matsumura rejected the Christian doctrine of original sin in favor of the Confucian understanding of human nature as essentially good (性善説 *seizensetsu*). Accordingly, he saw religious life as a process of self-cultivation that proceeds by stages, not as the once-and-for-all dramatic conversion so often emphasized in the Christian churches. Matsumura felt that his understanding was more suited to the Japanese psyche, and in 1916 published a short booklet explaining the famous Zen Oxherding Pictures as a guide to the path of spiritual cultivation and awakening to ultimate reality. At the same time, he insisted that such an understanding is not incompatible with the teaching of Jesus, who taught in the Parable of the Prodigal Son that individuals can come to their senses and return to God the Father on their own. The transformation that took place in the character of the son was the result of a gradual awakening and did not depend on an outside mediator or on any vicarious sacrifice.[18]

The standpoint taken by Matsumura and his successors is clearly indebted to the Neo-Confucianism of Ō Yōmei. There we see a strong faith in the divine and an emphasis on cultivating the inner insight (心の良知 *kokoro no ryōchi*), which is the innate capacity of each individual to follow the correct path and enter into union with the Great Void of the universe (太虛 *Taikyo*).[19] All persons, not just the saints and sages, are born with the same "true heart" that needs only to be stimulated and developed. The problem is that the average person is not aware of this inherent power to live according to the Way. One contemporary member expressed it this way: "Each person's heart is like a mirror that simply needs to be polished in order to choose the correct path." Worship, study, and seated meditation (静座 *seiza*) are all methods for polishing the mirror of one's heart. Only through these disciplined efforts can one rediscover one's true heart. As individuals advance through the stages of spiritual growth, sinful attitudes, desires, and actions gradually diminish and in their place love, beauty, loyalty, filial piety, righteousness, and faith naturally emerge. One who continues on this path will eventually experience union with God (神人合体 *shinjin gattai*).

3. Love of Neighbor (愛隣 *airin*)

Self-cultivation should not be misunderstood as a form of religious individualism. At their best, all religions teach us to live for others rather than to focus on individual or personal salvation. Our worship and respect of the "one lofty moon" requires that we love our neighbors. This is interpreted broadly to mean that each individual is responsible to live for emperor, nation, and humankind. In short, self-cultivation is not simply for individual liberation but the necessary first step in the wider process of bringing all of life—family, nation, world, universe—into harmony with the way. If we cultivate a heart of sincerity (誠 *makoto*), then we will naturally love our neighbor and contribute to the reordering of all things.[20]

4. Eternal Life (永生 *eisei*)

All religions teach that there is more to life than material existence. *Eternal life* refers to the indestructibility of the soul and life in the world to come. The Shinto tradition explains this as the process of becoming divine and entering the Plain of High Heaven (神になって高天原に上 がる *kami ni natte takamagahara ni agaru*). The notion of eternal life with God in heaven is also central to Christianity. Death may be inevitable but it is not the end. Our bodies may be burned or buried, but we are spiritual beings that continue to exist in the spirit world. This last teaching is the special gift of religion that enables us to live with hope.

Matsumura defined The Way as an association dedicated to putting these four beliefs into practice in everyday life. The vows that its members recite together at the conclusion of each religious service and in daily practice are expressions of commitment to follow this way:

We promise to hold fast to belief in God and always seek to serve him.

We promise to hold fast to the cultivation of virtue and always seek to improve and elevate our character.

We promise to hold fast to our belief in love of neighbor and always serve our nation, the universe, and humankind.

We promise to hold fast to our belief in eternal life and always live with hope.[21]

The Practice of The Way

As we have seen, Neo-Confucianism (more specifically, Yōmeigaku) provided the primary orientation for Matsumura's spiritual path of self-cultivation. The scientific theory of evolution and higher criticism laid the foundations for his critique and eventual rejection of traditional Christianity. In the early years of the movement, services and rituals were largely patterned after the other Christian churches in Japan. The Bible, the Protestant hymn book, and the organ were used in worship services; the sacraments of baptism and the Lord's Supper were observed. It was not long, though, before Matsumura came to realize that traditional Christian worship contained ideas contrary to his own fundamental beliefs. Since the words of most hymns contradicted what he was teaching, he decided to replace them with his own lyrics. He also experimented briefly with the use of traditional Japanese instruments in services. In the end, however, he returned to the organ, but only for a carefully selected number of hymns that were judged consistent with the teachings of The Way or for traditional tunes to which he had supplied new words.

Matsumura also realized that he could not simply imitate the rituals observed in Christian churches. Baptism in the name of the Father, Son, and Holy Spirit, for example, was clearly out of place as a rite of initiation for a movement that rejected the doctrine of the Trinity. Within two years, baptism was dropped as a requirement for membership and replaced with a signature and oath. Since Matsumura had thrown out traditional Christology with its doctrine of the atonement, it was inevitable that he would also discontinue the sacrament of the Lord's Supper. Christian influence remained, but borrowings from Shinto rituals were introduced to give a more authentically Japanese character to worship services.

In 1915 Matsumura secured a piece of land in Tokyo on which to build his headquarters. It was located in an area of Shibuya providentially named *Kamiyama*, God's mountain. A Shinto ceremony of purification (地鎮祭 *jichin-*

Followers of The Way with the founder, (second row, eighth from the right), in front of the Hall of Divine Worship.

sai) was held on the site, and by the following year several buildings had been erected there. The main structure was called the Haitendō (拝天堂), or Hall of Divine Worship, and was modeled on Japanese religious buildings rather than on Western-style churches. The dedication of this building in 1917 for worship and religious training, along with the publication of the *Dōkai Guidebook*, confirmed the establishment of the movement as a religion.

According to my informants, the founder felt that in its original form Shinto was a simple and pure reflection of Japanese culture and customs. It only stood to reason, therefore that Shinto traditions would play a role in shaping forms of worship. Matsumura had a Shinto-like altar placed in the Hall of Divine Worship, where a mirror and sacred strips of paper (御幣 *gohei*) were enshrined as the symbolic expression of ultimate reality (誠の表現 *makoto no hyōgen*). One member described the Hall as follows:

> It was built at a time when Japan was caught up in "worshipping the West." It was unusual to build such a Japanese building at this time. The outside was constructed in the style of a Buddhist temple, but the inside was designed according to the Shinto pattern.

The services also had a Shinto character. At each service, Matsumura performed the Shinto-style clapping of the hands (拍手 *kashiwade*) prior to reciting written prayers before the altar. Services included a period of quiet sitting, a scripture reading (from the *Dōkai Bible* or some Confucian text), and a sermon elaborating some aspect of the four basic teachings of The Way. The service concluded with a prayer, a collective recitation of The Way's oath, and a hymn. Although the Christian rituals of baptism and the Lord's Supper were dropped, weddings and funerals continued to be provided for members.

In addition to formal worship services, members were encouraged to recite the oath daily, and to observe times of prayer and meditation each morning and evening. Just as a Shinto-like altar was used as a focus for worship in the Hall of Divine Worship, Matsumura felt that individual members needed a similar focus for religious practice in their homes. For this purpose he prepared a hanging scroll inscribed with the name of God in Chinese characters: 皇天上帝. He instructed his followers to place it over a Shinto altar or in an alcove so that incense could be burned before it during daily prayer and meditation. One of my informants explained that many people regarded these hanging scrolls as protective amulets. Outsiders criticized the use of these hanging scrolls as no more than idol worship, but Matsumura considered that beginners needed a concrete symbol on which to center their religious activity.[22]

The Way in Process

The religious teaching and practice described above were characteristic of The Way until the end of World War II. Several of my informants who were active in

Inner sanctuary of the Hall of Divine Worship, at Matsumura's funeral (1939).

The Way as students during the war years insisted that they understood it as a separate religion and not as a part of Christianity. The building and worship were Japanese style, the Confucian classics and Eastern thought were always stressed, there were very few references to the Bible in lectures and sermons, Christian hymns were rarely sung, and one never heard the refrain "Amen" used at any of the services. In short, there was very little "smell of Christianity" in The Way.

Since the end of the war, the leaders of The Way have reemphasized the Christian roots of the movement. Matsumura's successor, in fact, referred to the movement as a form of "liberal Christianity."[23] A sign displayed outside the headquarters of The Way in Tokyo identifies itself today with the same phrase. This new self-understanding only gradually evolved in the postwar environment. The "anti-Shinto atmosphere" that followed Japan's defeat and the American Occupation persuaded the leaders that it was prudent to dismantle the Shinto altar in the Hall of Divine Worship and put in its place a simple table with flowers. In 1955 Bible lectures were resumed and the use of the Bible and hymns in religious services gradually increased. The postwar transformation was completed with the rebuilding of the Hall of Divine Worship in 1989, this time designed like a Western church with stained-glass windows and pews. On the surface, The Way looks very much like a Christian institution today, and its high regard for Jesus' teaching about the Fatherhood of God and love of neighbor reconfirm this impression. Other traditional Christian doctrines, however, are still dismissed and the emphasis continues to be placed on the Neo-Confucian teaching regarding self-cultivation.

KAWAI SHINSUI AND CHRIST HEART CHURCH

Matsumura was not the only Japanese leader to stress the importance of self-cultivation in the religious life. Another important illustration of this concern in Japanese Christianity can be found in the life and work of Kawai Shinsui (1867–1962), the founder of Christ Heart Church. Reinterpreting the faith through the lenses of Confucian and Buddhist traditions, this Japanese church maintains that Christianity offers a more complete path of self-cultivation and advocates traditional Buddhist disciplines of meditation to achieve a Christian *satori* (enlightenment), which is understood in terms of union with God. Although not as prolific a writer as Uchimura and Matsumura, Kawai did author a number of books, and his disciples edited and published a number of his lectures.[24] Although he shared their concern for the development of an independent Japanese expression of Christianity, his own understanding and expression of the faith differed significantly from the intellectualism of the Nonchurch movement, the liberalism of The Way, and the simplistic interpretation of Christianity he encountered in most of the mission churches.

Kawai's Religious and Intellectual Development

Like Matsumura, Kawai's early Christian formation began in mission churches and institutions. Born in the village of Onuma in Yamanashi Prefecture in 1867, Kawai's serious encounter with Christianity dates from a personal tragedy as a young man of twenty-two. Over the course of one year, five members of his family became seriously ill and died. His search for meaning in the midst of this despair led him to the New Testament. Comforted by Jesus' words in the Sermon on the Mount, "Blessed are they that mourn, for they shall be comforted," Kawai converted and received baptism in a Methodist mission church in 1890. Three years later he enrolled in Tōhoku Gakuin, a theological school related to the German Reformed mission, in order to prepare for Christian ministry. Although he received instruction from missionary teachers during his time at Tōhoku Gakuin College, his principal mentor was Oshikawa Masayoshi.[25] From Oshikawa he learned that deep religious experience and union with God (神人合一 shinjin gōitsu) through self-cultivation were important aspects of the Christian faith that its Western missionary representatives had overlooked. Although Kawai was not to establish an independent church of his own for several decades, a new understanding of the Christian faith was largely shaped during his time of study and work in Sendai (1893–1901).[26]

In his religious autobiography, My Spiritual Experiences, Kawai recalls how he began to reflect on the relationship between his Christian faith and the Asian religious traditions rooted from of old in the soil of Japan:

> While thus I was pursuing my study, a sudden idea came to me: What if Buddha, Confucius, Socrates should meet Christ? What if Wang Yang-Ming, Dōgen, Nichiren, or Hakuin should believe in Christ? I am sure they would discover something in addition to what Peter, James, John, and Paul had found. This being so, some greater truth beyond the Christianity conveyed from the West may be revealed by embodying the minds of these saints, and thus providing the West with the secret of truth found also in Japan.[27]

Kawai thus came to the realization that the Bible does not exhaust the teaching and richness of Christ. In fact, he reasoned, Jesus' message and teaching would have been different had he encountered Confucius or Buddha, rather than the simple peasants of Israel. To explain the teaching of Christ through an encounter with these saints from Asia became Kawai's mission.

In order to achieve an understanding of Christianity that could unite East and West, Kawai saw that more than academic study of ancient texts was needed—nothing less than an existential encounter with the wisdom of these Asian saints. While carrying on his theological studies, Kawai began to meditate every evening for five or six hours in a nearby field. After two years of serious practice, he experienced firsthand the reality of union with God, a teaching that his mentor Oshikawa had shared with him several years before. "At that instant," Kawai recalls, "I experienced and understood these words too: 'Blessed are the pure

Kawai Shinsui in his study at the Fuji-yoshida headquarters, (1954, age 88).

in heart: for they shall see God' (Mt. 5:8)."[28] This confirmation of faith provided Kawai with the confidence to develop his own independent expression of Christianity. "Once I had seen God with my own eyes, the logic of the learned was no match for my faith."[29]

Kawai's Interpretation of Christianity

In 1927 Kawai established Christ Heart Church within the grounds of Gunze Silk Manufacturing Company, where he had been head of the education department for almost twenty years. As he explained in one of his early lectures at Gunze, his reinterpretation of the Christian faith is based on thirty-six years of study, insights gained through intense meditation, direct revelations from God, and the wisdom of the saints of East and West.

As I pointed out earlier in the discussion of continuing revelation (chapter three), Kawai came to understand and elaborate the significance of Jesus for Japanese in terms of the "fulfillment" theology contained in the Gospel of Matthew. Like Uchimura, he argued that God had been actively at work in

Kawai with students from his Gakusei Shūdōin in Tokyo, 1919.

Asian history and culture long before the arrival of Western missionaries. This new understanding and conviction was expressed in the creed of Christ Heart Church as follows: "We believe the ways of the ancient saints are not destroyed but fulfilled by the coming of Christ." For Kawai, these "ancient saints" included Buddha, Confucius, the Neo-Confucianist Wang-Yang Ming, and a number of Buddhist saints (Hōnen, Shinran, Nichiren, Dōgen, and Hakuin).[30] Like John the Baptist in ancient Palestine, these Asian saints prepared the way for the coming of Christ and in essence constitute the "Old Testament" for Japanese Christians. Kawai writes that, while engaging in meditation in May of 1921, he experienced communion with the soul of Confucius and "reached the conviction that the mind of Christ and the spirit of Confucius were indeed similar manifestations." His elaboration of this fulfillment theology in relation to Confucius is worth quoting at length:

> *I revere your brightest life as a forerunner to Christ* with your seventy-four years on earth when you labored courageously. The great work you left behind you of saving the world depends now entirely upon us. Though you have been long in the realm of the unseen world, and I am here on earth, I will ask you to come to our help that we may together accomplish the sacred work to build up the Kingdom of Heaven.[31]

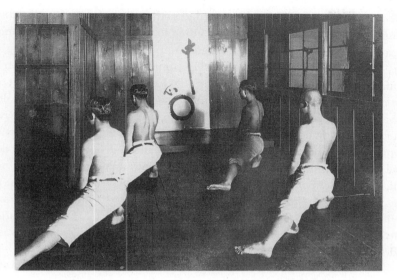

Students engaged in the morning practice of *kyōkenjutsu* (Tokyo, 1925).

In stark contrast to the displacement theology to which the missionaries appealed in their rejection of Japanese religiosity, Kawai stressed that the Confucian and Buddhist traditions offered much of value that could be incorporated into the lives of Christians. Accordingly, Zen meditation and *kyōkenjutsu* (強健術, another influential form of bodily training and discipline) became important means of spiritual development in the Christ Heart Church. Christianity does not require that we reject the goodness that appears outside of the Christian tradition; rather, we are called in Christ to "gather together all of the truth, goodness, and beauty from other religious traditions."[32] Kawai expressed a deep appreciation for the "riches" of Asian religions, but at the same time he was convinced that Jesus the Christ fulfilled and transcended these traditions.[33] What distinguished Jesus from the saints of earlier times and other places was his unique teaching that the spirit of the living God would dwell in us and guide us along the path of perfection, and the fact of his resurrection from the dead and promise of the world to come.

Two passages from the New Testament form the core of Kawai's interpretation of Christianity.[34] The first passage is from Philippians: "Let the same mind be in you that was in Christ Jesus" (2:5). This text constitutes the first pillar of Kawai's teaching and the inspiration for the name of his church. To be a Christian, Kawai explains, means to take on the "mind [heart] of Christ." In the

85

same way that Zen Buddhism is referred to as the religion of the Buddha-mind (*Busshinshū* 仏心宗), Kawai thought it fitting to name his way the Christ-mind religion (*Kirisuto shinshū* 基督心宗). Christianity is not just about "believing" in Jesus as savior, but involves discipleship, training, and practice in order to acquire the mind of Christ. Medical learning does not of itself cure illness if one does not follow the prescribed treatment. So, too, a knowledge of doctrine does not save without practice of the faith. In Kawai's words, "One cannot be saved by a faith based on doctrinal knowledge alone. There is no transformation without practice, and no salvation without transformation."[35] The transplanted doctrinal expressions of Christianity are like guidebooks to Mount Fuji sitting on a shelf. Their descriptions of slopes, trails, and peaks may all be correct, but the point is to climb and experience the mountain for oneself. Similarly, the aim of religion is to experience God directly and to undergo personal transformation. Instead of talking about salvation and union with God, Kawai's concern was to guide individuals to experience the reality firsthand.

The second New Testament passage emphasized by Kawai are the words of Jesus recorded in the Gospel of Matthew: "Be ye perfect, therefore, as your heavenly Father is perfect" (5:48). Christ requires perfection of his disciples, which can only be accomplished through serious spiritual training.[36] Commenting on the passage, Kawai explains that God's ultimate purpose is to bring all of creation to perfection, including human beings who have been created in the image of God. Just as the time it takes to complete a marathon varies from runner to runner, the time it will take each one of us to complete the path of perfection also varies. Those of us who fail to open our eyes and make progress on the path in this life will face the purifying fire of God's "education" in the world to come.[37] While we are reconciled with God through faith in Christ, the process of being remade in the image of Christ takes discipline and effort.

Borrowing the language of this New Testament passage, Kawai refers to his teaching of the way as the "Perfect Faith." God is perfect and his son Christ is both the perfect savior and the perfect teacher of humankind.[38] Kawai continued to affirm the traditional Christian doctrine of salvation from sin and eternal life through Jesus Christ.[39] He insisted, however, that this was not the whole of Christianity and that an exclusive emphasis on this teaching led to a shallow or superficial form of religion. I cite from the official translation:

> To take Jesus as a mere savior is to see His half side. To take Jesus as a mere master is also to see His other half. Both sides are of equal importance, and we should neither show any partiality nor weigh the importance of the two. As His way of salvation, plain and all-permeating, is necessary, so His way of instruc-

tion, solid and uplifting, is indispensable. In order that we may be saved, reliance would always suffice us; but in order that we may be educated, spiritual training is necessary.[40]

The way of Christ, therefore, includes both Other-Power and self-power.[41] One must persevere and complete the training process in order to become like the Master.[42]

Although Christianity is supposed to be a religion that unifies faith and ethical practice, Kawai observed that many Christians have fallen into a kind of "Pure Land Buddhist faith" that lacks a concern for moral training and discipline.[43] If all we do as Christians is pray and ask God for favors, we are in no position to criticize others for their religion of this-worldly benefits. This is precisely what he found troubling about the transplanted mission churches and the Protestant theology that accompanied it. Kawai argued that most Protestants followed the interpretation of the German Reformer Martin Luther and failed to understand and appreciate the Epistle of James and its teaching about practice or the "works" of faith. Luther thought this New Testament letter obscured the gospel of "grace" taught by the Apostle Paul and hence regarded it as an "epistle of straw." By doing so, however, Luther was only able to grasp half of the New Testament faith.[44] It is interesting to note here that Kawai spoke positively of the Roman Catholic tradition insofar as it affirmed the value of ascetic discipline in the lives of the saints and mystics.[45]

This special concern and emphasis on practice and self-cultivation is incorporated into the creed of Christ Heart Church, along with Kawai's fulfillment theology and affirmation of traditional Christian doctrines.

1. We believe in God the only Perfect Heavenly Father: Infinitely Great, Truly Sincere, Supremely Strong, Absolutely Good, Omniscient, Omnipotent, Supremely Beautiful, and of Divine Love; who made this heaven and earth and all things therein; and reigns, teaches, saves, judges, protects, destroys, and completes in the end.

2. We believe in Jesus Christ who represents and reveals this Heavenly Father in perfection, and *saves* and *educates* all the world, always working together with the Heavenly Father.

3. We believe in the Holy Spirit who develops, helps, comforts, and sanctifies us, working in our hearts all the time.

4. *We believe the ways of ancient saints are not destroyed but rather fulfilled by the coming of Christ.*

87

5. We believe that the practical way of serving our Heavenly Father and contributing to our fellowmen is to stand on the basis of sincerity which Christ valued most, and to aim at the perfection of the Heavenly Father which Christ indicated, and then, through perfect faith, to develop perfect character, do our duty perfectly, love men perfectly—thus each of us advance to perfection and thereby bring on earth the Kingdom of God.

6. We believe in the life everlasting and the existence of the world to come.[46]

On 1 January 1927, Kawai made a public declaration that he was establishing Christ Heart Church as a new and independent religious path.[47] That same year he published the final version of his poem, *A Eulogy on Jesus Christ*. These verses on the life of Christ, along with the *Seven Great Vows and Prayers*, became a part of the enlarged canon of the Christ Heart Church. Kawai had worked on the poem during his many years at Gunze and published an earlier and shorter version in Matsumura's magazine *The Way* in 1914. The revised version was based on "additional revelations from God." Written in classsical *kanbun* style, the text provided a concise synopsis of the life of Christ that could be memorized easily and used as a focus for daily meditation. It was also read in Sunday services along with the Bible.[48]

From the very beginning, Kawai made it clear that he had no intention of developing a popular movement for the masses; rather, his aim was to gather a small group of dedicated disciples who were committed to the path of self-cultivation and perfection. Enhancing the character of the few was regarded by him as more important than attracting a large number of mediocre or average members. The *Seven Great Vows and Prayers* (七大誓願 *Shichi dai seigan*), which define the meaning of membership and discipleship in the Christ Heart Church, reveal the high expectations and elitist orientation of the movement (what Max Weber referred to as "virtuosi religiosity").[49] Inspired by the Buddhist tradition in his development of these vows, Kawai expanded the four great vows "that all bodhisattvas make at the outset of their spiritual careers."[50] These vows were regarded as the perfect expression of the heart of religion and understood to be a "completion and fulfillment" of Buddhist wisdom in light of the revelation of Christ.[51] I reproduce the text of the vows here:

七大誓願	*The Seven Great Vows and Prayers*
天父神子誓願敬愛	We pray and vow that we may ever be loving and adoring our Heavenly Father and the Son.

聖霊良心誓願信従	We pray and vow that we may ever be faithful to the Holy Spirit and conscience.
罪悪迷執誓願悔改	We pray and vow that we may ever be repentant and void of all sin and all folly.
衆生万物背願救養	We pray and vow that we may ever be serving all men and cherishing all things in all the world.[52]
職分尊重誓願勤労	We pray and vow that we may ever be diligent in our day's exertions, thinking highly of our duties.
妙道完全誓願学修	We pray and vow that we may ever be learning, the mysterious perfect way pursuing.
神国清和誓願臨格	We pray and vow that the sacred peace of the Kingdom of God may come and abide with us.

Religious Practice in Christ Heart Church

Kawai instructed his disciples that to keep these vows and complete the path to perfection that ends with union with God requires the daily discipline of prayer, meditation, Bible study, and practice. He likened these four to "a four-wheeled carriage that runs on the rail of love and leads individuals to the Kingdom of God." If the carriage does not ride smoothly when one of the wheels is missing, neither can spiritual development advance without all its elements in place. Prayer and meditation are referred to as the quiet disciplines; Bible study and practice, as dynamic disciplines.[53]

Prayer marks the beginning of the religious life; it is the means whereby we express our basic faith in God and seek to understand his will for us. Care must be taken not to allow prayers to become shallow and self-centered by constantly asking special favors of God. Prayer is how we honor God and prepare our hearts for meditation.

Meditation guides us to personal transformation and enlightenment. Although the term *meisō* 瞑想 is used here, the Christ Heart Church bases its meditation on Zen, with some modification to allow sitting on church pews or chairs. Kawai also designated Romans 12:1 as the verse to use as a *daimoku* (題目, a repetitive prayer or chant) during meditation: "I appeal to you therefore, brothers and sisters, by the mercies of God, to present your bodies as a living sacrifice, holy and acceptable to God, which is your spiritual worship."[54] Meditation is understood as a duty to God and not simply as a means to enlightenment. Through it one loses the sense of separate existence and experiences oneness

Saint Takahashi Mutsuko laid out in state, with Kawai and three disciples (Fujiyoshida, 1947).

with God. Without it, one can only hunger for the heaven and eternal life Jesus Christ spoke, but not taste it. Not even prayer and good works are complete without the discipline of meditation.

Spiritual Bible study opens the faithful to knowledge of Jesus as savior and teacher, to the indwelling Spirit of God, the kingdom of God, and life in the world to come. The Bible is a book of faith and must be read with eyes of faith and internalized through quiet reflection.

Finally, authentic faith requires *practice*. Self-cultivation, personal spiritual advancement, and enlightenment are not the terminus of the religious life. Their whole purpose is to open one to live for others and for the kingdom of God. Those who seriously pursue the path and acquire the heart of Christ will be engaged in lives of service to humankind.

By following these methods for four years in Sendai Kawai "encountered the living Christ" and experienced "union with God" as a young man of thirty in 1896.[55] His debt to the wisdom of the East is clear, and yet Kawai insisted on a clear difference between the Zen enlightenment of *satori* and his own teaching and experience of "the perfect, wondrous way" (完全妙道 *kanzen myōdō*). Zen creates the sense of equality with ultimate reality, whereas the Christian path preserves the idea that God transcends all.[56]

During his lifetime, only five or six direct disciples were recognized by Kawai as having achieved this enlightenment experience. One of them, a

The *Seven Great Vows and Prayers* in Kawai's calligraphy.

The Holy Image used in the Christ Heart Church.

woman named Takahashi Mutsuko, took her asceticism to extremes. While serving as Kawai's secretary and personal assistant, Takahashi committed herself to lifelong religious training and celibacy. In spite of frequent illnesses, she fasted regularly and seriously pursued the fourfold disciplines advocated by Kawai. Upon her untimely death at the young age of forty-four, it was discovered that she had been engaging in more austere measures. Among her belongings were found a box containing Kawai's *A Eulogy on Jesus Christ* and no less than 115 copies of the New Testament. Every page of every book—about 30,000 pages in all—had been drenched in blood drawn from an incision in her side. Kawai was moved by Takahashi's "blood-stained sanguiscripts," and encouraged other disciples to imitate her spirit but not her methods. Clearly she had gone too far, but this did not deter Kawai from declaring her a saint, affirming that she had achieved *satori* and penetrated the inner mystery of Christ Heart Church.[57]

Like Matsumura before him, Kawai recognized the need for visible symbols on which to focus one's spiritual cultivation. He encouraged followers to keep a small copy of a portrait of Christ with them to remind them of the presence of Christ. The founder himself carried one in the sleeve of his kimono for many years as an aid to his own spiritual development. A larger version of that same "holy image" may be found today on the sanctuary walls of the movement's churches.

91

Despite the special stress put on individual spirituality in Christ Heart Church, various forms of community worship and training are also observed. Following the pattern of traditional Christian churches, services are usually held on Sunday morning and generally follow the Protestant order of worship, including hymns, Bible reading, a sermon, and prayer. In addition, services today include a reading from Kawai's *A Eulogy on Jesus Christ*, ritual bowing before the "holy image" and a photograph of the founder also hung in the sanctuary, and a group chanting of the Seven Great Vows. Baptism is observed as a membership ritual, but the Lord's Supper has never been observed. Curiously, Kawai's writings make no mention of this traditional Christian observance, either as a memorial or as a sacrament, and no one in the movement today seems to have any explanation for why it was left out of religious practice in the Christ Heart Church.[58]

The buildings used by Christ Heart Church are frequently referred to as a *dōjō*, since they serve as a place for religious training and not just as a sanctuary for worship services. Sunday services are frequently followed by meditation and study sessions. Since, as we saw, Kawai had come to regard the Confucian classics as a kind of Old Testament for the Japanese, these works are often studied along with his own commentaries and lectures.

In addition to local weekly and monthly meetings, a church-wide Cultivation Meeting is held for several days each summer at the Sōhonzan church located near the founder's birthplace in Fujiyoshida (Yamanashi Prefecture). These meetings contain lectures and worship services, teachers providing concentrated instruction in meditation and bodily training.[59] As a part of the training program participants clean the buildings, grounds, and grave sites. The annual retreat concludes with a memorial service for the founder.

Another feature of Christ Heart Church that distinguishes it from most other Christian churches in Japan is its flexible position regarding participation in the rituals of other religious traditions. Unlike the mission churches, which generally took a strong stand against such involvement with other groups, members are encouraged to show proper respect and to share in traditional customs as their conscience dictates. As a result, in addition to memorial services within the church, many members continue to participate in various Buddhist services for deceased family members and friends. For example, the church avoids conducting services during the annual period of festivals for the dead known as *obon* in order that members can freely participate in ancestral memorial rituals with other relatives.

The stated position of the church is that it is appropriate for Christians to show respect for those who have died, whether it be at church services, Buddhist memorials, or even Yasukuni Shrine (the Shinto shrine where many of Japan's war dead are enshrined). At one time Christ Heart Church was a member of the *Kirisutokyō Rengōkai*, an ecumenical association of Christian churches in Japan, but found it necessary to withdraw because of the strong opposition voiced by the association against taking part in rituals honoring the war dead at Yasukuni Shrine. The leaders of Christ Heart Church decided it could no longer remain a part of an organization that would discourage its members from showing proper reverence for their deceased relatives.

SOME COMPARATIVE OBSERVATIONS

In this chapter I have tried to highlight some of the major influences on Matsumura and Kawai in their development of independent Japanese expressions of Christian belief and practice. Both movements illustrate the complexity of the indigenization process and some alternative ways in which Western traditions and ideas (Reformed theology, higher criticism, and the new theology) have been interpreted and appropriated in light of diverse Asian or indigenous traditions (Neo-Confucianism, Zen Buddhism, Shinto). In response to the doctrinal emphases and rigidity of Western churches, Matsumura and Kawai stressed the importance of personal religious experience. Following in the steps of Uchimura Kanzō, these founders rejected the control of Western mission churches and shared a positive orientation toward different aspects of Asian religious and philosophical traditions, as well as a general disdain for priestly and sacramental traditions and rituals of Western churches (although Christ Heart Church has continued baptism as a rite of initiation). Matsumura's acceptance of higher criticism and the new theology distinguishes him from both Uchimura and Kawai.

Without denying the importance of faith in Other-Power, what distinguishes both founders and movements from Uchimura's Nonchurch movement is their conviction that self-power and moral cultivation are equally important aspects of the authentic religious life. This particular emphasis is hardly unique to these new Christian movements. It resembles in many ways the *Shingaku* 心学 movement that flourished in the Tokugawa period. As an earlier synthesis of Neo-Confucianism and Zen traditions, this movement similarly stressed cultivation of the mind or heart through meditation.[60] This movement was in rapid decline by the early Meiji period, but the concern for self-cultivation reappeared in a number of New Religions that were established over the course of Japan's modernization. This has been widely recognized with reference to such movements as Kurozumikyō, Hitonomichi Kyōdan, and PL Kyōdan.[61] The foregoing pages should make it clear that even the subculture of Japanese Christianity has been reshaped significantly by this important tradition.

CHAPTER SIX

Japanese Versions of Apostolic Christianity

C HRISTIANITY IN JAPAN has long had the reputation of being a difficult and demanding religion, one primarily for intellectuals and the educated white-collar middle class. In stark contrast to the scores of other New Religions that have emerged in Japan's modern century, Christianity has rarely been regarded as a viable alternative for the general population.[1] This image is no doubt related to the decision of the earliest Protestant missionaries to concentrate their attentions on Japanese from the samurai class, for whom popular folk religiosity was of little concern. In the Meiji period the samurai class, the most literate and intellectual class of Japanese society of the time, was overrepresented in the churches: the mere 5 percent of the total Japanese population in the 1880s and 1890s who were of samurai origins accounted for approximately 30 percent of total membership in the Protestant churches.[2] The image of Japanese Christianity as an intellectual's religion is further reflected in the fact that the greatest majority of church leaders were drawn from these same samurai families, where they had received a Confucian education that set them apart from the rest of the population.

Taken together, then, the preferences of the missionaries and the native orientation of those singled out for proselytization made it difficult for the new religion to appeal to the ordinary masses of Japanese. Ariga Tetsutarō describes persuasively the dominant place of this "elite" in the first Protestant churches and their disdain for the religiosity of the common people:

> Christian leaders of the Meiji period, being of samurai origin, had shared the samurai prejudice against Buddhism and Shinto. For precisely because these were the religions of the lower classes upon which the samurai looked down, they were bound to be more important factors of the society where all the former classes were mixed. This point they seemed to have missed. And here perhaps should be sought the chief reason why Japanese Protestantism has neither been able to extend its influence widely beyond the educated middle classes nor to answer successfully the challenges made by Buddhism, Shinto, and more recent popular sects.[3]

The similarly elitist indigenous versions of Christianity articulated by Uchimura, Matsumura, and Kawai—as we have seen in the preceding chapters—did little to remedy the imbalance. Like the majority of the foreign missionaries and the early Japanese Christian leaders, they tended to underestimate the strength and persistence of traditional and popular religious concerns, and hence failed to come to terms theologically with the needs of the broader population. This was to be the role of a second wave of indigenous movements organized in the 1930s and 1940s. Critical of both the mission churches and existing indigenous forms, these movements have succeeded in responding most directly to the needs of ordinary people and to the concerns embodied in folk religiosity.

Carlo Caldarola's study of Japanese Christianity included a worthy analysis of one of these movements, the Original Gospel (or *Makuya,* Tabernacle Movement), whose roots go back to Nonchurch movement, but concluded with a misleading generalization:

> Makuya is the only movement to indigenize Christianity—traditionally an upper-class religion—in the Japanese lower classes. By emphasizing its pentecostal aspects, the Makuya has ingeniously succeeded in fostering the continuity of a Japanese folk-religious tradition dominated by shamanism, magic, and miracles.[4]

The fact is, however, there are a number of other indigenous movements that have made similar cultural adaptations and attracted members from among the less educated layers of society. They include the Glorious Gospel Christian Church (1936), the Living Christ One Ear of Wheat Church (1939), Christian Canaan Church (1940), Japan Ecclesia of Christ (1940), the Spirit of Jesus Church (1941), Holy Ecclesia of Jesus (1946), and the Sanctifying Christ Church (1948). All of these movements show a common concern with recovering an "apostolic faith" that they consider missing in the transplanted mission churches. This chapter focuses on two of the larger movements from this second period, the Spirit of Jesus Church and the Holy Ecclesia of Jesus, and briefly reconsiders the Pentecostal version of the Nonchurch Christianity that was introduced in Caldarola's study.

MURAI JUN AND THE SPIRIT OF JESUS CHURCH

The founder of the Spirit of Jesus Church, Murai Jun, was born in 1897, the second son of a Methodist minister. Raised in a Christian environment, he went on to study theology at the Methodist-affiliated Aoyama Gakuin in Tokyo. At one point during his studies Murai became deeply troubled and was contemplating suicide. In 1918, while taking a ferry in Okayama Prefecture, he made up his mind to throw himself overboard and put an end to it all. At that moment he felt the presence of the Holy Spirit overpower him and he began to speak in tongues. The experience cleared his mind of all religious doubt and filled him with new strength and vision for the Christian mission.

Murai dropped out of Aoyama Gakuin and began evangelistic work. In time he assumed the post of pastor in the Japan Bible Church (the church that was to become the Japan Assemblies of God in 1949). In 1933, word of the pentecostal experience that had changed his life spread among the membership of his small congregation in Nishisugamo, Tokyo. But in 1941, after visiting the True Jesus Church in Taiwan, a Chinese indigenous movement that had been in existence for just over twenty years,[5] Murai decided to take leave of his congregation. It was in this same year that his wife, Suwa, received a revelation from God in which the name *Iesu no Mitama Kyōkai* (Spirit of Jesus Church) was given to designate them as a new church.

As we have already remarked in chapter two, Murai launched a rather strident critique of the existing mission churches and indigenous movements in the course of defending the establishment of his independent Spirit of Jesus Church. This is hardly surprising, given that conservative evangelical groups accused him of being a "servant of satan" for practicing tongues-speaking and sponsoring emotional healing services.[6] Speaking in tongues, in their view, was a mark of possession by an evil spirit, not the work of the Spirit of God. For his part, Murai insisted that he was restoring the authentic form of New Testament Christianity that was no longer practiced by churches in the West or in transplanted mission churches.

Unlike Uchimura and Matsumura, who were prolific authors, Murai left behind very few writings. As far as I have been able to determine, his only publications are *Biblical Theology* (聖書神学) and a short *Guide to Christianity* (基督教案内), both of which are still used for training pastors in the Spirit of Jesus Bible School in Tokyo. These writings elaborate traditional pentecostal traits (Spirit baptism, speaking in tongues, healing), the unitarian Jesus-only doctrine, the renewed emphasis on sabbath worship, the restoration of the New Testament rituals of foot-washing and baptism for the dead, and a strong eschatological orientation and emphasis on the doctrine of the Second Coming of Christ. Murai maintained that true Christianity is a religion of signs and miracles, and that the church today is called on to reproduce what went on in the early Christian movement in preparation for the triumphant return of Christ.

Spirit of Jesus Church pastors are fond of quoting from the Gospel of Mark (16:15–18) to define their basic mission. There the disciples are commanded to preach the gospel and baptize believers, and are promised the power to perform miracles, drive out demons, speak in strange tongues, and heal the sick. Pastors are also prepared to quote chapter and verse for all of the other practices enjoined by Murai. Baptisms, for example, are only performed in the name of Jesus Christ in accord with the example and teaching of the Apostle Peter (Acts 2:38; 10:48), rather than with the trinitarian formula of Father, Son, and Spirit that was adopted by the Western churches. Similarly, baptisms for the dead are conducted according to biblical teaching and precedent (1 Cor 15:29). Healing by prayer and anointing with oil is another New Testament practice (James 5:14–16) neglected by many churches but encouraged in the Spirit of Jesus Church. The ritual of the washing of feet performed by Jesus (John 13) has also been revived with pastors washing the feet of new members immediately following baptism. In colloquial Japanese the expression *washing one's feet of something*—roughly equivalent to the English expression *to wash one's hands of something*—is used by former Yakuza (gangsters) to express their decision to leave the underworld. In the same way, as one pastor explained to me, ritual footwashing in the church symbolizes that members have cut ties with the devil and embarked on a new life. In addition to these practices, the Spirit of Jesus

Church also preserves the sacrament of the Lord's Supper that earlier Japanese founders had all rejected.

Foreign Influences: Pentecostal and Dispensational Connections

Without gainsaying the personal charisma of Murai, it should be noted that the doctrines and practices he promoted were by and large the result of foreign influences. Prior to his encounter with the True Jesus Church on a visit to Taiwan in 1941, Murai had already aligned himself with pentecostal Christianity with its stress on Spirit baptism and speaking in tongues, but his subsequent emphasis on sabbath worship, washing of the feet, and "Jesus-only" (i.e., unitarian) doctrine was clearly prompted by what he found in the True Jesus Church.[7]

Actually, the genealogy is a bit more complicated. In his study of indepen-dent Christian movements in China, Daniel Bays has shown that many of the doctrinal peculiarities that attracted the attention of Murai were themselves of foreign origin. The anti-trinitarian "Jesus-only" teaching goes back to develop-ments within Christianity in the United States and was widespread among Pentecostals there and in Canada some years before the first Pentecostal mis-sionaries were sent to China.[8] Bays also suggests that the teaching regarding sabbath worship was probably due to the influence of early American Seventh-Day Adventist missionaries and their publications, which became increasingly evident in China after 1902.[9] In the light of these various influences, Bays describes the True Jesus Church as an "international transnational phenome-non."

Murai's eschatological orientation and emphasis on the Second Coming of Christ shows a similar reliance on outside developments, though I have not been able to document the immediate sources. In particular, dispensationalism has had an unmistakable impact on theology of the founder. A theological current that first emerged among Plymouth Brethren in England and Ireland during the 1830s and subsequently spread in North America, dispensationalism became the dominant model of scriptural interpretation in fundamentalist circles and is still popular in evangelical and pentecostal churches today.[10] Eschatological in focus, it divides biblical history into distinct periods, or dispensations, during which God deals with humanity through different covenants or conditions. In 1909 C. I. Scofield (1843–1921), an American pastor and Bible teacher, pub-lished his dispensational and premillennial Bible, in which he popularized the idea of seven dispensations: "Innocence (before the Fall), Conscience (from the

Fall to Noah), Human Government (from Noah to Abraham), Promise (from Abraham to Moses), Law (from Moses to Christ), Grace (the Church age), the Kingdom (the Millennium). The close of the Millennium ushers in the Eternal State."[11] It seems likely that Murai Jun was exposed to dispensationalism through his contact with American missionaries or Japanese Bible teachers who had adopted this approach to reading the scriptures.

An examination of Murai's publications suggests that Scofield's notes provided his study of the Bible with a frame of reference. Based on his writings, figure 4 depicts the dispensational and eschatological theology of the Spirit of Jesus Church. The period from the fall of humankind into sin until the time of the coming of Jesus covers a span of four thousand years. The death, resurrection, and ascension of Jesus are followed by the coming of the Holy Spirit, whose outpouring inaugurates a period of grace, salvation, the Holy Spirit, and the Church. Murai and his church maintain that the signs, miracles, and tongues that accompanied the coming of the Holy Spirit in the New Testament story are still present and will continue in effect until the end of the age of the church, when the rapture of true Christians will occur. After a seven-year period of tribulation, Satan will be cast into hell and Jesus Christ will return to earth with his followers to establish the millennial kingdom. At the end of this period, Satan is to be released for a brief period prior to the final judgment, at which time the human race will be divided into those who are to live eternally with God and those who will be cast into the lake of fire for eternal punishment. The old

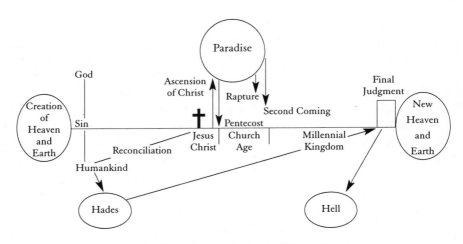

Figure 4. Cosmology of the Spirit of Jesus Church

heaven and earth will be destroyed as the new heaven and earth, the eternal home of the people of God, is at last revealed.

Those familiar with dispensationalism and pentecostalism in North America will hardly be surprised by Murai's theological scheme. Like other pentecostal groups, the Spirit of Jesus Church rejects intellectualism and emphasizes the importance of religious experience. Speaking in tongues, anointing with oil, dancing in the spirit, miracles of healing, and revelations from God are all basic components of everyday religious life. The symbolic world of the believer is filled with spirits, signs, miracles, and wonders. Miraculous healings and religious experience, rather than intellectual or theological sophistication, are the church's defining traits. Unlike many other Christian churches in Japan, the Spirit of Jesus Church does not engage in educational activities like running kindergartens or offering Bible classes in English. Only "biblical" ministry that focuses on sabbath and Sunday worship services and on home meetings during the week are regarded as legitimate church activities. While it does operate a Bible School for the training of pastors and evangelists, there is in effect no Christian education or Bible study for ordinary members.

The message is simple and clear: believe in Jesus Christ and receive the baptism of water and the Spirit. Virtually the only teaching that is offered has to do with what one must do to be saved and baptized.[12] Seekers are instructed—under not inconsiderable pressure, I would add—to repeat "Hallelujah, hallelujah!" over and over again until Holy Spirit baptism is experienced and the gift of speaking in tongues is granted.

The version of Christianity advanced by the Spirit of Jesus Church tends to appeal to those Japanese already deeply rooted in folk religious traditions. Considerable emphasis is placed on what is usually referred to as *gense riyaku* 現世利益, or the worldly benefits of religion.[13] In sharp contrast to the preoccupation with self-cultivation that marked earlier indigenous movements, sermons in the Spirit of Jesus Church tend to reiterate promises of spiritual and material blessing that await the true believer, and testimonials by the faithful bear witness to God's fulfillment of these promises. On one occasion, I heard Bishop Murai Suwa, the founder's wife, assure members of the congregation that God would bless their business enterprises. "For those of you who are shopkeepers," she explained, "God will lead customers past the stores of your competitors and through your front doors."

The promise of worldly benefits is complemented by the benefits of physical healing that are available to each member. A small flask of oil is kept on the pulpit beside the Bible for use in healing rituals that take place at many services.[14] Individuals frequently step forward toward the end of services to receive special prayer and anointing with oil for personal healing.

Unlike the earliest Japanese founders who looked for common ground between indigenous religious traditions and Christianity and tried to show the continuity from the one to the other, Murai's Spirit of Jesus Church sees itself engaged in "spiritual warfare" with traditional Japanese religiosity and condemns its practice as "idolatrous." In Okinawa, for example, church leaders pit themselves in an ongoing struggle against the Yuta (leaders of traditional religion) for spiritual control of the islands.[15] By conducting healing services and exorcisms, pastors claim to have proved their religious authority by surpassing the spiritual power of local religious leaders. In their aggressive evangelistic campaigns, pastors have instructed followers to destroy pagan idols and abstain from participation in pagan rituals. Despite these strict measures, however, the Spirit of Jesus Church has managed to establish more churches across Japan than any other indigenous movement. It has done so not by rejecting the religious needs of its members but by offering Christian alternatives designed to perform the same functions as traditional religious practices. Thus, for instance, members are forbidden to practice traditional rites of ancestor veneration while at the same time the church takes care of the dead by conducting vicarious baptisms and other special services throughout the year. In other words, the theology and practice of the Spirit of Jesus Church are far from exhausted by this-worldly concerns. Considerable attention is given to the dangers and fears associated with ancestors and the spirit world in both formal religious services and pastoral care. Clergy also provide "Christianized" rituals of land purification (地鎮祭 jichinsai) to protect members from evil spirits and make it safe for Christians to build homes and live in them. More than anything else it is the way Murai and his followers have directly addressed these folk religious concerns that distinguishes the Spirit of Jesus Church from Western pentecostal movements.

The Organization of Indigenous Christianity

In sharp contrast to Uchimura's rejection of Western church polities, clergy, and sacraments, Murai claimed to have rediscovered the strands of biblical tradition that legitimize a structure of authority with a special class of religious leaders. The Spirit of Jesus Church makes a clear distinction between the respective roles and responsibilities of clergy and laity. The bishop stands at the highest rung of the religious hierarchy, albeit in a largely symbolic role. The current bishop is Murai Suwa, the wife of the deceased founder. While she is respected as an authority by pastors and members alike, her role carries no "official" political power. As one pastor explained to me, "the function of the bishop is to provide spiritual guidance, not to rule or dominate." There are no church councils or meetings over which the bishop must preside, but Bishop Murai symbolizes the authority of the church and officiates at the communion service each year on the occasion of the annual conference. Similarly, the bishop often participates in dedication services for new church buildings and officiates at funeral services for pastors.

The actual control of the church is in the hands of the local pastors. A phrase one commonly hears among church members to express this sociopolitical reality is 牧師一任主義 *bokushi ichinin shugi,* which in essence means that the pastor of a local church is entrusted with its responsibility. No outside interference is permitted. The laity in each local church fall under the authority of the pastor and have no official role to play in the governing of the church. There are no congregational meetings and no lay leaders (elders or deacons). Neither is there a treasurer.[16] The pastor is in charge of the finances of the local church. Members, of course, are encouraged to tithe, but the use of church funds is determined by each pastor. In sum, the Spirit of Jesus Church is a streamlined religious organization with no committees or bureaucracy.

The responsibilities of the laity are summed up in the often heard expression 羊が羊を生み，そして牧師が養う, which literally translates as "Sheep give birth to more sheep, the pastor shepherds the flock." The choice of images is significant. As sheep, the laity have only a passive role to play in the organization. One leader explained to me that pastors view themselves as a family of priests, much like Aaron and the Levitical priests in the Old Testament.[17] They have been "set apart" from ordinary believers for their priestly activities. In order to train pastors for this high calling, a two-year program of Bible School is maintained in the church headquarters in Tokyo, with some ten to twenty students participating at any one time. The Bible and the writings of the founder form the content of the curriculum. After completing the two-year course, graduates assist in the work of the head church or engage in new church development.

We should note that the relatively high status and power enjoyed by pastors in the Spirit of Jesus Church has been a factor in its growth. Kinship ties have helped the church to spread in general, but this is particularly so among its leaders. Anzai Shin's study of the growth of the church in Okinawa noted that the founder of the church there had passed on the faith to his family so that after his death, his wife continued to work in the church, one daughter and one son became pastors, and two daughters became wives of pastors in this movement.[18]

Spirit of Jesus Church sanctuary, showing pulpit with flask of oil.

I discovered a similar pattern in my own study of a church in Shikoku. The pastor's father had converted to the Spirit of Jesus Church from an Assemblies of God congregation and became a leader in the movement. Two of her brothers and one sister also became pastors. At the time of the interview some years ago, three nieces or nephews were serving as pastors and two nieces were in the Bible School preparing for pastoral work. If this pattern is at all typical, it is not hard to understand the remarkable growth of the movement.

For all its foreign influences, the Spirit of Jesus Church clearly qualifies as an independent indigenous movement. In chapter two the defining characteristics of an indigenous church were given as self-government, self-support, and self-propagation. The Spirit of Jesus Church is self-governing and has adopted its own style of leadership and organization. It is completely self-supporting, receiving no financial support from foreign churches. In fact, this organization sends its own missionaries abroad. Finally, it is self-propagating and receives no assistance from foreign missionaries in evangelistic work. As a movement, it clearly emerged from a foreign-born or imported religion, but today those churches and Christian traditions are viewed as apostate. The Spirit of Jesus Church claims that it alone has truth and legitimacy. In terms of church-sect theory, it can only be characterized as an indigenous Christian sect: indigenous in that it has been transformed through contact with native culture and by virtue of its organizational independence from Western Christianity; sectarian in that it conceives of itself as the only true Christian way and continues to exist in tension with the larger society.

ŌTSUKI TAKEJI AND THE HOLY ECCLESIA OF JESUS

Another movement defining itself as a restoration of apostolic Christianity is the Holy Ecclesia of Jesus founded by Ōtsuki Takeji in the early postwar period. Ōtsuki was born in Ayabe City in 1906, and as a young man converted to Christianity while a student at Dōshisha Middle School, a private mission school in Kyoto. Ōtsuki was attracted to the faith through the evangelistic preaching of Kanamori Michinori during the daily chapel program and went on to receive baptism. Dissatisfied with Dōshisha's "liberal and socialistic" form of Christianity, Ōtsuki found his way into the Holiness Church in 1930.

The Holiness Church in Japan traces its origins to the early evangelistic work of the Oriental Missionary Society, organized by Nakada Jūji (1870–1939) and by Mr. and Mrs. Charles Cowman in 1901. Nakada had become acquainted with the Cowmans during a period he spent at the Moody Bible Institute in Chicago (1896–1898). Although the Oriental Missionary Society began as a nondenominational evangelistic movement, it changed shape over time until it became the Japan Holiness Church in 1917. From an initial membership of 1,600 and forty-six churches, it grew rapidly to a membership of 19,523 in 1932. A controversy erupted the following year around a shift in Nakada's teaching regarding eschatology, bringing the phase of growth to an abrupt halt. Apparently Nakada had received a new revelation from God during a special visitation of the Holy Spirit. Tetsunao Yamamori summarizes the change in doctrine as follows:

> The doctrinal emphases had always been placed on justification, sanctification, divine healing, and the Second Coming of Christ. To this list, Nakada now wished to add a fifth point, that Christ's Second Coming would be possible only through the restoration of Israel. Therefore, he admonished the members to pray for this to take place. To many it seemed as though Nakada believed that by praying for the salvation of the Jews the Japanese race might be saved. This was in direct conflict with the traditional view that salvation was an individual matter.[19]

As Bishop of the Holiness Church, Nakada expected all seminary teachers and pastors to accept his new vision, but many leaders rejected his authority, which in turn led to a schism within the ranks. Ōtsuki was among those who remained loyal to the end.

Nakada Jūji was a charismatic individual whose impact on Ōtsuki was enormous. Indeed, to this day Ōtsuki refers to Nakada as his teacher and a great prophet, adding that before meeting him he had understood nothing of the

Bible's teachings regarding personal sanctification, the restoration of Israel, and the Second Coming of Christ.[20] Ōtsuki completed his theological training at the Holiness Bible Seminary in Tokyo and engaged in evangelistic work in several locations around Japan before accepting appointment as a missionary to Manchuria in 1936.

Religious Experience and Direct Revelation

It was while serving as a Holiness missionary in Manchuria that Ōtsuki had a "direct encounter with the living Christ," a life-transforming experience that was to become the foundation of his independent ministry.[21] While praying in preparation for the New Year Convention (the first *seikai* 聖会 or revival meeting of the year) and asking God to send him a guiding motto, he was presented with the words of Jesus from the Sermon on the Mount, "Blessed are the pure of heart, for they shall see God." Ōtsuki explains that his belief in God was beyond question, even though he had never seen God. In his own congregation, however, a small girl named Kiyoko who testified that she had seen God went through a remarkable transformation before her short life came to its end. Inspired by the faith of this young girl, Ōtsuki asked God to purify his heart so that he might have the same experience. His prayer was answered on the evening of 9 January 1938. As Ōtsuki recounts, he lost all consciousness of himself and his surroundings and was confronted by the living Christ. He felt the "breath of God blowing on him" and saw a bright and beautiful light coming toward him until it entered his body. In seeking to make sense of the experience, Ōtsuki searched the scriptures and discovered that the Hebrew prophets and apostles had reported similarly moving experiences.[22]

As a result, Ōtsuki came to understand what the Apostle Paul meant when he wrote, "It is no longer I who live, but Christ who lives in me" (Gal 2:20). He saw that as individuals and as the church, we now form the body of Christ on earth, our bodies being the temple and dwelling place of the living Christ (2 Cor 6:16). This is why the early apostles did not merely preach Christ, but through the laying on of hands passed the living Christ to others. Through this same indwelling power Ōtsuki's life was transformed and healing became an increasingly important part of his ministry. (The church reports that over 8,000 individuals were healed during Ōtsuki's missionary work in China.) On the same evening that his personal transformation occurred, Ōtsuki also recorded specific revelations regarding the salvation of Israel and his future role in the fulfillment of the Bible's apocalyptic vision, which we will consider more closely below.

After returning to Japan in 1942, Ōtsuki engaged in evangelistic work and led revival meetings in various locations around Japan. In 1946 he received another revelation from the Lord in which he was instructed to establish an independent church to be named the Holy Ecclesia of Jesus. The mission of the church was to recover and spread the Apostolic faith in place of the Westernized version of Christianity that missionaries had planted in Japan. The motto of the church today emphasizes this concern to recover the apostolic faith:

キリスト者はキリストのごとく, 教会は使徒行伝のごとく.

Christians are called to be like Christ
and the Church to be like the Acts of the Apostles.

Obedient to these divine instructions, Ōtsuki left the Holiness Church with a small group of disciples and organized the Holy Ecclesia of Jesus. After a brief period based in Fukuyama City, Hiroshima Prefecture, Ōtsuki moved the head-quarters of the movement to Kyoto in 1949. This has been the organizational center for a nationwide evangelistic ministry, which has grown to include over 100 churches scattered across the country from Okinawa in the south to Hokkaidō in the north.

The Theology and Practice of Apostolic Christianity

The Holy Ecclesia of Jesus is a movement aimed at recovering apostolic Christianity and entrusted with a special mission regarding the nation of Israel in these "last days." Ōtsuki writes that "authentic mission is not to transmit the doctrine or theology of Christianity, but to manifest the living Christ in our lives."[23] The Holy Ecclesia of Jesus, understood as Christ's body on earth, is called to pass on the living Christ and to provide opportunities for individuals to encounter the living Christ. As an expression of apostolic Christianity, the movement emphasizes spirit baptism, healing, and continuing revelation from God as normative for Christians today.[24]

Reflecting on his experience in China and numerous other revelatory experiences, Ōtsuki came to the conclusion that he had rediscovered the truth of the biblical and apostolic teaching that it is by "calling on the name" that one encounters the living God. The invocation of the divine name, he claims, is the prototype of all religion. It can be traced back to the earliest human civilizations mentioned in the Bible (Gen 4:26), and is repeated throughout the biblical record. Important examples include these: "Everyone who calls on the name of the Lord will be saved" (Joel 2:32). "For there is no distinction between Jew and

Greek; the same Lord is Lord of all and is generous to all who call on him. For 'Everyone who calls on the name of the Lord shall be saved'" (Rom 10:12–13). Or again, the earliest Christians were also known as those who "called on the name of the Lord" (Acts 9:21). Unfortunately, this central teaching of the Bible disappeared from view as Christianity developed in Europe.[25]

Working his way systematically through the Hebrew Bible and the New Testament, Ōtsuki identified the ways in which God revealed himself through a variety of names. Today these names and expressions are studied, chanted, and prayed in both corporate and private worship in the belief that the God of the Bible will be present whenever his name is invoked. The founder's writings and numerous church publications list the following "holy names of God" (神の御名) for believers to use in devotional practice:

I am God almighty. 我は全能の神なり. (Gen 17:1)

I am who I am. 我は有て在る者なり. (Ex 3:14)

I am God. われは主なり. (Is 43:13)

I am the first and I am the last. われは始なり終なり. (Is 44:6, Rev 22:13)

The Word was God. 言は神なり. (John 1:1)

I am the bread of life. われは生命のパンなり. (John 6:35)

I am the light of the world. われは世の光なり. (John 8:12)

I am the resurrection and the life. 我は復活なり, 生命なり. (John 11:25)

I am the way, the truth, and the life. われは道なり, 真理なり, 生命なり. (John 14:6)

God is love. 神は愛なり. (I John 4:16)

According to Ōtsuki, God always reveals himself in a name and is actually present in his name. The actual practice of "calling on the name of God" closely resembles the sound and rhythm of the Buddhist practice of reciting the *nembutsu*. The center and climax of worship services in the Holy Ecclesia of Jesus comes when the entire congregation, following the direction of the minister, chants in unison one of the names of God—for example, *Kami wa ai nari* (God is love). In worship services a small bell is rung to mark the end of the chanting. It is by invoking the name of God collectively and in private that one is brought into a direct encounter with the living God.[26]

Given the centrality of this practice, it seems fitting to classify the Holy Ecclesia of Jesus as a form of *nembutsu kirisutokyō*. The tradition of the *nembutsu*, calling on the name of Amida Buddha for protection and salvation, was a practice that began in China and first flourished in Japan during the tenth and eleventh centuries.[27] It subsequently became an important part of the Pure Land

Ōtsuki Takeji, founder of the Holy Ecclesia of Jesus.

Buddhist sects. As many Japanese come from households belonging to the Pure Land tradition, the chanting of the *nembutsu* is a natural and common form of religious practice.[28] Ōtsuki himself was raised in a home that practiced the *nembutsu* as an expression of faith in the Other-Power of Amida Buddha. Against this religious backdrop, Ōtsuki suggests, his Christianizing of the practice is well-suited to Japanese sensibilities. Despite well-known similarities between the Buddhist and Christian dependence on Other-Power, Ōtsuki and other leaders of the Church are quick to point out that Amida Buddha was not a historical figure. "A being who does not actually exist," as one pastor put it, "cannot answer our prayers." The God of the Bible, by contrast, was revealed in human history in the person of Jesus of Nazareth. Through his life, death, and resurrection, Jesus is now the living Lord who has accomplished salvation on our behalf and can truly respond to our prayers.

As Ōtsuki himself noted, this practice of invoking the name of God is nothing unique to Japanese religion. William J. Jackson points out in his study of religious traditions in India that "devoted faith in the practice of calling on a divine name in prayer or incantation may be the oldest and most pervasive form of religious life in human history." He concludes that "in a wide range of Hindu traditions and circumstances the holy name was believed to have an inherent extraordinary potency, *bringing one in touch with the being or reality named.*"[29] I cite his words because this is the very claim that Ōtsuki and his followers make regarding the cornerstone of their devotional practice.

Recognizing that the God of the Bible is living and as active today as in first-century Palestine, the Holy Ecclesia of Jesus expects to experience miracles and God's healing power.[30] The outpouring of the Holy Spirit and indwelling power of Christ is thought as a matter of course to reproduce the miracles performed by Jesus and the early apostles. Healing is understood to be a sign of the indwelling of the Holy Spirit. Church altars typically display a Bible, a flask of oil, written requests for healing, and sometimes a handkerchief inscribed with a saying penned by the founder. This is also understood to be a continuation of the early Christian practice recorded in the New Testament with reference to the Apostle Paul: "God did extraordinary miracles through Paul, so that when the handkerchiefs or aprons that had touched his skin were brought to the sick, their diseases left them, and the evil spirits came out of them" (Acts 19:11–12). Prayers and anointing with oil for healing form a regular part of group worship services and pastoral ministry. In many homes one will also find an altar where the dead are memorialized and where oil is kept for prayer and healing of family members in the home.

In addition, the church has recently identified a healing spring (マリヤ泉) in Ayabe City, Kyoto Prefecture, close to the birthplace of the founder and to the site of the discovery of a "Maria-Kannon" figure.[31] The spring has since become a pilgrimage site for members. Members often fill containers with water from the spring and share it with persons suffering from all sorts of maladies. Those who are ill are encouraged to drink the water "while calling on the name of God" in the belief that God can heal them. Numerous healings have been reported by members during worship service testimonials and recorded in church publications. The Holy Ecclesia of Jesus is convinced that this healing spring was a providential sign meant to witness to a skeptical and doubting generation that the God of the Bible is still living and active today. Followers are reminded that healing does not occur because of some special properties in the water, but because of the supernatural power of God.[32]

Incorporation and Adaptation of Western Church Traditions

The Holy Ecclesia of Jesus, as we have noted, was established with the aim of restoring the practice of apostolic Christianity. Over the course of several decades, however, the movement has come to a reappreciation of many elements in Western church tradition. One sign of this more ecumenical orientation is the fact that it is the only independent movement in Japan that has recognized the Apostles' Creed as it own confession of faith. While continuing to recognize the mistaken policies and practices of many mission churches in Japan, the founder has been able at the same time to acknowledge the value of spiritual disciplines, symbols, and rituals that were developed within Roman Catholic and Greek Orthodox traditions.

One area in which the influence of these older Western traditions is particularly apparent in the Holy Ecclesia of Jesus is in the understanding and use of sacred space and religious symbols. The movement regards the sanctuary within church buildings as the "sacred space" for an encounter with the living God. Protestant mission churches in Japan, they feel, have largely failed to appreciate the need for buildings that create a sense of the sacred and an atmosphere for worship. As one pastor observed, "it is hard to distinguish many Christian churches in Japan from classrooms or a gymnasium—with their bare walls and folding chairs. Japanese need more symbols and atmosphere in order to sense that they are in a religious place." The same could be said, of course, of Uchimura's Nonchurch movement, which usually meets in rented facilities and lecture halls.

According to Ōtsuki and other representative leaders, the Japanese people need more symbol and form in order to experience religion. While these "forms" should not be mistaken for the reality to which they point, religious symbols are an important entrance way to authentic faith. In order to create this sacred space and religious atmosphere, the Holy Ecclesia of Jesus borrows extensively from the Roman Catholic and Jewish traditions. At the front of each church sanctuary behind the pulpit is always an altar on which is placed a Bible, candles, a menorah, and often a flask of olive oil. Above the altar is a crucifix and nearby usually hangs a sanctuary lamp. Stained glass windows often add to the visual effect. In addition to symbolically rich sanctuaries, church buildings and gardens are decorated with many other statues and images of the Holy Mother and St. Francis, who are regarded as models of Christian humility, discipleship, and spirituality. Leaders emphasize that the use of these symbols or images should not be interpreted as a form of idol worship, the misguided judgment to which most Protestant churches are prone.[33] Rather, they need to be understood as aids to worship that point individuals to a reality beyond themselves.

The sacraments of baptism and the Lord's Supper are observed with particular seriousness in the Holy Ecclesia of Jesus. Before individuals are allowed to receive baptism and admitted to church membership, they must have attended church as "seekers" (求道者) for a minimum period of six months, completed a basic course of instruction in the faith, and had a personal experience of baptism by the Holy Spirit. Each individual must write a detailed confession of sin before receiving baptism. In addition to this initial confession of sin, members and clergy are also encouraged to submit written confessions (罪の告白) periodically in preparation for receiving the sacrament of the Lord's Supper (communion services are usually observed four times a year).[34] This practice is based on the New Testament teaching that individuals should only "eat of the bread and drink of the cup" after self-examination (see 1 Cor 11:28). After reading an individual's confession, the pastor lays hands on the head of the member and declares absolution in the name of Christ. Some larger churches even maintain a special confessional room. While this kind of formal confession is standard religious practice in this movement, there is no requirement that individuals perform acts of penance, as is the custom in Roman Catholic churches.

The Holy Ecclesia of Jesus has also continued to observe traditional Christian services for confirmations, weddings, and funerals. In addition, the church provides Christian alternatives for a number of rituals traditionally observed by Japanese at Shinto shrines. On a Sunday nearest the annual *Shichi-go-san* festival in mid-November, for example, an occasion when girls of seven and three and boys of five visit a shrine with their parents, the church holds a special service for blessing infants and children (幼児祝福式). Parents bring their children to the front of the sanctuary and prayers are offered for their protection and growth. Similarly, the church holds a special "coming of age ceremony" (成人式) to sacralize the rite of passage to adulthood. Likewise, memorial services for the dead (死者の記念式) are provided as an alternative to traditional Buddhist services. All of these additional observances represent an effort by church leaders to show that Christianity is not just an individualistic religion with concerns for personal salvation, but a religion that cares for and supports the extended family and all of its needs.

In the process of institutionalization, Ōtsuki adapted the polity with which he was familiar in the Holiness Church and fitted it out with a tightly organized hierarchical authority structure. The Holy Ecclesia of Jesus is based on the biblical tradition of a priesthood "set apart" and invests considerable efforts in the selection and training of its ministers and evangelists.[35] Although this is a church with Protestant roots, Ōtsuki rejected the traditional Protestant approach to theological education and adopted elements from the Roman Catholic monastic tradition as the basis for training religious leaders. In Ōtsuki's view, most Protestant churches and theological schools fail to provide adequate attention to

Church altar with Bible, prayer requests, and handkerchief.

Holy Ecclesia of Jesus sanctuary, with Jewish and Christian symbols.

the spiritual disciplines required for ongoing transformation. Theological training in the Holy Ecclesia of Jesus is based on the conviction that each person is called to pursue the path toward sainthood and become another Christ. While Protestants emphasize salvation by faith, very few churches give notice to the biblical teaching that each person is to be transformed into the image of Christ.[36] This is the vocation of all Christians, but is said to be especially important for those who are training for religious leadership.

The four-year program of ministerial training at Logos Theological Seminary includes both biblical and doctrinal studies, referred to as intellectual formation, and attention to the disciplines that are necessary for spiritual formation. Following the Catholic monastic tradition, seminarians are called to purity, poverty, and obedience, and the church covers all tuition and living expenses. The day is divided into periods of prayer, study, silence, and work, but the center of communal life is clearly prayer and worship. Prayers are observed three times a day at the seminary chapel (6:30 A.M., 3:00 P.M., and 7:00 P.M.). Seminarians renew their vows at each of these services, chanting in unison their response to the question of why they are enrolled in Logos: that is, "to become a saint, to become another Christ."

Unlike other theological institutions in Japan, students at Logos also receive instruction in traditional Japanese arts. Women are taught flower arranging and the tea ceremony and men are trained in the art of calligraphy. These traditional Japanese arts are regarded as valuable disciplines for spiritual training that enable one to focus the mind and even experience union with the living Christ. Many churches maintain a tea room both to provide hospitality to guests and as a place for quiet meditation.

All students preparing for the ministry at Logos are single, and men and women are segregated for all activities. They sit at separate tables in the dining hall and on different sides of the classroom for lectures. In the chapel, too, the women sit on the left and the men on the right. During this four-year training period, private or personal communication between men and women is not permitted. This is what the founder refers to as the practice of "holy disinterestedness." At the end of the four-year training program, however, the Catholic tradition of celibacy is abandoned and the seminary director plays the role of matchmaker to arrange marriages for many of the men and women as they return to the world to begin their active ministry. Logos graduates are usually matched for marriage within one or two years of graduation, but as persons trained for the ministry they are not allowed to marry a lay person. Moreover, it is stipulated that marriage partners among the ordained are not to be selected on the basis of romance. Since the church only allows ordained members to marry within the "priesthood," many women recognize that they are destined to the single life as the number of women training for the ministry always outnumbers that of men. (In a recent year, for example, there were 26 women and 14 men enrolled at Logos.)[37]

Following completion of the Logos program, individuals must complete a three-year trial period as an associate teacher. In order to become fully recognized as a pastor or teacher, each candidate must pass a written examination and lead at least twelve individuals to the faith (which is understood to include both spirit and water baptism). The latter expectation reflects the strong evangelistic emphasis of the movement—a requirement that would no doubt quickly diminish the ranks of the ordained in most mainline denominations.[38]

Eschatology and Zionistic Orientation

As we have noted, the practice of apostolic Christianity and gradual incorporation of various older Western church traditions constitute important aspects of the Holy Ecclesia of Jesus. It is Father Ōtsuki's eschatological vision, however, that provides the central dynamic and an atmosphere of expectancy that characterize the movement. In these "last days," Ōtsuki explains, the Holy Ecclesia of Jesus has been set apart by God to play an important role as salvation history approaches its climax. This idea of a time of special "kairos" is based on Ōtsuki's reading of the Apostle Paul's teaching that after "the full number of Gentiles have come in... all Israel will be saved" (Rom 11:25). Although evangelism of Gentiles is understood as an important mission in order to perfect the "Bride of Christ" (ecclesia), it is the national and spiritual salvation of Israel that constitutes the special mission and ultimate goal of the movement.

Ōtsuki's concern for the nation of Israel clearly reflects the views of Nakada Jūji, his mentor in the Holiness Church, whose theology was dominated in his later years by eschatological concerns and the idea that Japan was somehow connected to the salvation of Israel.[39] Without denying this influence, Ōtsuki claims that he also received special revelation concerning the movement's responsibilities toward Israel while he was a missionary in China. He reports that the Lord instructed him:

1. to pray for the restoration of the nation of Israel;
2. to pray for the spiritual renewal of Israel, which is the condition for the return of Christ;
3. to pray for the peace of Jerusalem, which is the key to the peace of the world; and
4. to pray for the coming of the Messiah of Peace.[40]

Ten years after Ōtsuki received this revelation and began praying fervently for the restoration of Israel, the nation of Israel was reestablished as an independent state. This provided important confirmation for Ōtsuki and his followers at the early stage of this movement's development. This apocalyptic consciousness and concern for the nation of Israel pervades all aspects of this movement today.

Even though the movement is concerned with the salvation of Israel, it does not engage in evangelistic mission to the Jews as do a number of other Protestant mission groups. In light of the history of Christian-Jewish relations—persecution, murder, and the holocaust—the Holy Ecclesia of Jesus claims that Gentiles have no right to evangelize the Jews. Their calling is simply to pray for the restoration of Israel and peace in Jerusalem. Only then will the Messiah come again and establish peace throughout the world. At the present time, Ōtsuki explains, the church's primary concern should be to heal the wounds that Christians have inflicted on Jews over the centuries and to learn how to express selfless love. God will take care of the salvation of the Jews in his own time.[41] Although the cross and the star of David have usually represented separation and conflict, this movement combines them to symbolize their vision of reconciliation and harmony between Christians and Jews.

Symbol of the Holy Ecclesia of Jesus: the star of David and a cross designed with sakura flower petals.

Over the past several decades this movement has made numerous efforts to heal the past and forge good relations between Jews and Gentiles.[42] Several examples are worth mentioning here. Under the leadership of the founder's son, Ōtsuki Masaru, the Shinonome (Dawn) Choir was organized in 1970 to contribute to peace and improved relations through a ministry of music and a program composed of Hebrew and Japanese songs. Over the years the choir has made a number of concert tours to Israel and North America and has even performed in the Holocaust Museum in Washington, D.C. Some of these performances have been preceded by an apology for the past atrocities committed against Jews in the name of Christ. Many in the audience are visibly moved and after the concert some have indicated that it is the first time a Christian has apologized to them about anything. In 1995, to join in the celebrations commemorating the founding of the holy city of Jerusalem 3,000 years ago, the choir toured Israel and gave concerts in Tel Aviv and Haifa and at the Hebrew University of Jerusalem.[43]

In 1971 the Holy Ecclesia of Jesus also established the Bet Shalom (House of Peace) in Kyoto, where guests from Israel are accommodated for three nights free of charge. Another house is also maintained in Hiroshima. Over 10,000 Israelis and Jews have enjoyed the hospitality of these Bet Shalom guest houses during the past three decades. The 1972 terrorist attack on Tel Aviv's Lod airport—in which three Japanese participated—left twenty-four dead and another seventy-six wounded. In an effort to heal the damaged relations between Japanese and Israelis as a result of this tragedy, the movement established the Ōtsuki Peace Scholarship to assist students from Israel studying in Japan. Several years ago the movement also raised funds to support a professorship at the Hebrew University of Jerusalem.[44]

The most recent manifestation of this concern for the people of Israel is the Japan Holocaust Museum and Education Center, which was established in June 1995. The Holy Ecclesia of Jesus established the center in memory of the 1.5 million Jewish children and to contribute to peace education in Japan. Church members donated the 50 million yen required for the construction of the center and memorial hall. Materials on display in the museum were donated by Jews from twenty-two countries. During the first year of operation, the center received over eight thousand visitors, which included teachers and students from thirty different universities, sixty elementary and junior high schools, and representatives from various city government offices and human rights groups. One of the first visitors was Hannah Pick, a classmate of Anne Frank.[46] Through the displays, lectures, videos, and discussions, the director general of the center, Rev. Ōtsuka Makoto, challenges students to think about the Holocaust, the greatest tragedy of our century, as well as about the realities of Japan's exploitation of its Asian neighbors over the past century. Students are urged to become peacemakers. The activities of the center have opened up many new opportunities for this pastor to give public lectures and to speak to school groups about the holocaust and on pressing problems in Japanese society like bullying and discrimination.[47]

The close relationship to the people of Israel reflected in these various activities has had a significant impact on religious practice within the Holy Ecclesia of Jesus. In particular, the movement has been inspired to recover the Jewish roots of early Christianity. A number of leaders have been sent to Israel to study Hebrew and Jewish traditions and a Center for Judaic Studies has been established at Logos Theological Seminary in order to devote more attention to the Jewish foundation of Christianity. The Center often hosts Jewish rabbis and scholars for various lectures and special events. The orientation of the group toward Israel and Jewish traditions is also reflected in the official church calendar, which includes dates for Purim (March 5), a memorial day for the six million victims of the holocaust (April 16), Israel's Independence Day Anniversary (April 24), Anne Frank's birthday (June 12), the destruction of the Jerusalem temple (July 25), Yom Kippur (September 23), and Israel Day (October 10).

While churches do not observe special services on all of these occasions, concern for Israel is manifested in various ways throughout the church year.[48] Again, this orientation is evident in the Holy Ecclesia of Jesus hymnbook, which includes eleven hymns (41–51) dealing with the second coming of Christ, eight hymns dealing with the salvation of Israel (85–92), and twelve Jewish folk songs (202–13). The hymnal also contains a guide to prayer with eleven prayers related to the people of Israel, including prayers for Jews who are scattered throughout the world, for the peace of Jerusalem, and for the spiritual anointing of the 144,000 chosen ones who are destined to fulfill a special role in the final days.[49] Members are encouraged to offer these prayers on behalf of Israel three times each day.[50] The church has also been encouraging its members to observe a form of family worship based on the ancient Jewish sabbath tradition.[51] All of these connections with Israel have resulted in the majority of members setting themselves the goal of making at least one pilgrimage to the Holy Land during their lifetime. The founder, who has made three pilgrimages to Israel, wrote a number of poems and meditations regarding his own experiences for members to use for reflection on their pilgrimages to sacred sites in the Holy Land and Europe.[52]

At first glance, it may be difficult to appreciate the way in which all of these diverse elements—healing practices, chanting the names of God, Christian and Jewish symbols and rituals—can combine to form a coherent subculture for the participants involved in the movement. Ōtsuki's former colleagues in the Holiness Church are extremely critical of what he has created and tend to look down on it as so much kitsch. The founder's response is that, like the Apostle Paul, he is called to be "all things to all men." Ōtsuki believes that the Holy Ecclesia of Jesus must be an *ōburoshiki*, a cloth large enough to wrap up all the ingredients necessary to satisfy diverse human needs.[53]

TESHIMA IKURŌ AND THE ORIGINAL GOSPEL MOVEMENT

As we have noted at several points in the course of this study, Uchimura Kanzō's Nonchurch interpretation of Christianity has been influential in the development of various groups in the course of this century. The Original Gospel is a pentecostal manifestation of the Nonchurch movement and represents another Japanese effort to recover apostolic Christianity.[54] Dissatisfied with both the doctrinal rigidity of Western mission churches and the intellectualism of Uchimura's disciples, Teshima Ikurō (1910–1973) founded his movement in 1948. Since a considerable amount of information is now available in English, I will only draw attention to some key characteristics that distinguish this movement from other versions of Nonchurch Christianity and provide a basis for comparison with the other "apostolic" movements considered above.[55]

Uchimura had insisted that the Japanese were capable of reading the Bible by themselves, without depending on the confessions and commentaries of the mission churches. Operating on the basis of this Nonchurch principle, Teshima read the Bible and found that it was full of elements missing from both Nonchurch Christianity and the transplanted mission churches. The "original gospel," he discovered, was a charismatic form of religion and always accompanied by such phenomena as healings, spirit baptism, and speaking in tongues. These manifestations of the living Christ were no longer available in the trans-

Teshima Ikurō, founder of the Original Gospel movement, at one of the larger
Bible study meetings.

planted mission churches. In fact, Teshima observed, most church leaders no
longer even believed in the healing power of God. In short, the established
churches had exchanged the living apostolic faith for a doctrinal system about
Christianity. Teshima identified fully with Uchimura's effort to develop an independent and indigenous expression of Christianity by returning to the original
Scriptures. In the following statement Teshima explains his view that the
Nonchurch movement had also become a "stagnant" form of Christianity in the
hands of Uchimura's disciples:

> The followers of the Nonchurch movement attach great importance to the
> study of the Bible. Now this has become for them a substitute for faith. Some
> think they are saved as long as they study Biblical terminology, and in extreme
> cases, the meaning of Greek texts. But there is no salvation in the study of the
> letter. As it is written, "For the letter kills, but the Spirit gives life" (2 Cor 3:6).
> We cannot be saved until we encounter the living Christ, the great "I AM" who
> stands behind the Scriptures.[56]

Teachers in the Nonchurch movement may be good Biblical scholars, Teshima
acknowledges, but they lack the living faith of the New Testament.[57] As we
observed in chapter three, Teshima was extremely critical of the transplanted
mission churches and what is regarded as a misguided concern to present the

Western "shell" of Christianity (see page 37 above). He was also disillusioned with the lifeless form of Christianity into which the Nonchurch movement had degenerated. His harshest words, however, were reserved for Japanese Christian pastors who collaborated with the missionaries in order to stay on the payroll of mission churches. These pastors were unable to articulate the Gospel for the Japanese and simply parroted what the Western missionaries wanted them to say—"wagging their tails like dogs to please their masters,"as he put it—just to receive their stipend.[58] Teshima was determined to establish an independent and self-supporting form of Christianity that was both apostolic and indigenous.

The Jewish Roots of Apostolic Christianity

In 1948 Teshima began publishing his own magazine, *The Light of Life*, and began to elaborate his own understanding of Christianity in writing, as had been the tradition of most teachers in the Nonchurch movement.[59] In 1949 the pentecostal features of spirit baptism, healing, and speaking in tongues, which had initially only affected Teshima and his immediate disciples, spread throughout his Bible study group in Kumamoto. This event, which is now referred to as the "Makuya Pentecost," led to his break with the Nonchurch movement as a whole.[60] The term *makuya* 幕屋 is the Japanese term for the tabernacle, or tent, used as the portable sanctuary in which God dwelt among the Israelites in the desert. Teshima began referring to his movement as Makuya or the Original Gospel following the controversy with Nonchurch leaders over his pentecostal faith. Even though he continued to claim his faith was an expression of the Nonchurch tradition, he dropped the reference to the Nonchurch movement from the cover of his magazine in response to the continued criticism from Uchimura's successors. Yanaihara Tadao, for example, complained that within thirty years of Uchimura's death a "heretical" form of Christianity had been launched under the Nonchurch banner.[61] Takahashi Saburō similarly refused to recognize Teshima's as a legitimate movement since it had strayed from central Nonchurch emphases (forgiveness of sins, the resurrection, and the second coming of Christ) and had become enamored with healing and speaking in tongues.[62]

In addition to these charismatic and pentecostal features, Teshima's search for the "original gospel" also led him to a deeper appreciation of the Jewish roots of Christianity. In order to recover authentic apostolic Christianity, he felt that it was necessary to remove the effects of two thousand years of Europeanization and attempt to revive the earliest form of Christian worship. One of the most visible consequences of this decision may be seen in his adoption of the menorah in place of the cross as the central religious symbol of his movement. This seven-branched lampstand had been a common symbol for Jews since its use in the tabernacle of the Israelites to represent the presence of the living God. The New Testament indicates that this symbol was also important for early Christians. In the Revelation to John (1:12–20), for example, the Son of Man appears in the midst of seven golden lampstands, which indicates that the menorah was understood by the earliest Christians as the symbol of the living Christ (生きるキリストの象徴). It took centuries before the cross became widely accepted as the symbol of Christianity. According to my informants, Teshima's decision to adopt this earlier Jewish symbol was also motivated by the fact that most Japanese found the cross to be such a "cruel and tragic image" that it was unsuitable to serve as the symbolic focus for Christian worship in Japan.

In 1961 Teshima made his first world pilgrimage, traveling to India, the United States, Greece, and Israel. The Bible came alive for him during his visit to the Holy Land and this experience subsequently influenced the way he would train his own disciples.[63] True to the Nonchurch tradition, Teshima already placed considerable emphasis on the study of the Bible in the original Hebrew and Greek. His time in Israel convinced him that it was also important to live and study in the Holy Land in order to gain a deeper understanding and appreciation of the world of the Bible and the Jewish traditions that were so important

The menorah is the symbolic focus and representation of the presence of God at Original Gospel meetings.

121

to Jesus. Teshima felt that Japanese Christians could learn more about the Biblical tradition directly from Jews in Israel than from the Western church traditions and theological scholarship. He also thought it was important for young people to experience the patriotism of Jews in Israel and hoped it would serve to inspire and revive the Japanese spirit that had disappeared in postwar Japan following the military defeat in 1945.

In 1962 he began sending his younger disciples to study for a year or longer in Israel. To date over 700 students have studied Hebrew in Israel and worked part-time on a kibbutz. Some have also pursued academic degrees at the Hebrew University of Jerusalem.[64] Academic studies alone, however, were inadequate preparation for becoming an evangelist in the Original Gospel movement. In order to cultivate a spirit of total dependence on God, Teshima adopted the "biblical" practice of sending his disciples out two by two—with no money or change of clothes—with the expectation that God would guide them and supply all their needs as they traveled and preached the gospel. This approach to discipleship and training was based on the example of Jesus recorded in Mark 6:7–13. Teshima felt that trust in God could only be cultivated through difficult trials and personal experiences. This form of spiritual training continues today as the elders in the movement send out their disciples in the spring or fall on these missionary journeys.[65]

In addition to sending students to Israel, Teshima organized an annual pilgrimage to the Holy Land and through these trips cultivated ties with many Jewish leaders. He regularly invited Israeli dignitaries to Makuya meetings and hosted other Jewish leaders in Japan. Following the Six-Day War of 1967, Teshima initiated numerous activities to generate Japanese support for the state of Israel. As his son Isaiah explained not long ago, his father proudly "called himself a Neo-Zionist," which for him meant "a commitment to dialogue with the spirit of Israel for reviving the original spirit or values of the Bible in Japan as well as supporting the state of Israel in which the Holy History proceeds."[66]

Since Teshima's death in 1973, his wife and other leaders within the movement have strengthened the relationship with Israel and placed even greater stress on the Jewish roots of Christianity. Each year in February or March a two-week pilgrimage to the Holy Land is organized and usually attracts between 100 to 300 members. Several years ago, 1,600 members joined the pilgrimage in order to join in the celebrations surrounding the 3,000th birthday of Jerusalem. In 1988 the movement established a Makuya Center in Jerusalem to provide a community for members studying in Israel and to offer courses on Japanese language and culture.[67] The Original Gospel movement also operates a publishing company that specializes in books and resources for the study of Hebrew and produces translations of important works by Israeli scholars.

The ongoing relationship with Israel and contact with Jewish traditions has continued to reshape religious practice within the movement. One of the results of sending students to study and experience the religious life of Israel has been the gradual incorporation and adaptation of Jewish practices. A number of Jewish folk songs are included in the Original Gospel hymnbook and regularly sung at various services and events.[68] The Jewish Shabbat is also widely celebrated among Makuya members in Japan. In the early 1980s Makuya leaders also instituted a bar mitzvah initiation ceremony for young people in the movement. During spring break each year, anywhere from 50 to 100 junior high school students (aged 12–13) from all over Japan gather for three days of intensive religious practice at the "sacred sites" of Kumamoto and Mount Aso in Kyūshū. (Mount Aso is where the founder had his powerful encounter with the living God and experienced his call to religious work, and nearby Kumamoto is where he began the Original Gospel movement.) Young people stay in the Makuya retreat center at Mount Aso, but also visit the Kumamoto center and nearby gravesites of the founder and his early disciples. The program includes lectures on the history of the movement, videos of the founder, worship services, and various ascetic practices, such as *omisogi* (water ablutions for purification) and *hiwatari* (walking across a bed of hot coals). It is not surprising to learn that young people are rather preoccupied and anxious about this last ritual obligation and test of faith.

The Original Gospel and Japanese Spirituality

In addition to Teshima's concern to rediscover the charismatic and Jewish dimensions of apostolic Christianity, he was also committed to the process of indigenization and sought links between biblical faith and Japanese spiritual traditions. While other indigenous leaders had focused on the value of *bushidō* or Buddhist and Confucian traditions, Teshima was more concerned with the Japanese spiritual traditions prior to the arrival of foreign cultures. The beautiful, noble, sacrificial spirit taught by our forebears, Teshima claimed, is the key to the Japanese understanding of the cross of Christ. The *Kojiki, Nihon shoki*, and *Man'yōshū* are regarded as important resources for understanding the earliest Japanese spirit.[69] Already in Teshima's first book, *The Love of the Holy Spirit*, we see his deep appreciation for early Japanese spirituality in the life of Emperor Jinmu, who relied on the Sun Goddess in order to lead the Japanese people:

Makuya members doing *hiwatari* at one of the annual conventions.

I am moved by the legacy of the Emperor Jinmu who emerged from difficulties by depending on the power of the heavenly spirit, an appropriate lesson to be deeply engraved upon the hearts of the Japanese who are now groaning under the hard, postwar conditions. It is amazing that the ancient Japanese had such heightened spirituality. Whenever they met difficulties, they relied upon the *fuyū* (military authority, support, grace, merciful bestowal) of the divine spirit. They firmly believed that if only they had the merciful bestowal of the spirit upon them, they could break through any difficulties and that the spirit itself would crush down any enemies. With this firm belief they did *ukehi* (receiving of spirit) and *otakebi* (loud cries); such were their unique spiritual traits.[70]

Teshima's "Christianization of the pre-Christian past" included his interpretation that the ancient Japanese fellowship with the gods referred to in the *Kojiki* and *Nihon shoki* was in fact communication with the heavenly spirits referred to as angels in the Bible. These Japanese forebears not only provided exemplary models of spirituality and dependence on God, but also revealed what true humanity was intended to be.[71] This is also what the life of Jesus in the gospel reveals to us. It is the aim of the Original Gospel movement, Teshima explains, to join in Jesus' mission to restore this true humanity to all people. Although Teshima was particularly concerned with Japanese spirituality before the arrival of Buddhism and Confucianism from China, he also recognized the valuable contribution of Japanese Buddhists, such as Kōbō Daishi, Hōnen, Nichiren, and Hakuin and, like Kawai Shinsui, refers to this heritage as the Old Testament for Japanese.[72]

Makuya members participating in *omisogi* purification rituals.

This deep appreciation for ancient Japanese spirituality led Teshima to adopt certain ascetic practices from indigenous traditions for spiritual training within the Makuya movement. These include *misogi* water purification rituals, including *takiabi* (滝浴び) or standing under a waterfall, and *hiwatari* (火渡り) or walking across a bed of hot coals. The ascetic disciplines were regarded as important methods of bodily training and spiritual purification, and particularly important for individuals who had difficulty concentrating on spiritual matters. At the annual convention in March 1958 Teshima initiated the *hiwatari,* a common practice among Yamabushi, mountain priests, as a regular spiritual exercise for Makuya members.[73] He reasoned that if Christianity was truly the highest religion, its followers should be able to prove the power of the living God by walking across the burning coals. This became a standard practice at annual conventions and, as we noted above, became an important event in the mitzvah rite of passage for young people in the movement.

Recent Emphases and Nationalistic Tendencies

In spite of condemnation by various Nonchurch teachers over the past several decades, Makuya leaders have recently been reemphasizing their identity as an expression of the Nonchurch tradition. The Original Gospel magazine, *Light of Life*, for example, regularly carries articles about Uchimura and usually publishes a confession of faith that defines the movement in terms of Nonchurch principles.

The room where services are held at Original Gospel movement's Kumamoto Juku in Kyūshū. The appearance of the Japanese flag at Makuya meetings occurred after Teshima returned from a visit to the United States and found U.S. flags displayed in churches. He thought this was equally valid for Japanese Christians and encouraged Makuya members to show national pride by displaying the flag in services and on national holidays.

The Original Gospel Creed

私たちは, 日本の精神的荒廃を嘆き, 大和魂の振起を願う.

We lament Japan's spiritual desolation and long for the revival of the Japanese spirit.

私たちは, 日本人の心に宗教復興を願い, 原始福音の再興を祈る.

We long for the revival of religion in the hearts of the Japanese people and pray for the restoration of the Original Gospel.

私たちは, 無教会主義に立つ. したがっていかなる教会・教派にも属せず, 作らず, ただ旧新約聖書に学ぶものである.

We stand on the principle of Non-Churchism. Therefore, we neither belong to nor establish any church or denomination, and simply seek to learn from the Old and New Testaments.

私たちは, キリスト教の純化を願うが, 日本の他の諸宗教を愛し, 祖師たちの 人格を崇敬するものである.

We long for the purification of Christianity and at the same time love the other religions of Japan and venerate the character of the founders (saints) of Japan.

私たちは, 政党・政派を超越して, 愛と善意と平和をもって, 日本社会の聖化を期し, 社会正義と人間愛を宣揚するものである.

We transcend all political parties and with love, good intention, and peace we anticipate the sanctification of Japanese society and seek to promote social justice and love of one's neighbor.

It is undeniable that this movement shares many things in common with the Nonchurch tradition: independence from Western church traditions and rejection of the sacramental system and denominational polities, an emphasis on studying the Bible in the original languages, and the practice of meeting primarily in rented halls and members' homes, rather than investing in church buildings. Teshima and his followers also claim that their Zionistic orientation is also rooted in the views of Uchimura.[74] In spite of these shared features, Uchimura would undoubtedly be uncomfortable with the emotional nature of Makuya's pentecostal services and the recent neo-nationalistic tendencies evident in the movement.

In recent years the movement has been making special efforts to educate Japanese young people in the riches of early Japanese history. The movement's magazine *Light of Life* has been publishing a cartoon series dealing with the spiritual leadership of Jinmu Tennō, the first emperor, and the establishment of the nation of Japan.[75] This neonationalistic orientation is also evident in the articles written by key leaders in the movement. The founder's second wife and current symbolic head, Teshima Chiyo, for example, strongly urges Japanese to celebrate the national holiday honoring Emperor Jinmu as one way to reconfirm their identity and recover national pride.[76] She reminds her readers that the emperor was the father of the nation and ruled according to the will of heaven. While Japan's past may not be all glorious, it is necessary to educate the new generation of young people regarding the riches of the past so that they can have pride as Japanese. She expresses dismay at the recent trend in school textbooks that tends to interpret history in a negative light, stressing Japan's role in the modern period primarily as an invader of its Asian neighbors. Almost no attention is given, however, to the character and sacrifice of so many Japanese who died on behalf of the emperor during Japan's modern century.

The editor of the *Light of Life*, Nagahara Shin, similarly writes that it is necessary for Japanese to recover their "roots" in order to reestablish a positive Japanese identity. His article concludes with a photo of Yasukuni Shrine and a reference to the sacrificial spirit of those Japanese who were willing to give their lives for the nation. This spirit has been lost in modern Japan, but it can be recovered once again if the gospel is grafted onto this early foundation.[77] In a postwar educational system that has forgotten the riches of the Japanese cultural heritage, a significant dimension of the Makuya mission is to nurture a healthy Japanese nationalism among its youth. In short, it is time for the revival of the Japanese spirit (大和魂) according to the power of the original gospel.

CONCLUSION

In this chapter we have seen how diverse native and foreign elements have been combined to create several different Japanese versions of apostolic Christianity. We have only highlighted some of the distinguishing characteristics and sketched some of the complicated transnational relations (the U.S., Taiwan, Israel) and influences that have shaped the development of each of these movements. In sharp contrast to the indigenous groups examined in previous chapters, these apostolic movements have rediscovered the charismatic and pentecostal dimensions of the faith. In the case of the Spirit of Jesus Church and the Holy Ecclesia of Jesus, leaders have also rediscovered the strands of biblical tradition that legitimize an ordained and set-apart priestly order within Christianity and have created structures and polities that resemble Western churches in many respects. One area that deserves more detailed attention is the manner in which these movements have reinterpreted the Bible and adapted rituals in order to address concerns related to Japanese folk religion and the world of spirits and ancestors. It is to this fascinating development that we now turn our attention.

CHAPTER SEVEN

Japanese Christians
and the World of the Dead

T HE TRANSPLANTATION OF Western Christianity to Japan over the past
century has involved a fundamental clash between the missionary message and the religious consciousness and values of most Japanese. This
is particularly apparent in relation to the indigenous beliefs and practices related
to ancestors and the spirits of the dead. This area of difficulty is not unique to
the missionary experience in Japan, but something missionaries have struggled
with repeatedly throughout Asia and Africa. Some familiarity with these traditional beliefs and practices is required in order to appreciate the nature of the
clash that has occurred in the Protestant missionary encounter with Japan.
Following a brief introduction to this native tradition and the dominant
Protestant missionary response, this chapter will examine how Japanese

Christians, particularly those belonging to the independent and indigenous movements, have reinterpreted the Bible in a manner that more effectively addresses Japanese religious and cultural concerns.

THE PLACE OF ANCESTORS AND SPIRIT BELIEF IN JAPANESE CULTURE

In the context of Japan, the constellation of beliefs and practices associated with ancestors and the world of the dead is commonly referred to as folk religion. The somewhat ill-defined folk religious tradition represents the undercurrent of Japanese consciousness that continually reappears and reshapes other religious traditions. In fact, Hori Ichirō refers to folk religion as the comparatively stable "substructure" of Japanese religion.[1] Miyake Hitoshi elaborates on the point:

> It is within the frame of reference provided by folk religion that the organized religions have made their way into Japanese society. Only as they accommodated themselves to folk religion and its implicit norms did the institutional religions find acceptance and begin to exercise influence on people in their daily life.[2]

While the term "accommodation" here seems less than adequate to capture the complexity of the indigenization process, at the very least it must be recognized that a transplanted religious tradition that fails to address the concerns represented by this religious "substructure" will have serious difficulties in Japan. This is one of the serious dilemmas facing most transplanted Protestant mission churches.

It has long been recognized that the ancestral cult is a central feature of Japanese folk religion. In its classical or traditional form, the ancestral cult refers to the "belief in the superhuman power of the dead who are recognized as ancestors, and the rituals based on this belief."[3] Ancestors were originally understood to be founders of households (*ie*) and successive household heads. Thus ancestor veneration was essentially a patrilineal phenomenon. The interpretative framework for the ancestral cult is a cosmology that recognizes the interdependence between two spheres: the world of the living and the spirit world of the dead. The world of the dead, traditionally associated with mountains, is populated by various *kami* (gods), animal spirits, spirits of dead ancestors, and protective spirits. According to the worldview of Japanese folk religion, one's situation in this life is causally influenced by the spirit world. Health problems, business failures, and personal problems are frequently attributed to the failure of descendants to properly care for their ancestors. If the appropriate rituals are not performed, the ancestor suffers and cannot achieve lasting peace. Often wandering spirits "are said to be suffering from the emotional state of *urami*— bitterness, ill will, enmity, spite or malice."[4] Individuals suffering misfortune in this life often see the cause in the *urami* of some unpacified spirit. In order to pacify such spirits, individuals must perform memorial services and make special offerings; until the needs of the ancestors are met through rituals, they will more than likely function as malevolent spirits exacting retribution *(tatari)* upon the descendants.

Many observers predicted that these spirit beliefs and ancestral rites would disappear as a result of modernization and democratization. Two specialists in this field, Hoshino Eiki and Takeda Dōshō, however, maintain that "even today there is no sign that the Japanese concern for their ancestral spirits has diminished."[5] Although studies indicate that modernization and urbanization have significantly modified the family structure and the conception of ancestors,[6] the concern with ancestral rites and appropriate care for the deceased is still a dominant feature of contemporary Japanese religion and culture. Survey research, as well as studies of new religious movements and trends in popular culture, indicate the widespread persistence of these traditional concerns.

Survey Research

Although most Japanese do not have a clearly conceptualized religious commitment, the NHK Survey on Japanese Religious Consciousness discovered over a decade ago that many share certain religious feelings and common religious sensibilities.[7] The attitude of the Japanese toward ancestors is one important area explored in this study. Almost 60 percent responded affirmatively to the question, "Do you feel a deep spiritual connection with the ancestors?" The central place of ancestors in Japanese religiosity is also reflected in ritual behavior. Some 57 percent of respondents to this survey have a Buddhist altar, with 28 percent worshipping before it each day. Similarly, 69 percent regularly participate in Buddhist rituals at the family graves during *obon* or at the time of the spring and autumn equinoxes. The high rate of such ritual behavior suggests that there is still a relatively strong consciousness of the ancestors among many Japanese.[8]

Another question in the survey that sheds light on the place of ancestors in Japanese religious consciousness is, "What is the meaning of *shinkō* (faith or belief) to you?" The study classified the answers given to this question by those respondents claiming to have a personal religious faith (i.e., 892 individuals out of the total of 3,600 interviewed), and discovered that 12 percent of the responses indicated that faith was understood as showing respect for the ancestors.

131

This survey did discover that urbanization has had a negative impact on some of these traditional beliefs and practices: 71 percent of those living in rural or village communities "felt a close connection with the ancestors," but the number declined to 56 percent in the metropolitan areas of Tokyo and Osaka. Daily worship before a Buddhist altar is 37 percent and occasional worship is 64 percent in village communities or rural areas, but declines to 23 percent daily worship and 37 percent occasional worship in urban areas.

New Religious Movements

Urbanization has clearly contributed to the decline of traditional practices that were primarily based in rural communities and extended families. At the same time the population shift to urban areas has made possible the rapid growth of new religious movements during the postwar period. Although founders of New Religions have introduced "new" revelations, gods, and rituals, these movements are nevertheless often regarded as revitalized expressions of folk religion.[9] Without denying that there are "new" elements in the New Religions, their relative success in contemporary Japan is certainly due in part to their effectiveness in relating to the "old" concerns for ancestors and spirits of the dead.

Studies of many new religious movements reveal an ongoing concern for spirits and ancestors and an emphasis on rituals enabling their members to deal appropriately with the dead and transform malevolent spirits into protective ones. Helen Hardacre's research indicates that both Reiyūkai and Kurozumikyō stress the importance of ancestor worship in one form or another. Byron Earhart's study of Gedatsu-Kai revealed that the founder had provided innovative means of more effectively dealing with spirits and ancestors, such as the amacha (天茶) memorial ritual and the mediumistic technique of gohō shugyō (五法修行), both new methods of restoring harmonious relations with the dead.

Winston Davis, in his study of Mahikari, discovered a similar preoccupation with the dead: "Knowing how to feed and worship the spirits of one's ancestors has been the key to health and happiness for many Mahikari followers." Likewise, Ian Reader notes that the taizō (胎蔵) fire, one of the two gomagi (護摩木) fire rituals performed at Agonshū's popular Star Festival, is for the purpose of bringing peace to the restless spirits of ancestors and suffering souls who are causing physical and spiritual trouble for the living.[10]

We need to note here that new religious movements have also contributed to the transformation of the ancestor cult from a focus on a family's patrilineal forebears to a broader concern with the ancestors of both sides of the family. This "bilateral pattern of ancestor worship," Helen Hardacre observes, "is more congruent with the nuclear family."[11] The concern for the spirits of the dead has also been extended in recent years to the spirits of *mizuko* or aborted and stillborn children. Many traditional Buddhist sects as well as New Religions provide memorial services for *mizuko* in response to the felt needs of Japanese women who are struggling with a sense of guilt and condemnation associated with the spirits of the dead fetuses.[12]

Ancestors and Spirits in Popular Culture

In addition to New Religions, the mass media has become a crucial "carrier" (albeit a less stable one) of beliefs and practices related to spirits and ancestors. TV programs, for example, frequently feature popular spiritual healers and psychics who advocate the ritual care of angry or disgruntled spirits in order to achieve happiness, peace, and good fortune in this life. The printed media is even more important in transmitting these folk beliefs. In bookstores across Japan one will almost always find a section labeled "the spiritual world." Here one will find books, magazines, cassettes, and videos on a wide range of topics, including healing, astrology, divination, methods for controlling the spiritual world, and ways of communicating with the spirits of the deceased. While the influence of imported New Age phenomena is not without significance, the "new" syntheses of indigenous and foreign beliefs have not fundamentally altered the cosmology and framework of traditional folk religion. The message is essentially the same, and it is transmitted with the power of modern technology. Unhappiness, illness, and assorted life problems are still, for the most part, attributed either to bad karma from one's previous existence or to the spirits of the dead.

Numerous popular authors publish volume after volume of guides to the spirit world and to the manipulation of the spirits for one's own benefit. Kuroda Minoru, for example, a former member of Mahikari and veteran comic (*manga*) artist, began a religious movement called Subikari Sekai Shindan in 1980. Kuroda gathered a following (a large percentage of whom are junior-high and high-school girls) when he began publishing a series of "spirit world comics." A recent book contains cartoons that deal with the tormenting spirits of *mizuko* (aborted or stillborn fetuses) and the reality of the spirit world.[13]

Spirits of the Dead in the World of Business

New religious movements and the mass media are not the only "carriers" of traditional religious concerns. Religious shrines and rituals concerned with the

Scenes depicting the spirits of aborted fetuses from the Japanese comic book, *The Woman Who Sells Souls*.

dead have even appeared in what most people would regard as the most "modern" and "secular" of all places: the Japanese company and factory. This is an area receiving considerable attention in recent years, with scholars suggesting that in some cases business enterprises appear to be taking over certain of the roles traditionally played by religion.[14] Many of these companies not only have rituals for this-worldly health, safety, and financial success but also maintain company graves. At the well-known religious center of Mt. Kōya, for example, there are some 90 company grave sites. While some of these graves were established as early as 1938, most were not built until the late 1960s, when the extended family began to decline rapidly as a result of urbanization. Today these companies hold memorial services for the founder of the company and for individuals who died while in service to the company. (Colonel Sanders would no doubt roll over in his Louisville grave were word to reach him that in Japan Kentucky Fried Chicken celebrates a Broiler Thanksgiving Festival and a memorial service on his behalf.) Upper management and individuals who served on company boards are also often enshrined and memorialized after their death. In this way the company is providing many religious services once regarded as the exclusive domain of the extended family.

In spite of the processes of modernization and urbanization, beliefs and practices related to the ancestors and the spirit world are still relatively strong in contemporary Japan. It is hardly unreasonable for us to assume that these beliefs and practices were even more prominent in the early Meiji period during the first encounter between the Protestant missionaries and the Japanese. How did the earliest Protestant missionaries respond to this area of religious concern?

PROTESTANT MISSIONARY THEOLOGY AND THE ANCESTORS

As we discussed earlier, Protestant missionary theology and practice have tended to emphasize a total discontinuity between the Christian faith and Japanese beliefs and practices related to the dead. This was true for the earliest pioneer missionaries of the late nineteenth century as well as for the wave of evangelical Protestant missionaries that arrived in Japan during the postwar period. As noted in chapter three, the missionary view was that various indigenous traditions would need to be "displaced" to make room for the Gospel and authentic Christian faith. The gospel preached by most missionaries included the teaching that there is no hope for those who die without faith in Christ. Kazuo Yagi explains the "normative" missionary view as follows:

Protestants see human destiny as a separation to heaven or hell immediately after death. The first result of the Protestant view is that it is too late to pray for the dead, because their eternal destiny has already been determined at death. The second result is the unbearable estrangement of the heaven-bound Japanese Christian from his entire non-Christian ancestral line who are bound for hell.[15]

For individualistic Americans this was clearly not an issue, but for most Japanese the offer of personal salvation apart from the household and ancestral line represented an overwhelming existential crisis. In short, the Bible of the missionaries provided no basis for comfort or hope for the larger extended family.

The theological vacuum with regard to the ancestors was accentuated by the missionary demand for ritual purity on the part of Japanese converts. The first generation of Christians in Japan was under a great deal of pressure to comply with the iconoclastic policy of the missionaries. The early history of Protestant Christianity in Japan abounds with stories of individuals being cut off from their families or isolated in their communities because of their newfound faith and consequent refusal to participate in household ancestor rites or community festivals. It has not been uncommon for zealous new Christians, following the instructions of their missionary teachers, to burn their family Buddhist altars, ancestral tablets, and Shinto altars—understandably creating innumerable family conflicts.

It was not just the missionaries who took this uncompromising approach. In his social history of the early Protestant mission churches, Morioka Kiyomi reports that the leader of the Congregational Church and founder of Dōshisha University, Niijima Jō, following his return to Japan in 1874 after a decade of study in the United States, took a similarly hard line regarding these traditional practices.[16] When he returned to his own home, he explained to his parents that there was only one true God and that all gods made by human hands were simply idols. He promptly took down the *kamidana,* carried it out to the garden, and burned it. In subsequent lectures and preaching he explained that Christian commitment and faith required that one abandon the gods and buddhas and avoid participation in rituals before the *kamidana* and *butsudan.*

Morioka points out that it was extremely difficult for individuals to comply with the demand to dispose of the altars and memorial tablets unless the entire household converted to the faith. On the whole, it appears that Japanese converts found it much easier to get rid of the *kamidana* than the *butsudan* and *ihai,* since the latter represented the ancestors to whom the living were indebted. Morioka also notes that there was some variation in the responses of a main household (*honke*) and its branches (*bunke*). It was particularly difficult for the *honke*, given their stronger sense of family history and obligation to the ancestors, to comply with the demands of missionary teachers and Japanese Christian leaders like Niijima.

The clash between Protestant theology and Japanese religious sensibilities was rooted in the fact that the missionary carriers of the New Religion

> came from a culture that gave primacy to the nuclear family and to short-term separation rites for the dead. The Japanese receivers of the New Religion came from a culture that gave primacy to the *ie* system and to long-term liminal rites for the household dead.[17]

In the Japanese context, proper care and respect for the dead involved not only taking part in a number of rituals surrounding the funeral itself, but also the performance of annual festivals and memorial rites over the course of many years. The annual or *cyclical rites* are usually observed several times each year. On the spring and fall equinoxes (*higan*), families usually visit the household grave to clean the site and offer prayers and incense. In July or August (depending on the region of Japan) the spirits of the dead are believed to return to the home place for the several-day period referred to as *obon*. This is a time of family celebration that surrounds the welcoming and sending off of the ancestral spirits and that often involves visiting the household grave.

Linear rites, or memorial services (法事 *hōji*), are normally conducted over a thirty-three year period, and include services on the seventh day and forty-ninth day following a death, on the first anniversary and subsequent years (i.e., the 3rd, 7th, 13th, 17th, 23rd, 27th, and 33rd years following the death) in accordance with Buddhist tradition. Death anniversaries during the intervening years are often occasions for ritual observances before the family altar.

Ritual care of the dead beyond the funeral was clearly not a part of the Protestant tradition transplanted to Japan in the late nineteenth century. When the stark and simple Protestant funeral and burial service was compared with the traditional post-funerary rites extending over a period of many years, it is not surprising that many Japanese regarded Christianity as an "antifamily" religion that did not show proper concern for the dead.

MEMORIALISM IN INDIGENOUS CHRISTIANITY

For many Japanese, including the founders of most indigenous Christian movements, a religion that held out no hope for the salvation of the ancestors and prohibited members from showing respect towards them was, in effect, no religion at all. Eternal separation from those who preceded one in this life was regarded as unacceptable. As far as many Japanese Christians are concerned, there is still a vacuum in Protestant theology regarding the ancestors and relations between the living and the dead. Nor did Uchimura Kanzō, the founder of the Nonchurch movement, seriously engage the issues with which we are concerned here.[18]

It has been a number of indigenous movements that developed much later in the 1930s and 1940s that finally began to read the Bible in light of Japanese folk religious concerns. The most representative groups to address these issues are the Glorious Gospel Christian Church, the Spirit of Jesus Church, the Original Gospel, and the Holy Ecclesia of Jesus, all founded in the 1930s and 1940s. Many Protestant missionaries have regarded these indigenous developments as unfortunate expressions of syncretism and a deviation from normative Christianity. Indigenous leaders, nevertheless, regard their views as biblical and their elaboration of the Christian faith to be no less than the fulfillment of Jesus' promise to his disciples that "when the Spirit comes he will guide you into all truth" (John 16: 13).

This does not mean that indigenous leaders have disagreed with missionary teaching on all counts. Some continue to accept the missionary view that the native ancestral cult was to be shunned as nothing more than "idol worship." The Spirit of Jesus Church, for example, regards the Buddhist altar, ancestral tablets, and amulets from Shinto shrines as dwelling places of evil spirits. According to church representatives, the ancestral cult is a direct violation of the second commandment against worshipping false gods. Converts are usually assisted by pastors in burning the memorial tablets and other non-Christian religious paraphernalia. In spite of this symbolic rejection of traditional practices, the Spirit of Jesus Church by no means neglects the ancestors (as we shall see below).[19]

Most other indigenous movements, by contrast, have adopted a much more tolerant approach. Japanese leaders have come to view the missionary attitude toward these matters as an unnecessary stumbling block for potential Japanese converts and most have made concerted efforts to remedy the problem, which they regard as a misinterpretation of Christianity. In a very practical handbook published by the Holy Ecclesia of Jesus, for example, considerable attention is given to the problem of ancestors and care for the dead. A user-friendly question-and-answer format provides guidance on a number of topics for church members. The chapter entitled "Concerning Ancestor Veneration" explains the true Christian position with regard to the ancestors as follows:

In accordance with the Scriptures, the orthodox Christian church teaches that we are to respect our parents and truly honor our ancestors, and for this reason we reverently hold memorial services and festivals for the comforting of the spirits. Although we take special care of the dead and have high regard for our ancestors, in Christianity we do not *worship* the dead. As human beings, we should only worship the one true God who is the creator of heaven and earth and the source of our being; although we pray to God for the eternal peace of the dead, we do not worship the dead.[20]

A similar viewpoint is expressed in a special anniversary issue of the Original Gospel's monthly magazine *Seimei no hikari* (Light of life), which records the results of a symposium on the theme "Ancestral Rites and Memorial Services." The discussion is introduced with this explanation:

Christianity is misunderstood as a religion that does not show proper care and respect for the ancestors. One of the causes of this misunderstanding is that foreign missionaries taught Japanese that "they must get rid of their Shinto and Buddhist altar, since they represent nothing but idol worship."[21]

The editor goes on to explain that ritual care of the ancestors is not actually worship, but an expression of gratefulness and respect toward those to whom the living are indebted. While these explanations emphasize that it is "Christian" to show respect and care for the dead, we will show how these and other indigenous movements have moved far beyond the mere memorialism suggested by these publications.

Although these movements differ in their teachings regarding participation in the traditional practices, at the very least all have provided alternative and functionally equivalent rituals to remember and care for the dead (see table 5). Following a brief description of these ritual observances, we will consider the theological explanation for these practices in several representative groups.

In all the movements in which the founder has died, some memorial ritual has been institutionalized. In the case of the Nonchurch movement, there is a long tradition of holding memorial lectures and banquets in Tokyo and the Kansai areas on the Sunday nearest to 28 March, the death anniversary of Uchimura. The lectures are primarily regarded as opportunities for evangelism and outreach, but at the same time comprise ritual expressions of respect for Uchimura. Other groups hold actual memorial services on behalf of the founder. Christ Heart Church, for example, holds a service for the founder, Kawai Shinsui, in early August at the conclusion of a three-day retreat for study and training. The memorial service is preceded by several days of lectures, meditation, and

Table 5. Memorialism and Ritual Care of the Dead in Japanese Christian Movements

Indigenous Movement	Year Organized	Founder Memorials	Cyclical Rites	Linear Rites	Hymns	Extension of Salvation to the Spirit World	Family Altars (*butsudan* or Christian Equivalent)
Nonchurch movement 無教会	1901	▼		■			
The Way 道会	1907	■					
Christ Heart Church 基督心宗教団	1927	■					
Glorious Gospel Christian Church 栄光の福音キリスト教会	1936	■				■	■
Living Christ One Ear of Wheat Church 活けるキリスト一麦教会	1939	■					
Christian Canaan Church 基督カナン教団	1940						
Japan Ecclesia of Christ 日本キリスト召団	1940						■
Spirit of Jesus Church イエス之御霊教会	1941					■	■
Holy Ecclesia of Jesus 聖イエス会	1946	Founder living*			■		■
The Sanctifying Christ Church 聖成基督教団	1948	Founder living					
Original Gospel (Tabernacle Movement) 原始福音（幕屋）	1948	Founder living ■				■	
Life-Giving Christ 活かすキリスト	1966	Founder living					
Okinawa Christian Gospel 沖縄キリスト教福音	1977	Founder living					

Shaded cells indicate presence of phenomena in contemporary religious practice.

* The wife of the founder, referred to as 霊母様 (*reibosama*, spiritual mother), is remembered each year at a memorial service.

▼ In the case of the Nonchurch movement, memorial lectures are held on the Sunday nearest 28 March, the anniversary of the death of Uchimura.

Annual Memorial Lecture in honor of Uchimura Kanzō (Ōsaka).

cleaning of the head church facilities and graves. The church makes a point of not holding services in mid-August since it would conflict with the traditional *obon* observances, in which many members continue to participate with their non-Christian relatives. Teshima Ikurō, the founder of the Original Gospel movement, is also memorialized in annual services. In addition, the elderly members of the Kumamoto Original Gospel Church (where this movement began) clean the cemetery plot and offer fresh flowers every three days at the grave of Teshima and some of his earliest disciples. In the case of the Holy Ecclesia of Jesus, the founder, Father Ōtsuki (霊父様 *reifusama*), is still living, but his deceased wife, referred to as "spiritual mother" (霊母様 *reibosama*) for her important role as a counselor and guide to many women, is memorialized in the church calendar on 19 September (霊母記念日 *reibo kinenbi*).

While founders usually receive special attention, similar ritual care is provided for regular members and their families. All of the movements have Christianized the cyclical and linear rites for the dead observed by the majority of Japanese. The cyclical rites often involve an annual Common Memorial Service for Comforting of the Spirits (合同慰霊祭 *gōdō ireisai*) during the *obon* season or a congregational memorial service on Easter Sunday. Christ Heart Church holds such a service on 29 April, a national holiday, in remembrance of Emperor Shōwa's birthday. Since it is a holiday, it is easier for church members to gather at the head church near Mount Fuji. On the occasion of these services the founder's photograph is displayed and surrounded with flowers. In addition

Believers of the Christ Heart Church praying at the church grave sites following the annual memorial service for the Founder (Fujiyoshida).

to scripture readings and hymns, the service includes a reading of the names of all deceased members. The head of the church offers words of comfort and remembrance. This is followed by a tape-recorded sermon by the deceased founder. Following the service, members leave the church building to offer their respects at the grave of the founder and the crypt that holds the ashes of the deceased. The day concludes with a luncheon, a time of reflection, and a sharing of memories and stories regarding those who have passed away.

Annual memorial services also hold an important place in the Holy Ecclesia of Jesus. In addition to memorializing the dead according to the Roman Catholic calendar (on All Saints' Day in November, for example), leaders recognize that it is important for the church to provide services at times during the year when Japanese are most conscious and concerned about the ancestors, such as *obon* or *higan*. During these services members hold the photograph of the deceased family member on their lap until they are instructed to bring them forward and place them on a table at the front of the sanctuary for a pastoral prayer. The service concludes with a "vicarious mass" or Lord's Supper on behalf of the dead. The names of the deceased are read and the living receive the bread and wine on their behalf. This is a concrete manifestation of the "communion of the saints," and it is understood that the dead are receiving this communion spiritually in heaven.

Linear rites are also observed in various ways by most of these movements. These often follow the Buddhist custom of performing memorial services for the dead after so many days, months, and years (first-year anniversary, third, seventh, and so on). In response to requests from members, leaders or pastors of most of these movements hold memorial services in the church or in members' homes according to the usual schedule of linear memorial rites. In the weekly church bulletins of the Living Christ One Ear of Wheat Church, for example, there are announcements regarding the death anniversaries of various members that indicate how many years it has been since they were "called to heaven."[22] Several of the movements have also composed hymns commemorating the dead for these services.[23] Almost all the leaders and pastors of these movements regard such memorial services as prime opportunities for evangelism. While many Japanese would resist attending regular services at a Christian church, most friends and relatives find it difficult not to attend memorial rituals.

Memorial services are also quite common in the Nonchurch movement, but there is no set ritual or liturgy for such occasions. Some individuals hold family services in the home, while others organize memorial services with the Nonchurch group to which they belong. Sometimes a hall is rented for the occasion and a meal is shared together. Reflecting the Nonchurch movement's individualistic stance on matters of faith, there is considerable variation in both the content and timing of services. A Nonchurch group in Hamamatsu, for example, holds a special meeting on 15 August each year to remember the defeat of Japan that ended the war. This is, of course, during the *obon* season, a time when it is natural for Japanese to remember the dead. Although the primary concern of the meeting is to reflect on the responsibility of Christians with regard to world peace, it includes a communal memorial service for a number of individuals from their circle who died in the war. Another common practice in the Nonchurch movement is to honor the deceased through the publication of a special memorial volume of essays in a book or magazine.

In sharp contrast to Protestant missionary policy, many indigenous movements allow their members to maintain the traditional Buddhist altar in the home. Christ Heart Church, for example, sees no conflict between Christian faith and ancestor veneration. In fact, their members are encouraged to show proper respect toward traditional customs, and their participation in Buddhist ancestral rites with non-Christian family members is not regarded as problematic. Similarly, leaders in the Original Gospel movement encourage their members to pray where their ancestors prayed—in front of the Buddhist altar. When a meeting is held in the home of a member who has a Buddhist altar, the leader will simply place a menorah (the symbol of God and light used in Makuya worship) in front of the altar and hold the worship service with the doors of the *butsudan* opened. The Holy Ecclesia of Jesus encourages its members to maintain, as an alternative to the Buddhist altar, a Christian family altar as a focus for worship and prayer. Memorial tablets are replaced by small wooden crosses inscribed with the names or "spiritual names" of the deceased family members. This adaptation resembles the traditional Buddhist practice of giving a *kaimyō*, or Buddhist name, to the deceased. In this way the Holy Ecclesia of Jesus is providing concrete and visible means for their members to show their non-Christian relatives and neighbors that Christianity is a religion that shows special care and respect for the dead.

It would be wrong to leave the impression that only the indigenous movements have adapted to the needs of many Japanese to show special care and respect for the ancestors. In fact, many of the Christian churches related to denominations from Europe and North America have instituted a wide range of post-funerary rites over the course of the past century. There are a number of helpful studies documenting these ritual developments in various denominations. David Reid has analyzed the manner in which members of the United Church of Christ in Japan have adapted Christian practices to indigenous ancestral rituals. Similarly, Nishiyama Shigeru's study of the Anglican Church revealed that the ancestral cult has significantly transformed the practice of Christianity within this denomination. David Doerner's survey of a Roman Catholic parish likewise showed that numerous accommodations have been made to indigenous beliefs and practices related to the dead. As Berentsen notes, the Roman Catholic tradition has a more natural affinity to the ancestral cult than Protestant forms of Christianity because of its long practice of "offering liturgical prayers and Holy Mass for the dead."[24] More recently, Mark Luttio has shown how the Lutheran Church has created a funeral rite that is more compatible with Japanese religious sensitivities and concerns. Luttio also provides a helpful analysis of the funeral rite developed by the Japan Evangelical Church (JELC) in 1993, comparing this ritual not only with the JELC's first funeral rite of 1897 but also with traditional Buddhist rites for the dead. Faithful to the early missionary tradition, the 1897 rite consisted of only a funeral and burial (on the same day). The 1993 rite has adapted and incorporated many elements found in the protracted process of ritual care provided by the Japanese Buddhist tradition. Although these churches have made numerous ritual adaptations, for the most part they have failed to address the theological questions and concerns related to ancestors and various spirits.[25]

Typical family altars in the homes of Holy Ecclesia of Jesus members, with a wooden cross inscribed with the name of a deceased family member (left), and a more elaborate example (right).

READING THE BIBLE WITH JAPANESE EYES

The most significant development with regard to the dead is the theological view of many indigenous leaders that Christians have a legitimate mission to the spirit world (referred to in table 1, pages 14–15, as the "extension of salvation to the spirit world"). Upon reading the Bible for themselves, Japanese discovered that the New Testament contained a number of texts that were relevant to their concerns for the extended family and ancestors. Guided by their individualistic gospel, Protestant missionaries had apparently overlooked or effectively ignored these passages. Reading the same Bible as their missionary predecessors, the leaders of indigenous movements have all concluded that it is not only proper for Christians to show respect toward the dead but that there is hope for those who died without encountering the Gospel in this life. These leaders appeal to the same biblical texts when making claims regarding the potential salvation of the pre-Christian dead. The *locus classicus* is found in 1 Peter:

> For Christ also suffered for sins once for all, the righteous for the unrighteous, in order to bring you to God. He was put to death in the flesh, but made alive

145

in the spirit, in which also he went and made a proclamation to the spirits in prison, who in former times did not obey, when God waited patiently in the days of Noah, during the building of the ark, in which a few, that is, eight persons, were saved through water (3:18–22).

And in the following chapter:

For this is the reason the gospel was proclaimed even to the dead, so that, though they had been judged in the flesh, they might live in the spirit as God does (4:6).

The ministry to the world of the dead is understood as a continuation of the work begun by Jesus Christ when he descended into hades and preached to the imprisoned spirits who had rejected Noah's message from God in an earlier period of salvation

An ordained elder of the United Church of Christ in rural Shikoku, seated in front of the family altar, showing Buddhist memorial tablets standing next to the crucifix.

The church altar of a United Church of Christ congregation in rural Shikoku displaying photos of deceased members and a Buddhist memorial tablet at the annual memorial service on Easter Sunday.

history. This interpretation can best be understood with reference to the traditional worldview and familial orientation referred to above.

The Spiritualistic Worldview

Except perhaps for Uchimura's Nonchurch movement, these indigenous movements share what we might call a "spiritualistic worldview" not unlike the cosmology of Japanese folk religion. Their interpretation of the New Testament and their soteriological claims regarding the spirits of the dead must be understood in terms of their belief in the reality and interdependence of "this world" and another "spirit world" (i.e., the world of the ancestors). The lands of the living and the dead are regarded as interdependent and linked symbolically through prayer, preaching, and other ritual behavior. While this worldview may resemble that of the folk religious tradition introduced earlier, indigenous leaders maintain that it is also the worldview of Jesus and the early Christian movement.

Belief in the reality of a separate world of spirits and supernatural beings able to causally affect our world is hardly a novel idea or one foreign to the world of the Bible. As we noted in chapter three, Marcus J. Borg has argued that we cannot accurately understand the place of Jesus in the Judeo-Christian tradition without giving serious attention to the "world of Spirit."[26] While the notion of "another world" may be alien to post-enlightenment Westerners, Borg maintains that Jesus belonged to the charismatic stream of Judaism that took this worldview for granted, and that he served as a mediator between this world and the world of Spirit. The Japanese movements under consideration believe that they have been given the religious authority by Jesus Christ to continue this mediation between the two worlds. For some this interpretation is related to their reading of Matthew 18:18–20:

> Truly I tell you, whatever you bind on earth will be bound in heaven, and whatever you loose on earth will be loosed in heaven. Again, truly I tell you, if two of you agree on earth about anything you ask, it will be done for you by my Father in heaven. For where two or three are gathered in my name, I am among them.

This passage suggests an interdependence between this world and the spirit world and indicates that followers of Jesus have been authorized to influence the state of affairs in both worlds. According to Murai Jun, the founder of the Spirit of Jesus Church, the tragedy of Western Christianity is that it no longer recognizes that the church has been given the authority to forgive sins. This has apparently been forgotten along with all the signs, miracles, and wonders that characterized the early church.

Sugita Kōtarō, the founder of the Glorious Gospel Christian Church, encouraged his followers to pray on behalf of the ancestors with the understanding that the gospel of Christ could reach them in the spirit world. In volume 2 of *The Glorious Gospel*, Sugita writes, in rather Pauline fashion, that he is "certain in the Lord" that "offering prayers of intercession on behalf of the dead is a good and proper thing for believers to do. Although there is no Scriptural text stating that those prayed for will necessarily be saved, neither is there a text instructing us not to pray for the dead."[27] Sugita goes on to explain that God expressed his parental heart for all humankind in sending his son to die for the sins of the world. It is the height of selfishness and self-centeredness for us to think that God hated those individuals who lived before the revelation of Christ and only loves those of us who had the opportunity to encounter the Gospel over the past two thousand years. The fact that Christ descended into hell and preached to the imprisoned spirits is a clear indication that God cares for the dead as well as the living. He concludes that Christians should pray for the spirits of the dead, but should not assume that each person prayed for will necessarily be saved. While there are grounds for optimism, ultimately it is God who decides whose name will be written in the Book of Life.

The leaders of other movements indicate even greater confidence in the efficacy of their prayers for the dead and their preaching to the spirit world. According to the Original Gospel symposium referred to above, "Ancestral Rites and Memorial Services," the founder, Teshima Ikurō, taught that Christian memorial services were important rituals in the life of faith. Instead of chanting the Buddhist sūtras on these occasions, however, one should read from the Bible. As the Bible teaches, "Man does not live by bread alone, but by every word that proceeds from the mouth of God." Teshima explained that the spirits of the dead cannot eat material bread, but they can eat the word of God. That is why the most appropriate memorial rite is to read to them the word of God. Through our prayerful reading of the Bible, the "wandering spirits" receive guidance and are pointed in the direction of Christ. In contrast to the missionary tradition, Teshima taught that there is no need to throw out the Buddhist altar and memorial tablets. In fact, one should open the doors to the altar and preach the gospel to the ancestors. In this way, preaching and intercessary prayers on behalf of the dead are recognized as efficacious.

Imahashi Atsushi, a disciple of Teshima and founder of the Life-Giving Christ, explained to me that the first thing he did after his healing and conversion experience was to evangelize his ancestors.[28] He went before the Buddhist family altar and reported his conversion to the ancestors, praying that they would also receive the light of Christ. Because of the example of Christ recorded in 1 Peter, Imahashi has every confidence that the dead can hear the gospel preached to them and ultimately be saved. According to Imahashi, this is what it means to confess that Jesus Christ is Lord both of this world and of the spirit world.

This type of care for the dead has become a rather common ingredient of pastoral care in the movements under consideration. A seasoned pastor of the Holy Ecclesia of Jesus told me that he is often asked by members to pray for ancestors or family members who died without faith. On one such occasion he instructed them to place the photographs of the two deceased family members in the living room alcove, and they all joined together in prayer for their salvation. As the pastor prayed fervently, he could see the two spirits struggling in the world of darkness. "At that point," he explained, "the spirit of Christ within me proclaimed, 'I am the resurrection and the life.' At that moment these two spirits were indwelled by Christ and transformed into light. Then I saw them rise to heaven." Another leader described a similar pastoral visit as follows:

> One of the members of my church had recently lost her unbelieving husband and could not find peace. She felt that her husband's spirit was hovering like a dark cloud about the house, and she asked me to pray for him. I visited her home and she showed me her husband's photograph and the container holding his ashes. I clutched the container close to my heart and began to pray for him with the words of Christ, "I am the resurrection and the life." I called out his name and prayed that he would believe the gospel. When I finished praying she and I both felt great relief, and the Spirit confirmed in our hearts that he had been saved. After this pastoral visit, she was no longer troubled by his presence.

It is clear that concern for the dead is not abstract or philosophical, but a pressing existential matter. Furthermore, these examples illustrate the fundamental belief in the interdependence of this world and the spirit world and the power of the living to influence the world of the dead. In most cases, the salvific work of Christ in the other world is confirmed through visions, dreams, and the inward witness of the Holy Spirit.

Familial Orientation

As the foregoing examples suggest, notions of familial solidarity clearly shape the Japanese interpretation of the salvation of those already in the spirit world. The words of Paul and Silas to the Philippian jailer (Acts 16:31) are interpreted from a Japanese cultural perspective and taken very literally: "Believe on the

Lord Jesus, and you will be saved, you and your *household*" (emphasis added). The Japanese household (*ie*) is an extended family that includes both present and past members (ancestors). A Japanese expression that combines a Buddhist notion of merit with a Confucian familial orientation is often used to illustrate this interpretation of interdependence:

一人が出家すれば九族が天に帰る.

If one family member takes monastic vows, then up to nine generations of the whole household will be saved by virtue of his merit.

Commenting on this expression, one leader explained:

Since I have escaped the sin of Adam, so did my family. But this is not because of my virtue, but through the grace of Christ. I have confidence that my ancestors are saved, and I have been blessed by the fact that most of my living family members have also been saved.

Just as Abram was called by God and became a source of blessing for all the families of the earth (Gen. 12: 1–2), an individual's salvation in Christ can become the source of blessing to others, both the living and the dead.

CARE FOR THE DEAD IN THE SPIRIT OF JESUS CHURCH

The Spirit of Jesus Church links salvific work in the spirit world and the notion of "household" salvation to the long-forgotten ritual of vicarious baptism referred to in I Cor. 15:29, a key New Testament passage on the resurrection of the dead:

Otherwise, what will those people do who receive baptism on behalf of the dead? If the dead are not raised at all, why are people baptized on their behalf?

According to this church, it is through the ritual of vicarious baptism (先祖の身代わり洗礼) that the blessings of individual salvation can be extended to past generations as well. In a work entitled *Biblical Theology*, the founder, Murai Jun, placed considerable emphasis on this teaching. According to Murai, the biblical teaching of the salvation of the dead has been hidden from the church since the second century, when the church ceased to practice "water" and "spirit" baptism. "It is in these last days," Murai writes, "that this great mystery has been revealed to the Spirit of Jesus Church."[29] When newcomers visit one of the churches, they are presented with the Gospel and encouraged to accept it for their own salvation and, at the same time, informed that there is also salvation for the ancestors through vicarious baptism.

How does this work out in practice? Members can request that ancestors be baptized at the same time they are, or whenever they become concerned about the salvation of those who have gone before. A member simply states the ancestor's name, announces his or her relationship to the deceased, and then undergoes baptism by immersion on their behalf. It is significant to note here that the church also performs baptism for *mizuko* (aborted and stillborn children). In this way, the Spirit of Jesus Church is responding to the felt needs of Japanese women to deal with the sense of guilt and the curse associated with the spirit of a *mizuko*. Through this ritual the Good News of the forgiveness of sins is communicated to the dead, and their spirits are transported from hades to heaven.[30] Although their bodies decay in the grave, their spirits can be saved through the forgiveness of sins. Believers are assured that they may lay aside all their doubts and misgivings regarding the state of their ancestors following this ritual. A pastor in Okinawa explained to me that prior to the ritual of vicarious baptism many members have disturbing visions of the wandering spirits of the dead. Following this ritual care, however, the spirits are felt to be at peace and there are no longer any troubling spiritual encounters.

This understanding of vicarious baptism is expressed clearly in a hymn by that title in the church's *Spirit Hymns*.[31]

Vicarious Baptism

I

The spirits of our long-sleeping ancestors
    still now are weeping in sorrow.
Spring passes, summer comes, autumn goes and winter comes,
But hades is eternally winter's dead of night.

II

Like the never-ending shadowy darkness of hades
    tears are flowing.
Crossing over the river of death, the anguish of that day.
Even now they are in the bitter harbor.

III

The ship that goes out knows no bottom,
Sinking deeper and deeper in the depths.
Still now the salvation of our ancestors is closed,
Eternal spirits anguishing ceaselessly.

IV

Evil spirits come like a whirlpool,
Frantically seeking salvation.
Faintly hearing the splash of water,
The mysterious work of atonement in songs from heaven.

V

By and by the gates of hades are opened
Through the name of Jesus.
The substitutionary baptism of descendants in the world—
Oh, what immeasurable grace!

VI

Oh, the cries of joy reverberate!
Our ancestors have been saved!
The light of grace shines all around,
The songs of the angels thunder throughout heaven and earth.

Concern for the dead does not end with the ritual of baptism. The afore-mentioned Common Memorial Service for Comforting of the Spirits is also an important service in all Spirit of Jesus churches. According to one church repre-sentative, the significance of this service is that it allows living believers to join with the spirits of the dead in common prayer to Jesus Christ. In this it certainly resembles the Buddhist *obon* festival, a central motif of which is reunion and fel-lowship with the dead. There is some variation in the observance of this service from church to church. In one church on the island of Shikoku, for example, this service is held each August, and members bring a list of deceased family members for inclusion in prayer.[32] Memorial services are also performed numer-ous times throughout the year according to the requests of members (these ser-vices often follow the Buddhist custom to perform memorial services for the dead after so many days, months, and years). Although there is no incense, Buddhist altars, or ancestor tablets, the Common Memorial Service for Comforting of the Spirits is clearly the functional equivalent of the Buddhist memorial service that Japanese view as important for showing proper respect to ancestors and for assuring their eternal peace.

The concern for the dead is also manifested in the Daiseikai (大聖会), a meeting lasting several days that is held annually in each district or region. In eastern Japan, for example, a memorial service is observed during the Daiseikai each May for the founder and for pastors who have died. In addition to the gen-eral memorial services for the dead, the Tokyo church (headquarters) also observes annually in March a special memorial service for the founder and first bishop of the Spirit of Jesus Church.

THE JAPANESE CHRISTIAN RESPONSE TO INDIGENOUS SPIRIT BELIEFS

While many Japanese Christians are deeply concerned about the salvation of their ancestors, they also harbor fears about the possible misfortune (*tatari*) they may suffer at the hands of malevolent spirits of the dead known as *onryō* 怨霊. These concerns are deeply rooted in Japanese history, according to Hori Ichirō, and became widespread in the early Heian period (784–1185).[33] It has long been believed that individuals who die a violent or untimely death due to war or some unforeseen accident are filled with hate and bitterness and will return to cause harm to those in this world.[34] Missionary theology and practice provide little or no solace to Japanese Christians who are troubled by such fears. This is clearly an important dimension of pastoral care in the Japanese context, but something one will not find seriously addressed in the practical theology curriculum of any Protestant seminary in Japan. The leadership in most indigenous Christian movements, on the other hand, accepts these as "real concerns" and responds with prayers and ritual care that empowers many members to carry on with everyday life. Teachings regarding the efficacy of prayer, preaching to the spirit world, and vicarious baptism not only provide for the salvation of the dead but also help safeguard the living against these potentially dangerous spirits.

A participant in Original Gospel's symposium on "Ancestral Rites and Memorial Services" confided that she had been deeply troubled for years at the "bad death" of her parents resulting from the bombing of Hiroshima. She sought peace first in Seichō no Ie (a New Religion) and then through dedicated participation in a Christian church. Neither provided the solution for her spiritual distress. All of this changed when she encountered the Original Gospel movement and discovered the power of Christ over the spirit world. Her story is as follows:

> After joining the Original Gospel movement I was blessed with a happy marriage, and my husband and I began our life of faith together. However, when each of our children was born the spirits of my parents would appear, and my mother, in a rather mad and lunatic form, would demand, "Let me meet the children." These were my parents who had died of an illness resulting from the atomic bomb and had left me behind as a young child. I just could not bear this recurring image of my parents.
>
> One evening at the Original Gospel retreat on Mount Hiko I finally prayed fervently, "Lord, please save the souls of my parents who are wandering in the

spirit world." That night I had a dream of my father and mother encircled by light and accompanied by the elders of the Original Gospel. And with the most joyful look on their faces, I saw them moving through a tunnel of light. Through this dream I was convinced and assured that Christ had saved my parents. Since that time only my mother's happy face has appeared to me.[35]

Although concern for the dead is related most often to immediate family members and relatives, most of these movements extend their care to include the *muenbotoke* (無縁仏), the nameless or unknown dead who wander about with no descendants to properly care for their needs. Members of the Original Gospel movement in Okinawa, for example, were troubled by visions of the thousands upon thousands who died on the Okinawan islands as the Pacific War came to an end. These nameless ones had never received a proper funeral or memorial rites and were destined to wander about the spirit world. Through the founder's teaching they realized that these spirits could be saved by Christ in the spirit world. With this inclusive understanding of Christ's salvific work, members of the Original Gospel held a special service before a memorial stone for the war dead of Okinawa and prayed for their peace and salvation in the other world. Participants reported that they experienced a spiritual vision of these many suffering spirits being rescued as they joined in collective prayer on their behalf.

Another example is the care accorded the Catholic martyrs on the island of Kyūshū by the Holy Ecclesia of Jesus. In certain areas in Kyūshū popular religious beliefs regarding dangerous "wandering spirits" became associated with Christianity because of the large number of Catholics who were killed there in the sixteenth and seventeenth centuries. It is not uncommon to hear stories attributing suffering, illness, or *tatari* to these Christian ghosts. Father Ōtsuki, the founder, made a pilgrimage to Kyūshū with a number of pastors and visited the various sites of the martyrs. Recalling that these martyrs were killed without the opportunity to participate in a last mass, Father Ōtsuki poured wine on each grave site and held a memorial mass to comfort their spirits. The Holy Ecclesia of Jesus has now established several churches in Kyūshū in memory of these long-forgotten and largely ignored Catholic martyrs. Today scores of pastors and members make pilgrimages to Kyūshū in order to visit these sites and honor the faith and sacrifice of the martyrs through memorial services. For these Japanese Christians, the "communion of saints" is an experienced reality as they partake of bread and wine vicariously on behalf of the fallen martyrs.

CONCLUSION

In the various ways discussed above, indigenous Christian movements have extended the scope of salvation to the spirit world. Their ritual care of ancestors and wandering spirits brings peace to those already in the other world as well as protection for those still in the land of the living. While some may consider these spirits to be passively awaiting the final consummation of all things, others see them as taking on a more active role. According to the Spirit of Jesus Church, for example, vicarious baptism releases the spirits of the dead from hades and transports them to heaven, where they pray for family members remaining on earth. Just as a dead person is transformed into a benevolent ancestor through Buddhist memorial services, the Spirit of Jesus Church transforms their dead through baptism into benevolent ancestors who perform intermediary prayers (*torinashi no inori*) on their behalf. Similarly, some members of Spirit of Jesus Church refer to those in the other world as "protective spirits," and understand them to function much like guardian angels. In other words, the spirit world is populated with beings who provide protection and intercession on behalf of the living.

In this context it is interesting to recall Max Weber's view that one of the consequences of the Protestant Reformation was the "unprecedented inner loneliness" experienced by the single individual as a result of being cut off from the mystery and magic of medieval Catholicism.[36] This "disenchantment of the world" through rationalization left the lone individual responsible for his or her fate without the comforting resources of priests, sacraments, and saints. One could make the case that these indigenous Christian movements have contributed in a small way to the "re-enchantment of the world" through their recognition of the interdependence of the visible and invisible realms and the power of ritual over the living and the dead. In this way, their understanding of the unseen world has more in common with the Roman Catholic tradition than with Protestant Christianity.[37]

CHAPTER EIGHT

Comparative Patterns of
Growth and Decline

A S WE HAVE SEEN, since the reopening of Japan to the West in the late nineteenth century scores of denominations and sects have made their way from Europe and North America in an attempt to Christianize Japan, but institutionally affiliated Christians still amount to only about one percent of the population. When one considers the human and financial resources invested by both Roman Catholic and Protestant churches, as well as the efforts of indigenous Christian movements, it is hardly a picture of success. In a word, the story of Christianity in Japan is often portrayed as one of "failure" in comparison to the remarkable success of Christianity in Africa, Latin America, and nearby Korea. What is it about Christianity, or about Japanese society and culture, that has made the proselytization so difficult? This chapter will briefly introduce sociological research on patterns of "growth" and "non-growth" and consider some of the key difficulties related to the transplantation of Christianity in Japan.

THE SOCIOLOGY OF TRANSPLANTED CHURCHES

A review of research on church growth in Japan reveals that a large proportion of the studies focus on the early period of the Protestant missions. The most authoritative work in this regard is undoubtedly Morioka Kiyomi's *Japan's Modern Society and Christianity*. This study draws on earlier research by Morioka and his students, and provides a social history along with an analysis of mission work and church formation from 1852 to 1912. Morioka gives considerable attention to both the contextual factors (the sociopolitical climate, the legal situation, the struggle with indigenous religious practices) and the internal institutional factors (leadership, religious rivalry, higher criticism, and liberal theology) that shaped growth and decline patterns during the period studied.

Another helpful study, which draws on Morioka's earlier work, is Yamamori Tetsunao's *Church Growth in Japan: A Study in the Development of Eight Denominations, 1859–1939*. The author provides a comparative analysis of growth patterns in the Anglican, Presbyterian, American Baptist, Congregational, Methodist, Disciples of Christ, Southern Baptist, and Seventh-day Adventist churches during five historical periods. He examines both the socio-cultural setting (contextual factors) and institutional factors that influenced growth patterns in each period. For example, the author argues that between 1882 and 1889, the era of "openness to the West," the Congregational and Presbyterian churches made rapid progress because they sent more missionaries, trained national leaders at a quicker pace, organized more self-supporting churches, and emphasized education and work in strategic areas.

Robert Lee's *Stranger in the Land* develops a theoretical framework based largely upon national contextual factors. In a historical overview of Christianity in Japan (including the early Catholic period), Lee relates the growth and decline patterns to a typology of "responses" that range from periods of cordial welcome to times of hostility and persecution. While Lee provides a helpful perspective on early Christian activity in Japan, his primary focus is on the United Church of Christ (Kyōdan) during the early postwar period. The Kyōdan was actually quite successful at attracting new members during this period. From 1947 to 1951, for example, the Kyōdan recorded over 10,000 baptisms a year, compared with less than 3,000 for 1990. Membership retention, however, was more difficult. It seemed that scores were going out the back door as others came through the front door.

Several years after Lee's study appeared, the investigation of church growth became a major preoccupation of sociologists in North America. Serious discussions of church growth and decline in the United States began with the publication of Dean M. Kelley's *Why Conservative Churches are Growing* in 1972.[1] The basic thesis developed by Kelly in this controversial book can be summarized as follows: evangelical churches are growing because they fulfill the primary function of a religion, that of providing ultimate meaning to human life. Liberal or more ecumenical bodies, on the other hand, are declining because they tend to neglect this central function, focusing instead on various social issues. While Kelly does not fault the ecumenical churches for their social concerns, he maintains that failure "to undergird their activities with adequate grounding in ultimate meaning" has contributed to organizational decline. Kelley documents his argument with considerable data from both mainline (declining) denominations and evangelical (growing) churches in the United States.

Since the publication of Kelly's work, growing and declining denominations have been distinguished primarily in terms of their conservative or liberal theological orientation. Subsequent research has shown that church growth is related to a complex pattern of interacting factors and cannot be traced to a single cause. A volume edited by Dean R. Hoge and David A. Roozen under the title *Understanding Church Growth and Decline* provides a helpful antidote to simplistic explanations.[2] The researchers collaborating on this collection of case studies developed a more comprehensive framework for understanding organizational growth and decline, drawing attention to contextual factors that apply as much to religion as to any other institution.

About a decade after Hoge and Roozen's work, Wade Clark Roof and William McKinney provided another study of denominations in the United States that generally supported Kelley's earlier distinction between growth and decline in terms of theological orientation and further clarified the demographic factors that encourage these patterns.[3] Kelley's work focused on growth due to conversions, evangelistic outreach, and new church development. The size of a religious organization, however, is also dependent on the "natural growth" that occurs over time. Studies have shown that class, educational level, and theological heritage shape differential fertilities from group to group, and that upward mobility leads to a decline in fertility and birthrates. While more active membership recruitment and new church development on the part of conservative religious bodies cannot be discounted, Roof and McKinney's study as well as others indicate that higher birthrates and more effective religious socialization largely explain the current patterns of growth and decline.

These recent perspectives on the sociology of church growth have not yet been systematically applied to the study of Japanese Christianity. Nevertheless, we can at least observe that patterns of church growth in Japan today resemble those found by researchers in the United States. An examination of denominational statistics reveals that older Japanese churches, though not in decline like their counterparts in North America, are recording only modest church growth. For example, the United Church of Christ in Japan and the Anglican Church showed membership increases of approximately five percent over the past decade, while Japanese churches identified more closely with American evangelicalism recorded significantly higher growth rates of fifteen percent or more during the same period. These higher growth rates, however, are not significantly altering the overall picture of Christianity in Japan since the total numbers are small, amounting to only a few hundred new members each year.[4]

INDIGENIZATION: A CURE-ALL?

One frequently hears that the primary reason why churches have experienced only minimal growth in Japan is because they are still Western in orientation and have failed to develop indigenous forms of leadership, organization, and worship. Robert Lee, for example, concluded that the "Westernness" of Christianity represents a major obstacle to church growth in Japanese society. In one of the only articles on the sociology of missions, David Heise similarly pointed out that "foreign churches often are rejected if their social organization is too dissimilar to native patterns."[5] Hayashi Minoru more recently characterized the Christian movement in Japan as "a Westernized, non-growing, and weakened form of Christianity."[6] The general consensus appears to be that successful transplantation and church growth require indigenization. If indigenization is the "cure" for nongrowth, one would expect to find indigenous movements to be dynamic and growing. An overview of growth and decline patterns of representative organizations, however, reveals a more ambiguous pattern.

Nonchurch Movement

The Nonchurch movement has recorded significant growth since Uchimura Kanzō began his Bible meetings in 1900 with twenty-five students in his home. This initial group of disciples became the nucleus of other Nonchurch associa-

Table 6. Location and Number of Nonchurch Movement Meetings in 1967

LOCATION	HOME	RENTED ROOMS	HOSPITALS	SCHOOLS	WORKPLACE	TOTAL
Tokyo	48	20	6	8	9	91
5 Other urban centers	22	14	4	3	3	46
Other regions	187	25	13	13	9	247
Total	257	59	23	24	21	384

Figures taken from 高橋三郎 Takahashi Saburō, 無教会精神の探求 [In search of the Spirit of the Nonchurch movement] (Tokyo: Shinkyō Shuppansha, 1970), 196.

tions. By 1905 there were fourteen branches of the Kyōyūkai (Fellowship of Disciples), and supporters of Uchimura grew in number through his public lectures in rented facilities and the publication of his magazine, *Bible Studies*. A gift from a supporter in 1908 made it possible to build Imai Kan, a hall near Uchimura's home, which became the center for his ongoing lectures. In 1919 Uchimura moved his Sunday lectures to a rented hall in Ōtemachi, where 600 to 700 people attended each week. These numbers, however, do not adequately reflect the true size of Uchimura's following. In one of the earliest issues of his magazine he had already referred to his ideal of "a church on paper" to describe the relationship between himself and his growing number of readers. Uchimura reports that by 1928 *Bible Studies* had 4,200 subscribers, and his Sunday lectures had a "paying membership of 552, with a large waiting list" of individuals who wished to attend.[7]

Although some observers thought that the Nonchurch movement would decline and disappear after the death of Uchimura, it has in fact expanded as his disciples pursued independent evangelistic activities, organized groups, and published their own monthly magazines. On the basis of magazine subscriptions and attendance at Nonchurch meetings, John Howes suggested a Nonchurch membership of between 50,000 and 100,000 in 1957.[8] While this number seems rather high, the number of publications and organized groups does indicate a substantial following. On the basis of a survey conducted in 1967, Takahashi Saburō argued that Uchimura's prophetic spirit and mission had been effectively transmitted. Takahashi discovered over 50 different monthly magazines published by various disciples between 1920 and 1966, and found a total of 384 different groups throughout the country (see table 6).[9] Since well over half of these groups met in homes, it is not unreasonable to assume that most were small gatherings of five to ten people, though the statistics include several Bible lecture meetings held in rented halls with over one hundred persons in attendance. Although Takahashi did not estimate the actual number of participants, a decade later Carlo Caldarola's study placed the membership at about 35,000.[10]

If Caldarola's membership figure for the mid-1970s is accurate, it is apparent that the movement has experienced a steady decline for the past two decades, since, according to recent information, there are only about 300 Nonchurch groups active today. The number of charismatic teachers has declined considerably and many groups operate on the basis of a rotating leadership. Most groups are struggling to carry on with only five to ten members, though several larger groups still remain—the Bible lectures of Sekine Masao, for example, still attract over 100 people each week, and close to 1,000 still subscribe to his magazine. Similarly, Takahashi Saburō's weekly lectures are attended by 50 or more and his magazine is sent to almost 2,500. It is still very difficult to calculate the actual number of people involved in the Nonchurch movement, but 5,000 is probably a fair estimate.[11] A national meeting of Nonchurch groups has been held each year since 1987 to discuss the many critical issues the movement faces today. The first annual meeting was attended by 361 individuals and attendance in subsequent years has averaged about 300. According to the records of these meetings, the number of independent evangelists declined considerably during the third generation of the Nonchurch movement, and young people today generally do not find it very attractive. Furthermore, the members are struggling to meet the needs of aging followers who are without pastoral care as groups disband following the retirement or death of the leader. It remains to be seen whether these coordinated national efforts will be able to revitalize the movement.[12]

The Way

The Way, the second oldest indigenous movement, has experienced a similar pattern of growth and decline. Founded by Matsumura Kaiseki in 1907, it had a membership of 271 by 1911, with a main church in Tokyo and several branch churches around the country. Over the next two decades groups were organized on university campuses (Tokyo Imperial University, Keiō, Waseda, Tokyo Agricultural University) and branch churches were established in prefectures throughout Japan (from Kyūshū to Hokkaidō). In 1936, at the age of 78, Matsumura retired and appointed his adopted son and closest disciple to succeed him as head of the movement. That same year, The Way published a membership list of 309 pages with the names and addresses of some 4,300 members. This list included 101 members located overseas, for the most part in Japanese colonies such as Manchuria, and a few in immigrant communities in North and South America.[13] On the basis of the records I have been able to locate, this was the peak of the group's membership. Although it continued to record new members through the 1940s and 1950s, the number of deaths and the increasing number of "inactive" members has meant a steady decline in the postwar period. By 1970 the movement had declined to a membership of 2,343, affiliated with nine churches.[14] Although The Way continues to print 1,000 copies of its quarterly journal *The Way*, the actual membership nationwide is no more than 300. Most of these members are quite elderly, and there are no signs that an influx of young people will revitalize this group. While several small groups scattered around Japan still meet occasionally during the year, the only remaining church is the headquarters in Tokyo, where several meetings are held each month.

Christ Heart Church

Although it is difficult to find accurate statistics on the early development of Christ Heart Church, it seems to have followed a pattern of growth and decline not unlike that of the groups discussed above. The initial growth of Christ Heart Church was strongly influenced by its close relation to the Gunze Silk Factory in Ayabe City, Kyoto Prefecture. Hatano Tsurukichi (1858–1919), the President of Gunze, was a committed Christian who wanted to operate Gunze according to Christian principles. To that end he invited Kawai Shinsui, the founder of Christ Heart Church, to serve as the director of Gunze's education department in 1909, in which capacity Kawai served until 1935. During this time he led morning worship services, gave lectures, and directed Seishū Gakuin (Academy for the Cultivation of Sincerity), a school for training Gunze instructors. Kawai's influence spread across Japan as these instructors were sent to various branch factories around the country. By 1917 Gunze had grown to include 17 factories and 5,000 employees. The number of employees peaked at over 21,000 in 1934.

It is in this context that Kawai established Christ Heart Church in 1927. He first built a *dōjō* on Gunze property in Ayabe and shortly thereafter on the grounds of several branch factories. Services were usually attended by the president, factory managers, and numerous employees. Kawai would also visit factories that did not have a *dōjō* and give lectures from time to time.

At one point there were as many as 30 groups around Japan. Some insiders claim that at one time Kawai had 20,000 followers, but this number represents the approximate number of Gunze employees who were influenced by Kawai rather than actual church members. According to one observer, the membership in 1960 exceeded 3,000.[15] If that is an accurate number, it has seriously declined since that time. Although the church reports that it still has 27 groups around the country with a membership of 1,315, most are no longer active. While 900 copies of the church publication *The Mind of Christ* are printed each quarter, the de facto membership nationwide is no more than several hundred. The Tokyo church, which is the largest, has declined to a membership of 43 and has a regular attendance of only 15 to 20. Smaller branch churches usually have a gathering of only four or five people.

The aging process is clearly taking its toll. Many of the earliest members have already passed away, a number of elderly can only rarely attend services, and the church is largely unable to attract the younger generation. With only a handful of recognized teachers to provide instruction and lead religious activities, services at many of these branch churches consist of listening to tape-recordings of the founder's lectures or discussing Kawai's writings. The situation is so critical that at an annual meeting several years ago the founder's grandson, the organization's current head, indicated that within a matter of a few years it would no longer be possible to maintain the church buildings or publish the magazine.

Spirit of Jesus Church

The remarkable growth figure reported by the Spirit of Jesus Church was one of the factors that prompted my own initial research on indigenous movements. Organized as an independent group in 1941, this institution, like many other Christian denominations in Japan, did not see significant growth until after the Second World War. In 1950 the head church in Tokyo was built, and two years later a Bible school was established to train pastors. By 1958 the Spirit of Jesus Church had grown to a membership of 28,000 and become what Charles Iglehart referred to as the third-largest Protestant denomination in Japan.[16] The group continued to grow steadily on into the 1970s, and has reported phenomenal growth for the past decade. By the early 1990s the church claimed a membership of 420,000 (240,000 men, 180,000 women), with some 300 ministers (60 percent women), close to 200 churches, and over 400 evangelistic house churches. Anyone who has attended a meeting and received "water" and "spirit" baptism (the latter being authenticated by speaking in tongues) is counted as a member.

While case studies reveal that this church has experienced remarkable growth for the Japanese context, the membership figures are clearly inflated and cannot be accepted at face value.[17] As we noted in an earlier chapter, the Spirit of Jesus Church practices baptism for the dead, more specifically baptism for the ancestors of living members. Some observers have been overheard suggesting rather cynically that this practice is guaranteed to result in rapid church growth. On more than one occasion I have inquired whether the membership statistics include the baptized dead, but church leaders indicate that such baptisms are recorded in a separate category and have nothing to do with their membership statistics. The church has most recently clarified these statistics by indicating that there is an "active membership" of 23,283 individuals who regularly attend meetings and engage in church activities of one kind or another. Representatives maintain, however, that the larger figure accurately reflects the number who have been "saved" through the Spirit of Jesus Church.[18]

An examination of church attendance shows that the figure for "active membership" is the most helpful for understanding the actual strength of this movement. One rural church on the island of Shikoku which I visited reports a membership of over 600 (including four house churches). Regular attendance at weekly meetings in the mother church was from three to fifteen people, while close to fifty attended the annual memorial service for the dead in August. Similarly, the Tokyo district reports a membership of over 80,000, but attendance at weekly services in the main church averages around 500. In addition, there are some twenty house meetings on various days throughout the week with attendance ranging from ten to thirty. The Okinawa Spirit of Jesus Church reports a membership of 7,464, but the pastors informed me that regular weekly attendance is between 180 and 200, and 400 to 500 would attend the Christmas and Easter services. If one generalizes from these three examples, the active membership is probably less than ten percent of the total claimed.[19] Although the Spirit of Jesus Church continues to report thousands of baptisms, these claims are not accompanied by a serious increase in "active" members. It seems safe to assume that the "glory" days of the movement are over.

The Original Gospel Movement

As noted in an earlier chapter, the Nonchurch movement is also important for the other groups it has given birth to throughout its history. Largely because the

Nonchurch movement has no central authority or bureaucracy, it has functioned as the fountainhead of indigenous Christianity in Japan, giving rise to many other movements such as the Original Gospel. The latter, we may recall, is a Pentecostal movement started by Teshima Ikurō, one of several denominational founders dissatisfied with the intellectualism of Nonchurch Christianity. The Original Gospel is also organized on the home Bible study group model and meets in the homes of leaders and in rented facilities.

The Original Gospel, according to Carlo Caldarola's study, had grown by the 1970s to a membership of 60,000 and was organized into some 500 home Bible-study groups around the country.[20] Since the death of the founder in 1973, however, it has declined, like most other movements. The movement today consists of approximately 10,000 members, 100 teachers, and 94 Original Gospel groups (divided into 500 house groups).[21] This membership figure, however, does not represent a net increase of 10,000 new conversions to Christianity: according to church leaders, about 50 percent of the members were earlier associated with other Christian churches.

Holy Ecclesia of Jesus

The Holy Ecclesia of Jesus is one of the few indigenous movements that is still expanding in size today.[22] In 1946 Ōtsuki Takeji left the Holiness Church with a small group of disciples and began the Holy Ecclesia of Jesus in Hiroshima. Three years later he moved to Kyoto, which has been the center of the movement for almost fifty years. In the first decade, Ōtsuki and his followers organized 59 churches and attracted a membership of 1,172. The church has grown steadily under the charismatic leadership of Father Ōtsuki (as he is affectionately called by his followers), and today has over 100 churches, a trained leadership of over 224 evangelists and ministers, a total of 5,379 members, 1,601 associate members, 1,001 catechumens or "seekers of the way," 479 youth in the junior high school program, and 2,948 in the church school program for younger children. In sum, this is a movement involving some 10,000 people. Compared to other Christian churches in Japan, participation rates are very high, with over 7,000 people on average attending weekly services.

Although this is still a growing movement, demographic changes in Japanese society over the past decade are beginning to have an impact. Fifteen years ago young people involved outnumbered adults, but this is no longer the case. The number of young people involved in church school programs has declined significantly: junior high Sunday school attendance was 479 in 1986, but declined to 344 in 1995; elementary Sunday school attendance was 4,300 in 1986 but only 2,519 in 1995. The difficulty in recruiting youth for church programs is a problem that affects not only the Holy Ecclesia of Jesus. The declining birthrate and the heightened competition in Japan's educational system are having a negative impact on all Christian churches. Hugh Trevor points out that there has been a drop of approximately 50 percent in youth attendance for all denominations:

> The main reason has been the increasing pressure put upon even primary-school children (ages 6 to 11) to study at juku (entrance exam cram schools) to gain entrance to prestigious middle schools and some of the juku are on Sundays. Most of them are on week-days, but the children get so tired, they want to have Sundays free.... The loss of children is all the more serious because the majority of those who become Christians as adults usually tell of some favorable experience they had at a church when young, and fewer children in Sunday school now means fewer adults for the churches in the future.[23]

While Holy Ecclesia of Jesus churches may still be enjoying a period of growth at the present time, the overall drop in the numbers involved in the church school programs suggests that future growth—or even maintenance of the status quo—will become increasingly difficult.

When placed in historical perspective it is apparent that most of these groups recorded significant growth while the charismatic leader or founder was alive but tended to decline after his death. Most movements at present are barely holding their own or are in a state of rapid decline.[24] It is true that if we add up the membership of all of the indigenous movements, the total probably constitutes ten percent or more of the active Christian population in Japan. Nevertheless, in spite of their efforts most movements have not been able to sustain long-term growth. *The explanation that the general lack of response to Christianity in Japan relates to its failure to indigenize does not accord with the observable facts.*

In light of the overall pattern of decline, we must recognize that what is indigenous for one generation may appear strange or outdated to a subsequent generation. The fact that most indigenous movements are not recording significant growth today suggests that most hold little more attraction for the average Japanese than transplanted mission churches. Milton Yinger has pointed out that "what will give one generation a sense of unifying tradition may alienate parts of another generation who have been subjected to different social and cultural influences."[25] Commitment to an indigenous form that may have been meaningful half a century ago undoubtedly discourages the creation of new forms relevant to present-day cultural situations. An indigenous Christianity for contemporary Japanese, in other words, would look quite different from the forms developed much earlier this century.

A study of post-charisma decline patterns in indigenous movements also raises the question of whether groups can dig their own graves through "over-indigenization." Comparative studies of religious movements indicate that growing groups are the ones that maintain a "medium level of tension" with the larger society. Rodney Stark explains that a "movement must maintain a substantial sense of difference and considerable tension with the environment if it is to prosper. Without significant differences from the conventional faith(s) a movement lacks a basis for successful conversion."[26] Thus some indigenous Christian movements in Japan (The Way, for example), may have become so indigenous that there is minimal tension and ineffective mobilization of members for recruitment activities.[27]

Theories of church growth and studies of indigenization may show us how some churches more effectively mobilize members for recruitment activities, allocate resources for new church development, or attract members with an indigenous or contextual theology, but such studies do not really explain *why* Christianity has largely been rejected in Japan. We must remember that for decades approximately one percent of the Japanese have been church members. All the while, churches continue to report membership increases. Clearly, the "circulation of the saints" phenomenon is not limited to the religious scene in North America.[28] The hard reality is that the rate of defections, denominational switching, and the growth of the Japanese population have kept mainline, evangelical, and indigenous churches alike from gaining a larger share of the market in Japan's religious economy.

THE DILEMMAS OF CHRISTIANITY IN JAPAN

In considering the difficulties facing Christianity in Japan it is important to recall that it is a New Religion in this context and cannot be viewed and analyzed in quite the same way as Christianity in North America. As a foreign-born religion, Christianity has faced a number of obstacles in Japan that New Religions must struggle with in other countries. Rodney Stark has identified eight conditions for a New Religion to be successful in a given society. Here I would like to consider three that are particularly important for understanding the predicament of Christianity as a New Religion in Japan. Stark writes:

New religious movements are likely to succeed to the extent that they (1) retain cultural continuity with the conventional faiths of the societies in which they appear or originate; (2) maintain a medium level of tension with their surrounding environment; are deviant, but not too deviant; and (3) occur within a favorable ecology, which exists when (a) the religious economy is relatively unregulated and (b) conventional faiths are weakened by secularization or social disruption.[29]

Most scholars would agree that cultural "discontinuity" has been the defining characteristic of Christianity in Japan. Cultural discontinuity and the conflict between Christianity and Japanese religiosity can be traced back to the earliest period of missionary activity in the sixteenth century. Roman Catholic missionaries met with considerable success during their earliest work, but continually faced the difficulty of communicating their exclusivistic truth-claims in an environment that accepted multiple divinities and forms of religious practice.[30] Morioka Kiyomi, a leading sociologist of religion who has given considerable attention to the problems surrounding the transplantation and indigenization of Christianity in Japan,[31] explains that an understanding of a doctrinally pluralistic idea of god is embedded in the Japanese worldview. Consequently, Christianity necessarily encountered a negative reaction in Japan since its interpreters emphasize exclusive belief in one transcendent god. Indigenous Christian movements, in spite of significant cultural adaptations and a fulfillment theology, have also had difficulty in dealing with this basic Japanese religious orientation.

In a more recent study, Winston Davis contrasts the religious pluralism of the West, where individuals are faced with genuine alternatives, with the syncretistic religiosity that has evolved over the centuries in Japan.[32] While there have been "single practice" religious traditions demanding exclusive commitment from their followers (Sōka Gakkai, for example), this has been the exception rather than the rule. Most Japanese participate in annual religious events and life-cycle rituals associated with various Buddhist and Shinto traditions. Hence Japanese pluralism consists of a division of labor among the gods and is most accurately understood as a syncretistic system of "layered obligations," a model that Christianity has tended to clash with because of its claims to the sole possession of truth. Since most Japanese have been integrated into the system of household (Buddhist) and communal (Shinto) religious obligations, personal commitment to the Christian religion has remained extremely difficult.

As a proscribed religion for over two centuries (until 1873), Christianity was popularly understood and referred to as a heretical religion and evil teaching.

The exclusivism emphasized by early Protestant missionaries and their criticism of indigenous religious practices did little to alleviate this widespread perception. The history of Christian mission in Japan abounds with stories of individuals being cut off from their families because of their newfound faith. Refusal to participate as a household member in ancestor veneration or, following the instructions of missionaries, burning ancestral tablets or altars for the Shinto gods has led to innumerable family conflicts. For a variety of reasons, then, Japanese belonging to this "single practice sect" have had to live with the stigma of belonging to a deviant religion. With these "costs" of membership in mind, it is understandable why early converts to Christianity tended to be individuals who had lost their earlier status and position in society and were open to alternatives (for example, the dispossessed samurai class, particularly those from clans that had supported the Tokugawa government and had been excluded from positions in the Meiji government) or individuals who were in privileged positions—landowners and small industrial manufacturers—that made them less susceptible to community sanctions. In sum, Christianity has been "too deviant" for widespread acceptance by Japanese.

The fact that Christianity has been regarded as a deviant religion for much of its history in Japan is closely related to the political order within which it has had to operate. Reiterating Stark's third condition, in order for new religious movements to be successful the religious economy needs to be "relatively unregulated," and established religions must be in decline or "weakened by secularization or social disruption." Although Japan has not been without periods of social disruption and religious decline, the religious life of the masses has usually been closely monitored by those in political power. The brief success recorded by Roman Catholic missionaries in the sixteenth century, for example, was followed by strict measures of regulation ordered by successive military rulers during the Tokugawa period (1603–1867). Christianity became a proscribed religion, with Buddhism being used for registration and social control (i.e., for the identification of religious deviants). Consequently, many Christians were executed, and those who managed to survive did so only by going underground. While there were periods of relative openness and freedom after the Meiji Restoration, the overarching trend until 1945 was mass conformity to the civil religion of State Shinto and the emperor system (see chapter two).

With the defeat of the Japanese in 1945, political conditions finally became more favorable for the growth of Christianity. Under General Douglas MacArthur, the Supreme Commander of the Allied Powers (SCAP) during the occupation, a new "Bill of Rights" was issued that effectively dismantled the old social order. State Shinto was disestablished and reduced to a voluntary organization, while the Religious Bodies Control Law (which had both suppressed and used religious minorities for State purposes) was abolished.

Demographic changes related to postwar industrialization also helped to create a more favorable environment for Christian missionary activities. Since Christian churches were largely concentrated in metropolitan areas (unlike Shinto shrines and Buddhist temples), urbanization should have favored the growth of Christian organizations, but it now appears that Japanese new religious movements were the only ones effectively to capitalize on this population shift and deregulated religious economy.

INTERSOCIETAL RELATIONS: THE NEGLECTED DIMENSION

In order to understand the general failure of Christianity in Japan we need to consider more than the difficult internal political conditions or the failure of Western churches to indigenize. It is also important to recognize that intersocietal relations at the time of emplantation have been a major factor in determining the Japanese perception of Christianity as a deviant religion and the consequent course of church diffusion and growth. This is not to deny the importance of evangelistic zeal and missionary efforts, but to recognize that international political relationships also create either "inhibiting" or "facilitating" conditions for the spread of religions. As long as an imported religion retains its "foreign" character, it will more than likely appeal only to marginal individuals. For wider acceptance to be achieved the imported religion must be rooted in the culture of the receiving society to the extent that it is no longer perceived as an alien or deviant phenomenon.

This issue has received significant attention in Robert Montgomery's recent work on social identity theory, macrosocial relations, and the spread of religions. Montgomery proposes that we shift our focus away from the analysis of missionary efforts and strategies to the "perceptions" of the receivers, which are shaped largely by international political relations that divide groups into dominant or subordinate positions.[33] Montgomery's theoretical perspective is worth quoting at length:

> The underlying conditions affecting the acceptance of religions introduced from the outside are found in the quality of relationships between receiving groups and other groups, including groups from which New Religions are being introduced. A key factor in these relationships for acceptance of a New Religion is perception by the receiving group of the direction from which threat

or domination is coming. If a religion is introduced from a source not perceived as threatening, while at the same time there exists some threat for which the New Religion provides a resource for resistance, then a favorable condition is established for reception of the New Religion. Thus, if domination or threat is perceived as coming from sources other than the source of the New Religion, then the New Religion may be seen as a resource in establishing both group and individual identities that are important contributors to the maintenance of societies....

If, on the other hand, a group from which a New Religion is being introduced is perceived as threatening the existence or the distinctive identity of a society, then a condition encouraging resistance to the New Religion is established. Resistance may take several forms, depending on conditions. There may be a resurgence of traditional religion. If the traditional culture has been strongly challenged, there may be a variety of religious movements spawned that mix elements from the old culture with elements from a new culture.[34]

This analysis not only helps explain the receptiveness to Christianity of tribal or ethnic minority groups in certain societies, but also the divergent responses to Christianity in South Korea and in Japan. Christianity was initially perceived as a foreign religion in both Korea and Japan. In Korea, however, this perception was transformed by sociopolitical circumstances during the period of the nation's colonization by Japan. For Koreans the threat of domination was not from the source of the New Religion but from another occupying power. Although Protestant missionaries in Korea were largely "apolitical" and stressed personal salvation and piety, many Koreans discovered that Christianity also provided an "oppositional ideology" for resisting the Japanese government. As a result many Christians became deeply involved in movements for independence and refused to cooperate with the Japanese government in countless ways. Throughout this difficult period the affirmation of Christianity became a way for Koreans to assert their national identity over against the culture of their Japanese colonizers. In short, circumstances beyond the control of any mission strategist led to a positive linkage between Christianity and Korean culture, and provided the basis for the remarkable postwar growth of the Christian faith in Korea. This transformation of "perception" did not occur in Japan because the source of Christianity was also the source of the greatest threat to Japanese autonomy. Nor was there any substantive shift in this outlook during the postwar period; Christianity merely changed from being the religion of the enemy to being the religion of the Occupation government. David Martin makes the point succinctly:

The Korean experience is, in certain respects, the obverse of the Japanese; in other respects the two societies are very similar. The Japanese are the imperial nation for whom the Americans were rivals, and the Koreans are the colonized nation for whom the Americans were liberators.[35]

Some observers have suggested that slow church growth in postwar Japan may be due in part to the fact that Japanese Christians have been less open about their personal faith and less aggressive in proselytization than their counterparts in Korea. Perhaps this is just another example of Christians being "real" Japanese by exercising restraint in talking about themselves in public. There are many situations, however, in which Japanese do not feel so compelled: members of many new religious movements actively proselytize in a variety of public places, including train stations, parks, and busy commercial streets. The fact is, the Japanese are quite capable of being open and aggressive. The reason Japanese Christians tend to be less demonstrative about their faith is that there is still a degree of stigma attached to Christianity. An individual's cultural identity as a "Japanese" seems to be threatened by membership in a Christian church, whereas such difficult questions of "identity" do not arise in the case of indigenous New Religions.[36]

THE TRANSPLANTATION OF KOREAN CHRISTIANITY TO JAPAN

With approximately one-quarter of the population now belonging to Protestant or Catholic congregations, South Korea is a country in which transplanted Christianity can almost be considered an indigenous religion. Over a decade ago, for example, when the Korean Protestant churches celebrated their 1984 centennial, the Presbyterians among them already outnumbered their counterparts in the United States. Dynamic church growth has been accompanied by increasing involvement in international mission. While there were just under a hundred Korean missionaries serving overseas fifteen years ago, a 1995 survey discovered that the number had grown by then to 3,272 in 119 countries.[37]

One of the most significant developments in Korean Christianity since the Second World War has been the organization of the Full Gospel Central Church by Paul Yonggi Cho. Cho was educated in the Assemblies of God Bible College in Seoul and ordained as an Assemblies of God minister several years after beginning his evangelistic work. Although Cho was deeply influenced by the Assemblies of God and maintains close ties with Pentecostalism worldwide, the Full Gospel Central Church (now called the Yoido Full Gospel Church) is essentially an independent and indigenous church, and represents the most influential stream of Korean Pentecostalism. This church has been actively engaged in mission work in Japan for approximately two decades. As an Asian and experiential expression of Christianity, it represents a clear alternative to the transplanted Western churches that dominated the earlier phase of Protestant mission to Japan, and as such deserves serious attention.[38]

The Yoido Full Gospel Church

Beginning in 1958 as a tent church with just five members, the Yoido Full Gospel Church has experienced rapid growth over the past three decades and now claims a membership of 620,000 members, making it not only the largest Pentecostal church in Asia but also the largest in the world. After collapsing from overwork and stress in 1964, Cho learned the importance of delegating responsibilities to others. Under his charismatic leadership there are now 633 pastors, 400 elders, and 50,000 deacons or deaconesses shepherding his burgeoning flock. The church operates a Sunday school program with an enrollment of over 26,000, a ten-week training course for home cell leaders, a sixteen-week training course for church officers and lay leaders, and a three-year Bible Institute for training pastors. The Bible Institute already has close to 300 graduates and a current enrollment of 294.

Yoido Full Gospel Church is now a finely tuned organization with its membership divided into 50,000 home cell groups in 406 subdistricts throughout Seoul. These cell groups are centered on prayer and Bible study and constitute the major means of pastoral care and evangelism.[39] It is probably most accurate to view Yoido Full Gospel Church as a distinct denomination since it includes nine satellite churches, affiliated churches, and educational institutions, and has sent over 250 missionaries overseas. On a given Sunday several hundred thousand members will worship in one of the seven services at the main sanctuary (seating 25,000), by closed circuit television in one of the nine overflow chapels (seating another 25,000), or by video in one of the nine satellite churches. Over one hundred buses transport members to services from throughout Seoul and outlying areas. Thousands of Sunday School children and teachers can be found meeting in small groups throughout the halls and rooms of either the ten-story Christian education center or the thirteen-story world mission center. Foreign members and international guests, who receive special care, are provided with headsets and instructions for locating the channel with simultaneous interpretation in their own language. (One can choose among English, Chinese,

German, and French.) Sunday services are also broadcast throughout Korea from twelve radio stations and four television stations.

Church growth is clearly a major concern of Cho and the Yoido Full Gospel Church. In 1976 Cho established Church Growth International (CGI) to sponsor conferences and seminars aimed at promoting church growth worldwide. According to a recent Yoido Church publication, 1.3 million pastors and church leaders from forty countries have participated in CGI seminars.

Sung Rak Baptist Church and Berea Academy

Another important Pentecostal influence in present-day Korea is the Sung Rak Baptist Church in Seoul. Its founder, Ki Dong Kim, experienced a conversion accompanied by healing, baptism in the spirit, speaking in tongues, and prophetic visions. In 1961, at the age of twenty-one, Kim began his ministry as a lay evangelist with a primary emphasis upon healing and exorcism. Eight years later Kim founded Sung Rak Baptist Church with a small flock of seven members. Although officially a Baptist church, it has been Pentecostal in nature from its inception. All-night prayer gatherings, revival meetings, exorcisms, healings, and speaking in tongues are the regular fare at this Baptist Church. Jae Bum Lee explains:

> Ki Dong Kim's ministry is well known as a ministry of exorcism in Korea. He has led nine hundred exorcism meetings since 1961. During the same time he has reportedly raised seven people from the dead.... He healed 120,000 people who were crippled, blind, deaf, cancerous, and demon possessed. Kim states that he has cast out demons from four hundred thousand people and that fifty-nine of those were completely crippled people.[40]

By the mid 1980s Sung Rak Baptist Church had grown to a membership of nearly 25,000 and had a pastoral staff of 73. Like the organizational structure of the Yoido Full Gospel Church, Sung Rak provides pastoral care and outreach through 1,300 home cell groups. Although not nearly as large as the Yoido Church, the Sung Rak Baptist Church, Lee maintains, is the "fastest growing superchurch in Korea today."

The influence of this stream of Pentecostalism extends far beyond the walls of the Sung Rak Baptist Church. Believing that all Christians can be miracle workers and exorcists, Kim began Berea Academy in 1978 to train and cultivate these gifts in lay people. Very quickly, however, the student body of Berea Academy came to include seminarians training for the ministry as well as pastors dissatisfied with their own denominations. The curriculum of study is based upon Kim's practical experience with exorcism and his biblical exposition of demonology (subsequently published as a three-volume work, *Demonology*, in 1985 and 1986). By 1985 graduates of this training program had reached 1,119. Some of these graduates have gone on to start similar schools. Hahn Man-Young, for example, a professor of music at Seoul National University, who systematized the theology (demonology) of Ki Dong Kim, established Grace Academy and a new church in Seoul. Similarly, Tai-Ka Lee, a disciple of both Ki Dong Kim and Hahn Man-Young, started another academy in Masan and is reported to have a thriving church of over 10,000 members. The pattern of church growth through schism is clearly not confined to Korean Presbyterians and their 32 denominations.

THE SHAMANIZATION OF KOREAN CHRISTIANITY

It is not by mere chance that all-night prayer meetings, exorcisms, prayer mountains, and healing services are found in Korean churches. Although Pentecostal church leaders would deny the influence of "pagan religion," most scholars agree that shamanism has been the central force in shaping the development of Korean Pentecostalism.[41] Byong-Suh Kim explains that "shamanism is the belief system of this-worldly blessings—material wealth, good health, and other personal and familial well-being."[42] In Korean society the shaman *(mudang)* serves as a link between ordinary people and the spirit world, which is populated by numerous gods, ancestors, and spirits. Through rituals and offerings shamans can control the spirit world (transforming malevolent spirits into protective spirits), perform healings and exorcisms, and bring about concrete benefits for individuals in this world. Whether regarded as "syncretism" or "contextualization," this shamanistic orientation has undeniably permeated Korean Christianity. In *The Korean Minjung in Christ*, David Suh expresses this view forcefully:

> Korean Protestantism has almost been reduced to a Christianized *mudang* religion. That is, the form and language of the worship service are Christian, but the content and structure of what Korean Christians adhere to are basically *mudang* religion. Although missionaries rejected shamanism and thought that it had been destroyed, Korean Christianity has become almost completely shamanized.[43]

The influence of shamanism is apparent in the theology of Pentecostal leaders as well as in the practices associated with prayer mountains.

175

Paul Yonggi Cho's theology might best be viewed as a synthesis of Korean shamanism, Robert Shuller's "positive thinking," and the pragmatism of the Church Growth school of missiology associated with Fuller Theological Seminary's School of World Mission (Pasadena, California). The shamanistic orientation of Cho's theology is clear in his exegesis of 3 John 2: "Beloved, I wish that thou mayest prosper and be in health, even as thy soul prospereth." This passage is the foundation for what Cho refers to as the Threefold Blessing of Salvation:

"Thy soul prospereth" means that by believing in Jesus Christ we live an abundant life spiritually and "thou mayest prosper" means that we are blessed with material things through a life in which all things work together for good; "thou mayest be in health" means that believers who have received salvation are blessed to be delivered from the pain of sickness because Jesus paid the price of healing at Calvary.[44]

According to Bong Ho Son, professor of philosophy at Seoul National University, this "triple meter faith" (as it is popularly referred to) leads to an "excessive emphasis on earthly blessings."[45] If one does not experience healing or personal prosperity then there must be some unconfessed sin or lack of commitment to religious duties. More active participation in religious services, trips to prayer mountain centers, or speaking in tongues will surely bring about the desired results. As Grayson has observed, "Attendance at church and fervent prayer are believed to create a condition in which the person will be blessed."[46]

The influence of the shamanic worldview can also be seen clearly in the demonology of Ki Dong Kim and the Berea Academy. Kim teaches that this world is hades and that individuals who die without Christ become evil spirits and wander about in this world and possess people. Suffering and various kinds of illness are caused by these unclean spirits, who enter a person and use their energy. Exorcism, then, necessarily becomes a central concern of Kim's church. Healing involves calling the spirit of the dead person by name and casting it out in the name of Jesus Christ.

Kim's etiology of illness is essentially that of traditional Korean shamanism. Kwang-il Kim explains that, according to early shamanistic diagnosis, one of the primary causes of sickness is "a wandering spirit, the spirit of an ancestor, any dead person, or any evil spirit."[47] Traditionally, the shaman discovers the identity of the ancestor or spirit responsible for causing the illness through trance or divination. In the case of Christian shamans or exorcists, this seems to occur primarily through dialogue with the possessed person.

The prayer-mountain centers *(kido-won)* established by churches all over Korea are another concrete expression of shamanistic Christianity. According to Yohan Lee's study, there were only two Christian prayer-mountain centers in Korea before 1945; by 1982 the number had increased to 289.[48] The Yoido Full Gospel Church established Osanri Prayer Mountain Sanctuary in 1973 under the leadership of Cho's mother-in-law Choi Jashil. Today the Osanri center consists of a main sanctuary seating 10,000, two smaller sanctuaries seating 5,000 each, 300 private prayer grottoes, and Western-style dormitories accommodating 3,000 people. Free shuttle bus service from Yoido Church to the Osanri center is provided daily on an hourly basis. Sung Rak Baptist Church also maintains three prayer-mountain centers, although none of them is as large as Yoido's Osanri center. Religious activities in these centers include mass prayer meetings as well as private regimens of prayer and fasting. Koreans stream to these mountain centers seeking baptism in the Holy Spirit, personal healing, and answers to prayers for health, wealth, fertility, and success in this life. These centers also cultivate the charismatic gifts. Yohan Lee, for example, reports that "to practice speaking in tongues, some prayer mountain centers push the participants in the prayer meeting to repeat 'Hallelujah' seven hundred times or nine hundred times."[49] In addition to prayer-mountain centers related to specific churches or denominations, there are many independent centers with pastors who specialize in healing particular illnesses.

THE EXPANSION OF KOREAN PENTECOSTALISM TO JAPAN

Since the late 1970s, Paul Yonggi Cho's Full Gospel Church has been actively engaged in missionary outreach to Japan, and is rapidly becoming one of the most visible and influential forms of Pentecostalism in the country. This is a particularly significant development in light of the long history of difficult relations between Korea and Japan. Cho probably expressed the feelings of most Korean missionaries to Japan when he wrote:

> You must realize how hard it was for me to go to Japan. After knowing about the millions of people massacred by the Japanese before 1945, I had a great hatred toward the Japanese people. However, God healed my heart when I confessed my sin. I now travel to Japan every month.[50]

The mission to Japan began in 1976 with the organization of a church in Osaka. Two years later another church was established in Tokyo, and numerous branch churches and home cell groups have been organized since that time. By

1989 the Japan Full Gospel Mission consisted of twenty missionaries, nine churches, and a membership claimed to be over five thousand.[51] Cho began television evangelism in 1978 and currently broadcasts a half-hour "Invitation to Happiness" program each week on seven different stations across Japan. His version of Pentecostalism is also spread through Japanese translations of his books and a monthly newsletter. His book *The Fourth Dimension,* for example, has already sold 20,000 copies.

Along with television evangelism and church planting, Cho has placed considerable emphasis upon training people for pastoral work and mission in Japan. In 1985 Cho established a Tokyo campus of the Asian Church Growth Institute (ACGI) and, two years later, another branch in Osaka. Students attend regular classes or enroll in the correspondence course and use taped lectures. The ACGI is essentially a three-year course and involves a six-month internship in Korea during the final year of the program. In a recent year there were approximately two hundred students in the Tokyo program and thirty in the one in Osaka.

HEALING SERVICES AND TESTIMONIALS IN THE JAPAN GRACE ACADEMY

On a much smaller scale Berea and Grace academies have also made their way into Japan through pastors, itinerant evangelists, healers, literature, and tapes. One base for the Japan Grace Academy is a thriving Gospel church in Yokohama. The pastor of this church and director of the academy belonged to a Presbyterian church in Korea before coming to Japan for the first time as a missionary many years ago. Because of the slow growth of Christianity in Japan he returned to Korea disheartened, but a time of study at Grace Academy gave him the "power" to continue his missionary work. Since his return, the church has grown to approximately one hundred members through his ministry of "signs and wonders."

One evening I attended a special healing service at a Gospel church in Yokohama that featured Kei-Fa Kim, a "shamaness" from Hallelujah Kitō-in, one of the prayer-mountain healing centers in Korea. Kim appeared in a striking white dress and was introduced by the pastor. The service began with a video tape showing her, with thousands in attendance, engaged in her successful healing ministry in Korea. The video was rather graphic, showing her perform surgery with only her hands and fingernails on patients suffering from a variety of infections, skin diseases, growths, and tumors. The video and lively hymn singing created a climate of expectation. During this time forms were distributed to the audience so that individuals could indicate whether they wished to receive healing at the close of the service. The form required a signature acknowledging that Kim would bear no responsibility and explained that "healing" can often take several weeks. In the meantime one should attend church, pray, and use the medicine Kim provided (olive oil and holy water from the Hallelujah Center). One should not go to a hospital or see a doctor during this time.

Her preaching was punctuated with stand-up testimonies by individuals and families who had benefited from her healing touch over the past several years. At considerable expense they had gone to her prayer-mountain healing center and spent days (in some cases even weeks) in search of healing. In one testimonial, a man indicated that he had made three such trips to Korea for relief from back trouble (taking a gift of some 700,000 yen on his last visit). After several days at the Hallelujah Kitō-in (prayer center) he still had not been healed. The shamaness indicated that lack of faith and spiritual problems at home were preventing the cure. He called Japan to check on the situation at home and learned that his daughter had just performed a *mizuko kuyō* (memorial service for an aborted fetus) in front of the family Buddhist altar. On hearing this, the Korean healer informed him that he must have his family shut the doors to the room containing the Buddhist altar in order to control the evil spirits. This they apparently did: the man gained the faith required for healing and returned to Japan.

Another testimony was given by a father who stood at the front of the sanctuary with his young daughter, whom he had taken to the same Hallelujah Prayer-Mountain center for healing after doctors in Japan had failed to cure her unusual illness. At the center in Korea, the girl's parents were instructed to chant the Apostles' Creed while a special ingredient placed on the child's stomach burned for several minutes. According to the father's testimony, the girl was miraculously healed and the family returned to Japan. Although not nearly as visible as Cho's brand of Pentecostalism, the Berea and Grace academies are slowly making their way into independent and charismatic churches in Japan through a network of itinerant evangelists and faith healers.

THE FUTURE OF KOREAN PENTECOSTALISM IN JAPAN

Since the late 1970s Japan has been undergoing what sociologists and journalists refer to as a "religion boom" or a "revival of magic and occultism." An important dimension of this so-called revival has been the development of numerous New Religions with a shared emphasis on religious experience, spirits, and exorcism. The future of Pentecostal Christianity in Japan must be considered in light of this postmodern revival of folk religiosity.[52] An important feature of Japanese folk religion is the importance placed upon rituals oriented to "this-worldly benefits." Hori Ichirō explains that "the magico-religious needs and emotional associations of the Japanese people are important factors of receptibility in the process of borrowing or selection of foreign religions in Japan."[53] Protestant Christianity in Japan, which, for the most part, has been isolated in an intellectual middle-class ghetto, has been highly critical of what might be called mass religiosity. Pentecostal forms of Christianity, on the other hand, share a great deal in common with the New Religions flourishing in contemporary Japan, as both tend to emphasize religious experience and this-worldly benefits. In an interview, one Japanese Pentecostal leader explained it this way:

> Evangelicals have long taught the message of salvation from sin, but failed to teach the biblical message of healing and economic blessings from God. This emphasis on material blessings is something emphasized by Cho and is an important part of the Gospel.

Generally speaking, the experience-orientation of religious "seekers" today does not predispose them toward participation in most Japanese Christian churches, which tend to be "clergy-centered institutions"[54] characterized by intellectualism and predictability. In contrast, Pentecostal churches, particularly those recently imported from Korea, tend to be "member-oriented" groups marked by high rates of active participation on the part of believers, and by the effective employment of lay leaders in recruitment work. This is not to deny the high status of charismatic pastors in Pentecostal churches, where powerful, miracle-working ministers are frequently "idolized" by the laity. The point here is that Pentecostal churches tend to "empower" members through instruction and gifts of the spirit. Whereas established religions and churches tend to monopolize spiritual power in the hands of an elite clergy, Pentecostal churches and New Religions provide opportunities for rapid upward spiritual mobility. Charismatic or shamanistic powers are not restricted to the founder or pastor. Winston Davis refers to this tendency as the "democratization of magic" in the New Religions.[55] With only a few days of training, any member can achieve power over the spirit world and perform acts of healing and exorcism.

In his study of Japan's New Religions, Hayashi Minoru argues:

> The Christian movement in Japan, which largely represents a Westernized, non-growing, and weakened form of Christianity, can become biblically dynamic and culturally relevant if it becomes more willing to learn critically from the growth dynamics of the New Religions.[56]

A critical factor in the acceptance and growth of a religion in Japan, he explains, is the "spiritual power"—not the academic qualifications—of a religious leader. This power enables the leader to meet the practical needs of Japanese people. In this context, Hayashi advocates "power evangelism" and suggests that Christianity needs to recover the "signs and wonders" of the New Testament if it is to make progress in Japan. Apparently, only a Christian "shamanism" can compete with the shamanism of the New Religions.

In many ways the Pentecostal churches from Korea embody the approach advocated by Hayashi, but so do many of the homegrown movements considered earlier, where shamanistic leaders perform signs and wonders on a daily basis and assure the faithful of God's blessing upon the living (and sometimes the dead). It is undeniable that some of these churches are growing faster than Western-oriented churches and often serve a social class largely untouched by other Protestant denominations, and that they represent a dynamic stream of Asian Christianity deserving of serious attention. Nevertheless, as indicated earlier, their significance should not be overestimated. Recent statistics indicate that of the less than one percent of the Japanese population represented by the country's 1,057,088 Christians, probably no more than one-tenth belong to Pentecostal churches or to charismatic congregations within the Roman Catholic Church or conventional Protestant denominations.

A decade ago Paul Cho Yonggi wrote, "God has now given me a promise that ten million Japanese are going to be saved in the decade of the eighties."[57] While Full Gospel Churches in Japan have recorded significant progress over the past decade, the results are far short of Cho's optimistic forecast. In spite of their many efforts, these churches still consist largely of recent Korean immigrants or spouses of interethnic marriages. Cho is busy training evangelists in Japan who will likely contribute significantly to the expansion of Full Gospel Pentecostalism in the years ahead. Still, as we approach the end of the 1990s, the cumulative membership amounts to no more than the smallest fraction of the grandiose predictions of its leader.

Pentecostal Christianity may "fit" the current social climate better than the intellectual expressions of Christianity associated with Western churches. This fact alone, however, hardly assures church growth in the Japanese context. The decline of indigenous Pentecostal movements has shown us that much. Daniel Adams also helpfully reminds us that church growth in Korea is related to a unique historical experience and is not readily transferred to other situations:

The differences between Yoido Full Gospel Church and churches in other countries is not so much the presence or absence of the Holy Spirit as it is the process of indigenization and the unique blending together of syncretism, nationalism, and utopianism in Korea.[58]

Unlike the Koreans, many Japanese still tend to regard Christianity as a "stranger in the land" and incompatible with Japanese cultural identity. Furthermore, many still regard Koreans as an inferior race and are unlikely to seek religious solace in churches dominated by religious leaders from a former colony. Homegrown New Religions, on the other hand, since they are rooted in indigenous religious traditions and emphasize cultural continuity, are more likely to meet the needs of the urban masses and revitalize the spiritualistic worldview of the Japanese.

CHAPTER NINE

The Broader Context
of Japanese Christianity

S INCE THE INITIAL transmission of Roman Catholicism to Japan in the sixteenth century, Christianity has generally been regarded as an intrusive
force in Japanese society and often referred to as a "foreign" and "evil"
religion. Despite the seemingly insurmountable obstacles—cultural discontinuity, social stigma, and, until fifty years ago, strict government control—numerous transplanted and independent churches have managed to establish an
organizational presence in Japan. In this study I have tried to look at this process
not through the eyes of the foreign missionaries but from the perspective of the
Japanese, who were not mere passive recipients of transplanted Christianity but
active agents who reinterpreted and reconstructed the faith in terms that made
sense to them. Over the years most representatives of Protestant mission

churches have regarded these indigenous developments as unfortunate expressions of syncretism and a deviation from normative Christianity. As we have seen, however, to the Japanese founders themselves their elaboration of the Christian faith was nothing other than the fulfillment of Jesus' promise to his disciples that "when the Spirit comes he will guide you into all truth" (John 16:13).

However much the views of these Japanese leaders may have clashed with Protestant missionary theology, their approach was firmly rooted in Christian tradition. As early as the second century a similar process of Christian interpretation was advanced by Justin Martyr (c. 100–165), whose primary concern was to relate his faith to the Greek philosophical and cultural traditions. Although Justin did criticize many ideas in Greek philosophy, there were others he esteemed as compatible with his understanding of Christianity. In fact he accorded certain elements of truth in Greek philosophy a position similar to that of the Old Testament. These "pre-Christian" truths in Hellenistic culture were regarded as a "preparation" for the coming of Christ, the divine Logos. According to Justin's *First Apology*, the pre-incarnate Logos not only was working through the Greek philosophers, but they were also Christians to the extent that they lived according to the Logos. The implications of this interpretation were far-reaching, as Jean Danielou has suggested:

> To renounce idolatry and to accept Christianity ceases for the Greek to be a betrayal of his tradition, and becomes instead an act of loyalty to the best elements of it. Socrates is a forerunner of Christ no less than Moses, and Christianity is the plenary manifestation of something which sages had possessed only in a partial revelation.[1]

Like Justin Martyr, the indigenous leaders we have considered played a similar role in providing Japanese Christians with a sense of cultural continuity. Commitment to Christ for them did not necessitate a total rejection of the past or a "betrayal" of Japanese traditions, as many Protestant missionaries maintained. Rather, the best elements of this pre-Christian past could be affirmed as a part of the Christian way. Particulars aside, the mere phenomenon of these indigenous movements testifies to the fact that a number of Japanese have succeeded in disengaging Christianity from its Western orientation and the negative associations with which it has been encumbered for several centuries. It is not that they set out to gainsay the contribution of Western Christian traditions and missionary efforts, but simply to recognize that the influence of that contribution is subject to limits in other religious histories and contexts.

THE "WAYS" OF JAPANESE CHRISTIANITY

In the course of the previous chapters we have seen how differents streams of foreign influence have blended in diverse ways with indigenous elements to produce a number of alternative Japanese Christian traditions. It has become clear that, despite certain ingredients shared in common by these movements, each of them represents a distinct gestalt and subculture. Notwithstanding the popular myth of the homogeneous Japanese, these movements point to a considerable degree of cultural and religious diversity beneath the surface harmony and order for which modern Japan prides itself. In a largely unknown work published over three decades ago (which I found buried in the archives of the United Church of Christ in Japan), a certain Miyazaki Akira insists that in order to make sense of the development of Christianity in Japan one must take into account the cultural pluralism of Japanese society . "Japanese culture is not a single unified culture," he writes, "but a complex of cultures."[2] Given this pluralism, Miyazaki argued that we should expect indigenous Christianity to appear in diverse forms as a result of its encounter with the native traditions of Shinto, Buddhism, Confucianism, Shugendō, and Bushidō. Our own studies have borne this out. Any simple caricature of "a Japanese Christianity" is quickly confounded by the diverse patterns of appropriation that have appeared over the course of Japan's modern century.

Just as Europeans and North Americans require diverse cultural expressions of Christianity, the Japanese also have different tastes and dispositions. It is hardly surprising that, alongside a variety of denominations and sects of Western origins, an equal variety of indigenous Christian groups—high church, low church, evangelical, pentecostal, shamanistic, and so on—should flourish in Japan. Carlo Caldarola's reference to the Nonchurch movement as *the* Japanese Way of Christianity needs qualification. It may be the way for a small group, a predominantly highly educated elite, but there are many other ways to be Christian and Japanese. In this sense, our microsociological studies of rather marginal indigenous Christian movements has provided substantial support for the macrosociological understanding of Japan as a more heterogeneous society than is often recognized in many popular characterizations.

Indigenous Christian movements not only differ in their theology, practice, and style of worship but also in their models of organization and definition of gender roles. Uchimura adopted the Confucian educational model based on a personal relationship between teacher and disciple as the most suitable approach for organization of the Nonchurch movement. This male-dominated

Confucian model was largely adopted by a number of other movements, including The Way, Christ Heart Church, Original Gospel movement, the Japan Ecclesia of Christ, and the Life-Giving Christ. All these groups rejected Western church polities, the notion of an ordained clergy, and the accompanying system of sacraments.[3] A number of other movements, however, have accepted (with some adaptation) the distinction between clergy and laity, and have established Bible schools or seminaries to train individuals for the ordained ministry. These include the Christian Canaan Church, the Spirit of Jesus Church, the Living Christ One Ear of Wheat Church, and the Holy Ecclesia of Jesus. Among these movements we also find observance of the traditional rites of baptism and the Lord's Supper, as well as of other rituals related to care of the dead. Interestingly, these latter movements all share a charismatic or pentecostal orientation and tend to be egalitarian, allowing women to take an active part in the ordained ministry rather than confining them to domestic duties or to supportive roles behind the scene.[4] In contrast to the dominance of male teachers in the Nonchurch movement, for example, 60 percent of the ministers in the Spirit of Jesus Church are women, perhaps reflecting their central role in traditional folk religion and shamanism.

Although the Nonchurch movement has been known to represent a "manly expression" of Christianity, in recent years women have taken on a more active role by offering alternative activities and critical perspectives on the conservative Confucian orientation of the movement. Today there is a Women's Planning Group based at the Imai Hall, a center that functions as the national headquarters for the Nonchurch movement. This group sponsors regular weekday meetings that include panels and lectures by women on a wide range of topics, including the modern family, education, and the liberation of women. In a lecture I attended, a feminist scholar and active member spoke plainly about how far behind the Nonchurch movement was with regard to recognizing the rights and gifts of Japanese women. Male teachers have dominated the Nonchurch movement since Uchimura's day, she explained, and very few men have expressed interest in the lives and concerns of women. The centrality of male teachers has created a strong hierarchical structure in which women have been expected to take the passive role as students. Even though Nonchurch Christianity rejects the clergy-laity distinction, the elevation of male teachers within the movement in reality undermines the principle of the priesthood of all believers. In recent years, women have been allowed to participate more actively in Nonchurch meetings, but they are still only allowed to give informal talks, while the formal Bible lectures continue to be monopolized by the men.[5]

CHARISMA AND LEADERSHIP SUCCESSION

The fact that there are diverse "ways" and subcultures within Japanese Christianity should not blind us to the common features shared by many movements. Comparative analysis has revealed an interesting and recurrent pattern that has appeared in many movements as the founder's charisma has been institutionalized along the lines of the traditional household (*ie*) system. Although this family system has been regarded as a factor discouraging some Japanese from converting to Christianity, a study of leadership succession in indigenous movements indicates that once conversions do occur, the social organization of the new-found faith is often patterned on the household system. This principle of social organization and leadership succession has a long history in Japan. Religious authority in major Buddhist sects, for example, has been transmitted through father-son blood lineage (血脈相承 *kechimyaku-sōjō*) since Shinran (1173–1262), the founder of the Shinshū sect of Pure Land, married and had a family.[6]

Most Japanese Christian movements, with the exception of those following the principles of the Nonchurch movement, have adopted or adapted this traditional pattern of leadership succession to various church polities (see figure 5). Although religious authority is not always passed from father to son, it tends to stay in the family of the founder. Matsumura Kaiseki and his wife were childless but adopted a son to take over as head of The Way. The adopted son's wife, and then daughter, succeeded him as head of this religious body. Leadership of this movement only transferred outside of the family when ill-health forced the daughter to resign from this position. Christ Heart Church is now in its third generation of leadership. The founder, Kawai Shinsui, was succeeded initially by his son; almost a decade ago, leadership was transferred to his grandson. In the Spirit of Jesus Church, religious authority was transferred to the founder's wife, who has served as bishop for many years now. According to my informants, their daughter is expected to be the next bishop. The wife of Matsubara Kazuhito, founder of the Living Christ One Ear of Wheat Church, similarly assumed leadership following her husband's death. The same thing occurred in the Glorious Gospel Christian Church. Even those movements that adopt elements from imported organizational forms tend to institutionalize charisma within the founder's family. The founder of the Holy Ecclesia of Jesus, Ōtsuki Takeji, is still living and a powerful influence on the movement, but he has officially retired. Two years ago his son was elected to the position of *Shiboku* (司牧, bishop or president). Representatives of all of these movements would

187

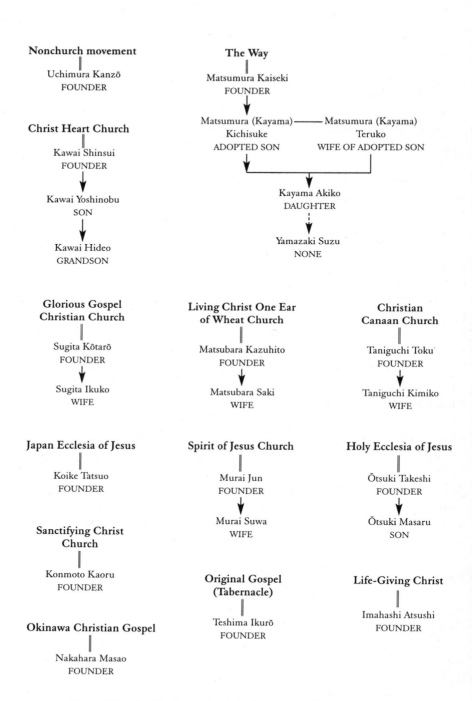

Nonchurch movement

Uchimura Kanzō
FOUNDER

Christ Heart Church

Kawai Shinsui
FOUNDER

Kawai Yoshinobu
SON

Kawai Hideo
GRANDSON

The Way

Matsumura Kaiseki
FOUNDER

Matsumura (Kayama) ——— Matsumura (Kayama)
Kichisuke   Teruko
ADOPTED SON   WIFE OF ADOPTED SON

Kayama Akiko
DAUGHTER

Yamazaki Suzu
NONE

**Glorious Gospel
Christian Church**

Sugita Kōtarō
FOUNDER

Sugita Ikuko
WIFE

**Living Christ One Ear
of Wheat Church**

Matsubara Kazuhito
FOUNDER

Matsubara Saki
WIFE

**Christian
Canaan Church**

Taniguchi Toku
FOUNDER

Taniguchi Kimiko
WIFE

Japan Ecclesia of Jesus

Koike Tatsuo
FOUNDER

**Sanctifying Christ
Church**

Konmoto Kaoru
FOUNDER

Okinawa Christian Gospel

Nakahara Masao
FOUNDER

Spirit of Jesus Church

Murai Jun
FOUNDER

Murai Suwa
WIFE

**Original Gospel
(Tabernacle)**

Teshima Ikurō
FOUNDER

Holy Ecclesia of Jesus

Ōtsuki Takeshi
FOUNDER

Ōtsuki Masaru
SON

Life-Giving Christ

Imahashi Atsushi
FOUNDER

Figure 5. Leadership Succession in Indigenous Christian Movements

insist that leadership is not based on blood or heredity (*seshū* 世襲), but this seems to be the most natural form of religious succession in the Japanese context.[7] This pattern, while rather common in indigenous movements, is by no means unique to Japan.[8]

The Nonchurch movement, which rejected both Western church polities and religious succession based on the household principle, is now facing a number of difficulties related to its loose association of Bible study groups organized around the Confucian teacher-disciple relationship. As we noted earlier in this study, Uchimura established the principle that a group would disband upon the retirement or death of the teacher. No arrangements were made for the continuation of a particular group or for the formal education of successive leaders for the movement. It is not surprising to discover that the Nonchurch movement, as well as Christ Heart Church and The Way, which have also relied on the informal relationship between teacher and disciple for their future leadership, are now having to cope with a shortage of leaders. If the history of religious movements teaches us anything it is that charisma tends to be short-lived. Some religious groups effectively prepare for the eventual disappearance of this powerful force, while others fail to face the reality in time. The Way and Christ Heart Church seem almost resigned to their fate of continual decline. The Nonchurch movement, on the other hand, is making some efforts to meet the new challenges that have accompanied the post-charisma stage of development.

Uchimura would probably be dismayed to find that the movement he founded has undergone considerable institutionalization in its struggle to survive. In 1986, the Imai Hall Library and Nonchurch Archives were opened next door to the building where Uchimura once lectured and now serves as a resource center for the movement. The following year the first nationwide Nonchurch meeting was held. This has now become an annual event and is usually attended by more than three hundred members from around the country.[9] Leaders have realized that groups must coordinate their efforts and resources in order to insure the survival of a movement with a majority of elderly members.[10] Even though the need for mutual support and collaboration is widely recognized, many of those involved expressed concern that the holding of national annual meetings may give the false impression that Nonchurch Christianity is just another denomination or sect. In deference to Uchimura, the organizers have been careful to point out that the annual meeting has no official status and is simply a free association of "brothers and sisters in Christ who simply wanted to deepen their fellowship with each other."[11]

Current leaders have recognized that the movement is in crisis as it makes the transition from the third to fourth generation. During the second generation immediately following Uchimura there were many active leaders engaged in evangelistic work. The number declined considerably with the third generation in the postwar period, and indications are that the number of teachers and evangelists will decrease even more rapidly with the fourth generation. The continual replenishment of the movement by charismatic leaders that had been envisioned in the early phase of the movement has simply not materialized. The shortage of evangelists has obliged leaders to search for alternative ways of cultivating successors. In 1992 the Nonchurch Study Center (無教会研修所) was established in order to provide for the continuing education of members and training of evangelists. The program began with 110 applicants.[12] It is interesting to note that, whereas two decades ago, as Carlo Caldarola observed, Nonchurch leaders regarded "seminary classes as useless,"[13] today's leaders have realized that a more formal program of theological education is necessary for the long-term growth—perhaps even survival—of the movement. The curriculum resembles that of almost any denominational seminary and includes lectures and seminars in Old Testament Language and Literature, New Testament Greek, Christian Theology (with a focus on Theology of Japan), Christian Ethics, New Testament history, Faith and Society, and Nonchurch History.[14] The only components apparently missing from a typical seminary curriculum are courses in homiletics, pastoral counseling, and church government or polity.

At the same time as these efforts are being made to train more leaders, one also hears widespread criticism of the traditional "teacher-centered" pattern of leadership in the movement.[15] Dissatisfaction is not confined to women and younger members. A number of elderly members find that their needs are not adequately addressed by the fluid form of social organization Uchimura favored. What does an elderly member do when his teacher retires or dies and the group dissolves? Who provides pastoral care for the elderly who are unable to attend meetings? Who will provide a Christian funeral if one outlives one's teacher? According to one report, the anonymity of the larger Bible study meetings can sometimes even mean that a person's illness, or even death, can go unnoticed. Overdependence on a declining number of elderly teachers is also regarded as a major cause for the failure of the movement to attract young people and reach out to children and women.

As noted in chapter four, the Nonchurch movement has always met in rented facilities or homes. For the most part, this was regarded positively because it freed members from the heavy financial burdens of purchasing property and building in Japan. Today, however, numerous Bible study groups are reporting that it is becoming increasingly difficult to rent appropriate facilities for holding regular meetings. Members also complain that dependence on rented quarters usually means that not enough time is available for fellowship and discussion among members following the Bible lecture. These and other inconveniences have led some members to be so bold as to suggest the radical idea that it might be good for Nonchurch groups to invest in their own buildings.[16]

The dilemmas currently faced by the Nonchurch movement serve to remind us that indigenous movements cannot be viewed in static terms. Indigenization is an ongoing process and movements must cope with changing generational needs and cultural concerns. Indigenous movements "are seldom standing still in their understanding of God, themselves, and others. They are continually evolving and trying new ideas and forms."[17] As movements seek to address new situations, they can evolve in various directions—even in the direction of rapprochement with established church traditions.

ALTERNATIVE PATTERNS OF APPROPRIATION

At the conclusion of my study, I am persuaded that the story of the transmission and cultural diffusion of Christianity in Japan does not lend itself to a simple face-off between the acceptance of transplanted Christianity on the one hand and the development of alternative indigenous Christian movements on the other. The range of responses and patterns of appropriation is much broader and more complex. I agree with Wendy James and Douglas Johnson, who argue that "Christianity does not necessarily spread as an organic entity; partial elements, themes, symbols, practices, are characteristically taken up by a particular culture or civilization, ethnic class, or interest group, at a particular time."[18] While my own studies have focused on indigenous movements, the influence of the Christian tradition is not confined to organizational forms such as these. After all, the number of Japanese belonging to either transplanted churches or indigenous Christian movements represents less than one percent of the population. In one sense, this seems to suggest that the vast majority of the Japanese have had little time for the evangelistic appeals of either Western missionaries or indigenous Christian leaders.

At the same time, a much higher percentage of Japanese have appropriated elements of Christianity or tried to make sense of Jesus on their own terms apart from organized forms of religion. In the deregulated religious economy of the postwar period, attitudes toward Christianity have generally become more favorable and encouraged many Japanese to widen the scope of their eclectic orientation to include features related to this foreign-born religion.

Although based on data gathered over ten years ago, the NHK Survey of Japanese Religious Consciousness provides helpful information for understanding how Japanese perceptions of Christianity have been gradually changing in recent decades.[19] The findings of the survey presented a slightly more optimistic picture of Christianity in Japan than provided by denominational statistics: two percent of the Japanese identify themselves as Christian and twelve percent feel a certain empathy for Christianity. Jan Swyngedouw has noted that while empathy for Buddhism and Shinto increase with age,

> Christianity shows a completely reverse trend. In the 16–19 age bracket, it reaches a favorable claim of 29.7 percent to go gradually down to 4.5 percent and 5.4 percent for, respectively, the 60–69 and the over-70 age brackets. Moreover, Christianity evokes empathy among 14 percent of the "unbelievers," almost equal to Shinto, but this drops to about 5 percent with the believers.[20]

Within a decade of this survey, these more positive attitudes toward Christianity have resulted in new patterns of ritual behavior. As noted in the opening chapter, Japanese religiosity is characterized by a stronger emphasis on ritual than on doctrine. As a rule, Japanese do not commit themselves to one particular religious organization; rather, they participate in the annual festivals and rituals of both Shinto shrines and Buddhist temples throughout the year. A religious division of labor also characterizes the rites of passage: Shinto dominates rituals associated with birth and Buddhism monopolizes rituals connected with death. Although an exclusive commitment to Christianity is still rare among Japanese, in recent years many have begun to accept the ritual contribution of Christianity (on their own terms) into the traditional division of labor. Until the Taishō period (1912–1926), Japanese weddings were performed without religious officials. Shinto priests began to perform wedding ceremonies after this time, modeling their services to a certain extent on Western church weddings. Today, however, Christian churches are becoming a significant competitor for this role in the Japanese religious division of labor.[21]

The fact that Christian weddings are becoming increasingly popular among young couples today suggests that the stigma associated with Christianity may be declining. A survey conducted in 1991 discovered that the percentage of Christian or church-related weddings was 35.9 percent in the Kantō region and 23.8 percent in the Kansai region. Similarly, a survey conducted the following year found that 31 percent of the weddings conducted in Japan were Christian.[22]

To a certain extent, the growing popularity of Christian weddings has been promoted by the highly publicized church weddings of TV personalities and movie stars. For whatever reasons, Christianity seems to be finding a niche for itself in the complex of Japanese folk religion by performing this fashionable if compartmentalized role. This trend of "Christian" weddings represents a natural Japanese appropriation of another religious tradition into the rites of passage in contemporary society.

A significant number of church representatives, both Japanese and foreign, have been critical of this piecemeal adoption of Christianity, which takes over ritual without engaging the individual in a serious faith commitment. At the same time, many others argue that wedding services provide one of the few positive points of contact between churches and younger Japanese. To this end many pastors and missionaries have devoted themselves to the "wedding ministry" as a way to present Christian perspectives on human relationships, family, and marriage to people who would otherwise know nothing of the church. The wedding ministry has also become a significant business enterprise, providing a source of income for clergy, missionaries, churches, and major hotels fitted out with Western wedding chapels. It remains to be seen if this approach will have long-term benefits for increasing membership in the churches of Japan. At the very least, the fact that scores of younger Japanese are choosing Christian weddings indicates that the present environment is much more open to Christianity and that much of the social stigma attached to the Christian faith has declined during the postwar period.

In addition to this selective ritual adaptation, there are numerous other examples of the appropriation of Jesus into Japanese religious culture outside the established churches. One of the most interesting examples is the folk tradition, passed down in a legend by the people of Shingō village, Aomori Prefecture, that links the historical Jesus to Japan. They claim that after growing up in Galilee, Jesus traveled to Japan and stayed in their village until he returned to begin his public ministry in Judea at the age of thirty-three. He returned to Japan after a dramatic escape that had his look-alike Japanese brother Isukiri crucified in his place. As the legend goes, Jesus died at the age of 106 and was buried in Shingō village. There is a large cross erected on a mound to mark the burial site of Jesus, which is also where villagers observe the tradition of an annual *Bon* Festival dance, though the lyrics used in the song to accompany the dance differ from those of other regions.[23] In an effort to stimulate the local economy, the government tourist bureau now prints Japanese and English brochures to publicize its claim to fame.[24]

Grave of Jesus in Aomori, Japan.

The selective appropriation of elements from the Christian tradition is also a prominent feature of a number of Japanese New Religions. Many of the Japanese New Religions have felt compelled to find some place for the Christ figure in their mythologies.[25] Here it is worth looking briefly at several examples of how Jesus has been understood by some New Religious Movements. Tensokōkyō (天祖光教) is a messianic movement based in Nagoya that draws on both Buddhist and Christian traditions. It does not use the Bible in worship or teaching, but its sacred text, *La Voco de Sfinkso* (*The Voice of the Sphinx,* written by the founder), is permeated by biblical themes and ideas (particularly from Genesis and Revelation), and the teachings of the movement draw on many doctrines and practices of the Christian church. The founder is understood to be a manifestation of the second coming of Christ and the future Buddha (Maitreya), thus superseding both Buddhism and Christianity.

Dancing *(bon-odori)* in front of the grave of Jesus.

Although Tensokōkyō has a low profile and is relatively unknown, two other movements that have been the focus of considerable media attention over the past decade have also freely appropriated ideas from the Christian tradition. Asahara Shōkō, the founder of Aum Shinrikyō, began his movement with an initial emphasis on traditional Buddhist teachings and ascetic practices aimed at personal liberation and enlightenment. To this Asian tradition he added apocalyptic ideas from the Bible and came to regard himself as a messianic figure who was destined to lead his followers in the establishment of an ideal society referred to as the Kingdom of Shambhala. With the publication of two small books, which declared his messianic identity, Asahara's character became increasingly authoritarian as he elaborated an apocalyptic vision with himself as a central character in the unfolding drama.[26] It is still difficult to fathom, but what began as a loose association of yoga practitioners evolved into a movement bent on mass destruction. He and his followers are now on trial—many of them already serving prison terms—for their involvement in the sarin gas attack on the Tokyo subway system on 20 March 1995, which resulted in twelve deaths and thousands of injuries. Since the arrest of Asahara and some of his key followers, numerous other violent crimes have been confirmed by confessions and or evidence presented at the ongoing trials.

One final example is provided by Ōkawa Ryūhō, a prominent new age figure, who founded the Science of Happiness Association (Kōfuku no Kagaku) in 1986 when he was only thirty-three years old. A graduate of the University of Tokyo and former salaried worker, Ōkawa began to attract a following through the publication of his "spirit world" books. In a period of four years he published almost 150 books, which together sold around 4 million copies. Ōkawa claims to communicate in trance with spirits from the "other world" and writes down the messages he receives. These have been published as collections of spirit revelations and consist of messages from such luminaries as Buddha, Jesus Christ, Edgar Cayce, Swedenborg, Newton, and Picasso. Jesus Christ is a significant figure, but just one of many spirits sending messages to this world. From all of these guiding spirits Ōkawa has synthesized an eclectic vision for building a New Age Civilization that integrates personal and public happiness.[27]

The place of Jesus Christ in Japanese New Religions requires a full-length study of its own. I mention these examples only in order to locate the movements documented in this study in their wider cultural context and to show that interest in Jesus (or even Christianity) in Japan extends far beyond the boundaries of established churches and indigenous movements. While many Japanese New Religions find a place for Jesus Christ or incorporate beliefs or ideas from the Judeo-Christian tradition, they also claim to be establishing new paths that transcend or supersede Christianity. In contrast to these New Religions, the movements considered in this book were founded by Japanese who identify themselves as a part of the Christian tradition, though independent of the Western churches. What all of these examples indicate is that established churches in the West cannot control how the Christian tradition will be appropriated in other times and places.[28]

THE GLOBAL CONTEXT

For many years Western scholars assumed that a spiritualistic worldview would soon be a thing of the past as the process of modernization extended throughout the world. Rodney Stark, for example, remarked as recently as 1990 that "during the last century only one social science thesis has come close to universal acceptance among Western intellectuals—that the spread of modernization spells doom for religious and mystical beliefs."[29] Secularization was regarded as an inevitable global process explaining the consequences of modernization for religious institutions and individual religiosity. The appearance of scores of new religious movements worldwide and the growth of Pentecostal-Charismatic Christian movements has forced sociologists and historians of religion to rethink this rather simplistic interpretation of the changing nature and role of religion in modern societies.

The sociological study of religion has clearly been burdened by a Eurocentric orientation for many years. Just as Western church leaders often expected the younger churches to simply accept their authority and theological traditions, there has been a tendency for academics to assume that the Western experience of modernization and secularization would be definitive for all humankind. Peter Berger's *The Sacred Canopy*, one of the few best sellers in the sociology of religion, played a leading role in disseminating this point of view. In this important and popular work, Berger concluded that "it is safe to predict that the future of religion everywhere will be decisively shaped by the forces that have been discussed in this and the preceding chapters."[30] In a word, non-Western countries were expected to follow the Western pattern of development with only minor variations.

We have slowly begun to recognize that masses of humanity are likely to live on the margins or outside of the benefits of societal modernization for many years to come and, more than likely, will remain embedded in local cultural traditions for the foreseeable future. Of those who have reaped the benefits of modern technology, many have chosen not to adopt the modern secular frame of mind that characterized the European experience of modernization. It is becoming increasingly clear that the human capacity to combine various elements from traditional and modern technological cultures has been profoundly underestimated. Over three decades ago, Herbert Passin noted perceptively:

> Modernization does not mean the complete and instant displacement of the traditional. The process is not uniform; it affects the separate cultural elements, areas of thought, and population groups that make up a nation in different ways. Certain elements of traditional culture may remain completely unaltered.... The result is that a modern sector grows up alongside the traditional one. *Although the modern sector tends to expand, it is by no means certain that the final culmination of this process is the complete obsolescence of the traditional. At the very least, for long periods they can co-exist side by side.*[31]

Passin's remarks were not originally made with reference to religion, but his nuanced understanding of the impact of modernization is certainly more accurate for religion than the many "tired" theories of secularization. This is not to suggest that the Japanese are extraordinarily religious or that Japanese society is more religious today than in premodern times, but simply to point out that modernization has ambivalent effects on religion.[32] In short, the sociological theory regarding modernization and secularization developed on the basis of Western or European history does not fit the case of Japan's modernization. A unilinear conception of modernization and religious decline cannot adequately account for the course of development in many non-Western regions of the world.

The world has changed a great deal over the past thirty years and Peter Berger has been willing to admit that he got it wrong. In more recent years, he has written that "a theory that sees secularization as inextricably linked with modernity runs into serious difficulties.... There are vast regions today in which modernization has not only failed to result in secularity but has instead led to reaffirmation of religion." While holding to his earlier views with regard to the secularization process in Northern Europe, he now points out that "the rest of the world is as furiously religious as ever, and possibly more so."[33]

In their attempt to make sense of this "big picture," Irving Hexham and Karla Poewe suggest:

> The "re-religionization" of the world has something to do with the global breakdown of modernity, most obviously since the 1970s. The five world religions, Judaism, Islam, Buddhism, Hinduism, and Christianity, have inspired

folk or urban popular movements that seem to criticize a widespread sense of inner disintegration, anomie, dislocation, and most important, an absence of an overall perspective.[34]

It is not surprising to find that many of these movements are particularistic (ethnic, nationalistic, and religious) and seek to provide some kind of symbolic anchor in the cultural flux and ambiguity of modern society. The indigenous and independent Christian movements are an important part of this larger global phenomenon.

In the Japanese context, we have found that most movements have been unable to sustain long-term growth in spite of indigenization. The transplantation and diffusion of Christianity is a complicated process that cannot be reduced to the simple formula, "Missionary efforts and investments + indigenous cultural adaptations = numerical success." This is not to deny the importance of indigenization for the successful diffusion of a foreign-born religion. By comparing the situation of Christianity in Japan with that of South Korea, we noted a number of important political and cultural factors that have discouraged the widespread acceptance of this new faith. The different patterns of development in Korea and Japan, for example, indicate that macropolitical relations at the time of emplantation is a critical factor shaping the subsequent trajectory of religious diffusion. While indigenous movements in both countries have made similar cultural adaptations, it has been the Korean movements that have grown dynamically and become active in global cross-cultural mission.

Since the time when Protestantism was first transplanted to Japan, Christianity in the West has undergone significant changes. Today most Protestant missionaries recognize the need to develop contextual theologies and forms of worship appropriate to different cultural contexts. Efforts in this area have moved far beyond earlier concerns with establishing "self-supporting" local churches to a consideration of new ways of conceiving and interpreting the Christian faith. The Roman Catholic Church has also expressed a deeper sensitivity to the needs and concerns of non-Western Christians under the banner of "inculturation." In spite of these developments in missiological circles and Western theology, it remains to be said that most of the theologizing that occurs in indigenous and independent Christian movements in Asia and Africa has been ignored or simply written off as syncretistic aberration. With the exception of the Nonchurch movement, the groups taken up in this study are largely unknown either inside or outside of Japan. Although Christian ecumenism today recognizes the importance of interfaith dialogue and mutual understanding among the world religions, the views and perspectives offered by indigenous Christian movements are usually not accorded similar respect or taken seriously.

Indigenous movements in Japan and elsewhere represent serious efforts to make sense of the Christian faith in light of local cultural traditions and concerns. These movements have remained relatively small in Japan, but the issues and questions with which they have struggled are suggestive of what is occurring among the developing churches in other non-Western societies. "When Christianity is taken out of the European cultural tradition," George R. Saunders observes, "the nature of kinship, lineage connections, and the role of ancestors often become problematic."[35] These new theological concerns are patent in the development of Christianity both in East Asia and the African continent.[36] There is no escaping the fact that post-Enlightenment European or North American Christianity can no longer be regarded as the measuring rod for defining a "normative" Christianity.

For some years the more astute observers have been telling us that it is no longer accurate to think of Christianity as a Western religion. David Barrett has noted, for example, that for eighteen centuries over 90 percent of the Christian population was Caucasian. The decline in European churches and the growth of Christianity in the non-Western world over the past century have changed the face of Christianity. We may still be prone to think of Christianity as a Western religion, but by 1981 non-whites formed the majority of all Christians and by the late 1980s 56 percent of the Christian population was located outside the West in Sub-Saharan Africa, Latin America, and Asia.[37] Andrew F. Walls writes about the implications of this demographic shift:

> Within the last century there has been a massive southward shift of the center of gravity of the Christian world, so that the representative Christian lands appear to be in Latin America, Sub-Saharan Africa, and other parts of the southern continents. This means that Third World theology is now likely to be the representative Christian theology.[38]

We are only beginning to grasp what this new definition of "center" and "periphery" will mean for religion in the coming century, but there is already clear evidence that dynamic new forms of Asian and African Christianity are already having a significant impact on the Western churches.[39]

For some time professional theologians have been attempting to address the issues that have emerged from the encounter with the "great traditions," but it is primarily the leaders of indigenous movements who are involved in a serious Christian engagement with the "little traditions" (i.e., folk or primal religious traditions) that shape the concerns of the masses throughout Asia and Africa. Almost a decade ago Donald Dayton made an appeal to open the ecumenical door and "let the riff-raff in," referring to the contributions that the Holiness and Pentecostal movements have to make to the larger Christian community.[40] These marginal movements in the United States were on the cutting edge of the antislavery movement in the 1830s and affirmed women in ministry well in advance of the established or mainline churches. And, as we remarked above, Christian ecumenism all but systematically excludes the views and perspectives offered by indigenous Christian movements. Perhaps if the door were opened a little wider, Western churches would find there is something to learn from the many indigenous and independent movements that are developing throughout the non-Western world.

Whether or not the established churches will accept these movements as equal partners in dialogue remains to be seen. Those of us engaged in the comparative study of religion, in any case, must take these movements more seriously, however bizarre and anachronistic they may appear at times, however much they may disturb our own religious—or secular—sensibilities. Bruce Lawrence has put it well:

> At the end of this century religion remains feisty and fissiparous, pragmatic and progressive, this-worldly and other-worldly. It will persist as a major social force into the next century, and among the believers whom it might count in its fold may be a new generation of social scientists willing to observe more closely and categorize with new respect what an older generation had first spurned as outdated and then mislabeled as "damaged goods."[41]

For my part, I doubt that in the coming century the religious fold will be teeming with social scientists who are "true believers." But whatever our deepest convictions as scholars may be, one things seems clear: if we are going to provide an accurate and reliable guide to the world of Christianity in the years ahead, we must be willing to cast our nets more widely to include the kinds of movements and new forms of faith considered in these pages.

Bibliographical Guide to
Indigenous Christian Movements

T HE PURPOSE of this appendix is to provide an introduction to the basic
literature available on each of the movements considered in this study.
Brief resumes are also provided for the groups that did not receive systematic attention in chapters 4 to 6. Additional details scattered throughout the
various chapters may be garnered by consulting the Index for the names of
founders or particular movements. For those who wish to pursue personal contact, addresses and contact persons for each movement may be found in the
Christian Yearbook, which is published annually in Japanese by the Kirisuto
Shinbunsha of Tokyo.

The groups are arranged chronologically, according to the year of their
founding.

NONCHURCH MOVEMENT 無教会

FOUNDER: Uchimura Kanzō 内村鑑三
YEAR ORGANIZED: 1901
TREATMENT: Chapter 4

GENERAL BIBLIOGRAPHIES

Resources on Uchimura Kanzō and the Nonchurch movement are abundant and extensive holdings may be found in the archives of the Imai Hall and the International Christian University Library.

今井館図書資料センター蔵書目録 [An inventory of Imai Hall Resource Center holdings]. Tokyo: Imai Kan Seisho Kōdo Kyōyūkai, 1990.

内村鑑三記念文庫目録 [An inventory of the Uchimura Kanzō memorial collection]. Tokyo: International Christian University, 1997 (third edition).

PRIMARY SOURCES

Uchimura Kanzō. 内村鑑三全集 [Complete works of Uchimura Kanzō]. Tokyo: Iwanami Shoten, 1981–1984.

The Complete Works of Kanzō Uchimura, with notes and comments by Taijiro Yamamoto and Yoichi Mutō. Tokyo: Kyō Bun Kwan, 1971.
This is a seven-volume collection of Uchimura's English writings, including his diary "How I Became a Christian," and various other essays and editorials published between 1886 and 1924.

無教会史 I, 第一期: 生成の時代 [Nonchurch history, vol. I: The first period: The formative years], edited by the Nonchurch Historical Research Association. Tokyo: Shinkyō Shuppan, 1991.

Tamura Kōsan 田村光三, ed. 1985 年無教会夏期懇話会記録 [Proceedings of the 1985 Nonchurch summer colloquia]. Tokyo: Mukyōkai Kaki Konwakai Jimukyoku, 1986.

第 1 回 (1987) 無教会キリスト教全国集会記録 [Proceedings of the first Nonchurch Christianity national meeting]. Tokyo: Mukyōkai Kirisutokyō Zenkoku Shūkai Jimukyoku, 1988.
This is an important resource for understanding the Nonchurch movement today. Published each year since 1988, the proceedings record lectures, regional reports, and summaries of various group discussions.

SECONDARY SOURCES

Caldarola, Carlo. *Christianity: The Japanese Way*. Leiden: E. J. Brill, 1979.

Howes, John F. "The Non-Church Christian Movement in Japan." *The Transactions of the Asiatic Society of Japan*, Third Series 5 (1957), 119–37.

———. "Uchimura Kanzō and Traditional Japanese Religions." *Japanese Religions* 2/1 (1960), 23–30.

———. "Japanese Christians and American Missionaries," in Marius B. Jansen, ed. *Changing Japanese Attitudes toward Modernization*. Princeton: Princeton University Press, 1965, 337–68.

———. "Japanese Christianity and the State: From Jesuit Confrontation/Competition to Uchimura's Noninstitutional Movement/Protestantism," in Steven Kaplan, ed. *Indigenous Responses to Western Christianity*. New York: New York University Press, 1995, 75–94.

Jennings, Raymond P. *Jesus, Japan, and Kanzō Uchimura: A Brief Study of the Non-Church Movement and its Appropriateness to Japan*. Tokyo: Kyō Bun Kwan, 1958.

Miura, Hiroshi. *The Life and Thought of Kanzō Uchimura, 1861–1930*. Grand Rapids, Michigan: William B. Eerdmans, 1996.

Moore, Ray A. ed. *Culture and Religion in Japanese-American Relations: Essays on Uchimura Kanzo, 1861–1930*. Ann Arbor: Center for Japanese Studies, The University of Michigan, 1981.

Norman, William H. H. "Kanzo Uchimura: Founder of the Non-Church Movement." *Contemporary Religions in Japan* 5/1 (1964), 34–44.

Ohara Shin 小原 信, 内村鑑三の生涯 [The life of Uchimura Kanzō]. Tokyo: PHP Kenkyūjo, 1992.

THE WAY 道会

FOUNDER: Matsumura Kaiseki 松村介石

YEAR ORGANIZED: 1907

TREATMENT: Chapter 5

PRIMARY SOURCES

Matsumura Kaiseki 松村介石. 信仰五十年 [Fifty years in the faith]. Tokyo: Dōkai Honbu, 1926; 1989 revised edition.

———. 道会栞 [Dōkai guidebook]. Tokyo: Dōkai Jimusho, 1917.

———. 道会問答 [Dōkai catechism]. Tokyo: Dōkai Jimusho, 1919.

———. 新宗教 [New religion]. Tokyo: Dōkai Jimusho, 1925.

———. 道会バイブル [The Dōkai bible]. Tokyo: Dōkai Jimusho, 1928.

———. 諸教の批判 [A critique of religions]. Tokyo: Dōkai Jimusho, 1929.

———. 道会の信仰 [The Dōkai faith]. Tokyo: Tōhō Shoin, 1934.

Matsumura Kichisuke 松村吉助. 暗夜を憂うること勿れ: 言志四録抄 [Lament not the dark night: Selections from *Genshi shiroku*]. Tokyo: Dōkai Jimusho, 1949.

Magazine: 道 [The way], published quarterly.

SECONDARY SOURCES

Akiyama Shigeo 秋山繁雄, 明治人物拾遺物語: キリスト教の一系譜 [Stories of Meiji figures: One lineage of Christianity]. Tokyo: Shinkyō Shuppansha, 1982.

Katō Masao 加藤正夫, 宗教改革者・松村介石の思想－東西思想の融合を図る [The thought of Matsumura Kaiseki, religious reformer: An attempt to unite eastern and western thought]. Tokyo: Kindai Bungeisha, 1996.

Ōuchi Saburō 大内三郎, 松村介石研究序説 [An introduction to research on Matsumura Kaiseki]. 日本文化研究所研究報告 [Bulletin of the Institute for Japanese Culture, Tōhoku University] 12 (1976), 1–18.

———. 松村介石: 内村鑑三との関連において [Matsumura Kaiseki: His relationship to Uchimura Kanzō], 内村鑑三研究 [Uchimura Kanzō studies] 8 (1977), 68–82.

近代文学研究叢書 [The library of modern literature], vol. 45. Tokyo: Shōwa Joshi Daigaku Kindai Bungaku Kenkyūshitsu, 1977.

This is a particularly helpful resource that includes an overview of Matsumura's life and writings (199–208) and a chronological bibliography of his publications (209–68).

CHRIST HEART CHURCH 基督心宗教団

FOUNDER: Kawai Shinsui 川合信水

YEAR ORGANIZED: 1927

TREATMENT: Chapter 5

PRIMARY SOURCES

Kawai Shinsui 川合信水. 耶蘇基督讃 [A eulogy on Jesus Christ]. Tokyo: Kōbundō, 1927. The English version is available as *A Eulogy on Jesus Christ*, trans. Yoshinobu Kawai, Tokyo: Christ Heart Church, 1961.

Kawai Shinsui 川合信水. 孔子の教育と吾が体験 [The education of Confucius and my experience]. Tokyo: Kirisuto Shin Shūdan Shuppanbu, 1946.

———. 大人と小人 [The superior man and inferior man]. Tokyo: Kirisuto Shin Shūdan Shuppanbu, 1953.

————. 神の誠と吾が体験 [The sincerity of God and my experiences]. Tokyo: Kirisuto Shin Shūdan Shuppanbu, 1956. The English version is also available as *My Spiritual Experiences*, trans. Kawai Yoshinobu. Tokyo: Christ Heart Church, 1970.

————. 労働問題の宗教的解決 [The religious solution to the labor problem]. Tokyo: Kirisuto Shin Shūdan Shuppanbu, 1964.
This booklet addresses labor problems from the perspective Kawai developed as director of education at the Gunze Silk Factory.

————. 川合信水先生の論語講話 [Kawai Shinsui's lectures on the *Analects* of Confucius]. Edited by 安井英二. Tokyo: Kirisuto Shin Shūdan Shuppanbu, 1970.

————. ガラテヤ書玄義 [The mysteries of Galatians]. Fujiyoshida: Kirisuto Shinshū Kyōdan Jimukyoku Shuppanbu, 1965.

————. 完全訓講話 [Lectures on the perfect teaching]. Tokyo: Kirisuto Shin Shūdan Shuppanbu, 1977.

————. 山月川合信水先生御教話覚書 [A memorandum of talks by Sangetsu Kawai Shinsui], edited by Yasui Eiji 安井英二. Tokyo: Kirisuto Shin Shūdan Shuppanbu, 1969.

————. 押川方義川合信水両先生復書翰集 [A collection of correspondence between Oshikawa Masayoshi and Kawai Shinsui]. Edited by Kawai Michio 川合道雄. Tokyo: Kirisuto Shin Shūdan, 1981.

Magazine: 基督の心 [The mind of Christ], published quarterly.

SECONDARY SOURCE

Ōtsuka Eisan 大塚栄三. 郡是の川合信水先生 [Kawai Shinsui Sensei at Gunze]. Tokyo: Iwanami Shoten, 1931.

GLORIOUS GOSPEL CHRISTIAN CHURCH
栄光の福音キリスト教団

FOUNDER: Sugita Kōtarō 杉田好太郎
YEAR ORGANIZED: 1936

Sugita Kōtarō converted to Christianity as a result of reading the Bible during a long illness following a period of military service. In preparation for the Christian ministry, he enrolled in the theological seminary of the Holiness Church in Tokyo. Following graduation and ordination, he was sent by Bishop Nakada Jūji to serve as the pastor of the Holiness congregation in Aso, Kyūshū. Sugita could not accept the hierarchical structure of the Holiness Church and established the Glorious Gospel Christian Church as an independent movement in 1936. The name of the church was taken from 1 Timothy 1:11, which makes a specific reference to the "glorious gospel of God." Although he rejected the religious authority of the Holiness tradition, he continued to observe the sacraments of baptism and the Lord's Supper and maintained the Holiness Church emphasis on divine healing.

Like Uchimura in his Nonchurch movement, Sugita rejected the clergy-laity distinction. All Christians are expected to be witnesses of the gospel and those who are called to be evangelists must be self-supporting like the Apostle Paul (who was a tentmaker). Sugita supported himself as a math and English teacher and received no regular salary from the church. The church does not require a membership fee or tithe, but simply encourages members to support the church as God leads them.

Over the years, a number of members donated their land or homes to establish 10 churches around the country. The membership peaked at approximately 3,000 in the late 1970s, but has declined rapidly over the past decade and is down to 1,000. The founder's wife, Ikuko, succeeded him in 1972, but no clear program for training leaders was ever established. Worship services today follow the typical Protestant pattern of hymns, Bible reading, and prayers, but members listen to a taped sermon by the founder since no one has been properly trained to continue this role. The annual convention held in August is still attended by 200 to 300 members, but observance of the Lord's Supper has been abandoned since it is too much trouble to distribute bread and wine to that many people. This ritual has now been modified and is called a "spiritual Lord's Supper" (霊的聖餐式); no elements are distributed but a brief time of meditation is observed. Like the founders of other indigenous movements, Sugita took a hopeful approach to the fate of the ancestors who died without hearing and responding to the gospel of Christ in this life. He was also more tolerant of his followers participating in Buddhist memorial rites and provided alternative memorial services to meet the felt needs of Japanese and to indicate that Christians also showed care and respect for the dead (see chapter 7, pages 105, 114).

PRIMARY SOURCES

杉田好太郎. 栄光の福音大衆版 [A popular introduction to the glorious gospel]. Aso, Kyūshū: Eikō no Fukuin Kirisuto Kyōkai Shuppanbu, 1952.
A simple introduction to the basic teachings of this church that follows a question-and-answer format.

———. 栄光の福音前編 [The glorious gospel, part 1]. Aso, Kyūshū: Eikō no Fukuin Kirisuto Kyōkai Shuppanbu, 1954.

———.、栄光の福音後編 [The glorious gospel, part 2]. Aso, Kyūshū: Eikō no Fukuin Kirisuto Kyōkai Shuppanbu, 1961.

———. 栄光の福音説教集上巻 [Sermons on the glorious gospel, vol. 1]. Aso, Kyūshū: Eikō no Fukuin Kirisuto Kyōkai Shuppanbu, 1955.

———. 栄光の福音説教集下巻 [Sermons on the glorious gospel, vol. 2]. Aso, Kyūshū: Eikō no Fukuin Kirisuto Kyōkai Shuppanbu, 1958.

———. 栄光の福音聖歌集 [Hymns of the glorious gospel]. Aso, Kyūshū: Eikō no Fukuin Kirisuto Kyōkai Shuppanbu, 1941.
This is a hymnbook of 82 pages; all of the lyrics were written by the founder, with the exception of one by his wife, but melodies were borrowed from various Christian hymns and Japanese songs.

WRITINGS BY THE FOUNDER'S WIFE

Sugita Ikuko 杉田伊久子. エデンに帰る人々 [People who return to Eden]. Aso, Kyūshū: Eikō no Fukuin Kirisuto Kyōkai Shuppanbu, 1964.
This volume records the story of the founder's faith, relationships with other Christian churches, and the development of the independent Glorious Gospel Christian Church.

———. 聖霊の諸教会に対する警告 [The Holy Spirit's admonitions to various churches]. Aso, Kyūshū: Eikō no Fukuin Kirisuto Kyōkai Shuppanbu, 1980.

———.、栄光の福音キリスト教会: 創設者の信仰の証 [The Glorious Gospel Christian Church: The faith and witness of the founder]. Aso, Kyūshū: Eikō no Fukuin Kirisuto Kyōkai Shuppanbu, 1972.

LIVING CHRIST ONE EAR OF WHEAT CHURCH
活けるキリスト一麦教会

FOUNDER: Matsubara Kazuhito 松原和人 (1905–1966)
YEAR ORGANIZED: 1939

The founder of the Living Christ One Ear of Wheat Church, Matsubara Kazuhito, first came into contact with Christianity through the Mino Mission while a junior high student. While a student at Kyoto University he began to study Christianity more seriously after hearing lectures on science and religion by Satō Teikichi, a Christian professor. Following graduation from university he moved to Kōbe and became an elementary school teacher. He converted to

Christianity as a result of attending services led by an evangelistic group related to Barclay Baxton (1860–1946), a low-church Anglican who served as a missionary in Kōbe and Matsue from 1890 to 1891. Matsubara subsequently felt a call to be an evangelist and attended Bible school (Shioya Seisho Gakusha) for one year to prepare for the ministry. He began independent evangelistic work in 1939. During the postwar period, the Ichibaku Church has grown to include 18 churches (primarily in the Nagoya and Kansai areas) and a membership of over 1,000. The founder died in 1966 and his wife, Saki, has led the church since that time.

This is an independent and indigenous church, but the evangelical and Holiness mission traditions provide the primary theological foundation for the church. Like the Holiness traditions, the church emphasized baptism of the Holy Spirit and healing; speaking in tongues, however, is not recognized as a legitimate practice for public worship, although some members exercise the "gift" in private. The founder emphasized divine healing and often anointed individuals with oil and held special healing services. This is much less common today, but occasionally a healing service is held. The church observes both baptism and the Lord's Supper.

A memorial service is held for the founder each May and for other deceased members on Easter Sunday and in the fall on a Sunday preceding the autumn equinox (秋分の日). Various Christian memorial services are also held in the homes of members on special death anniversaries in accord with Japanese tradition. These services are regarded as an excellent opportunity for evangelism. A common practice of church members is to divide the ashes (分骨) of the deceased between the church cemetery and the Buddhist family grave in an effort to accommodate the needs and concerns of non-Christian relatives.

At the head church in Nagoya average Sunday attendance is over 200 and sign-language is provided for a small deaf group in the front of the church. The church service has a Biblical and evangelical orientation, with members following the sermon with their Bibles opened. The church actively supports revivals and crusades directed by various evangelical groups in Japan, making its identity as a distinct and separate subculture weaker than other indigenous movements.

PRIMARY SOURCES

一麦: 松原和人の信仰と生涯 [One Ear of Wheat: The faith and life of Matsubara Kazuhito]. Nagoya: Ikeru Kirisuto Ichibaku Kyōkai, 1972.
This is a memorial volume that contains the founder's own brief autobiography, numerous photographs of the founder from childhood through his adult ministry,

several of his sermons, and reflections by various leaders and members from various congregations of the Living Christ One Ear of Wheat Church.

Matsubara Saki 松原 向, ed. 一粒の麦もし死なば [If one grain of wheat dies]. Tokyo: New Life, 1986.
A collection of sermons by Matsubara Kazuhito, edited by his wife and current head of the church.

活けるキリスト一麦 [Living Christ one ear of wheat], a monthly newsletter.

CHRISTIAN CANAAN CHURCH 基督カーナン教団

FOUNDER: Taniguchi Toku 谷口とく
YEAR ORGANIZED: 1940

The Christian Canaan Church was founded by Taniguchi Toku, who converted to Christianity through contact with Plymouth Brethren missionaries from England. After his conversion he experienced the baptism of the Holy Spirit and formed this independent Japanese Pentecostal Church. The group began with house meetings in 1940. The headquarters of this church is in Sakai City south of Osaka and churches are concentrated in the Kansai area. As the Church is too small to maintain its own theological school, its pastors are trained at various Bible colleges and seminaries in the area. According to a recent *Christian Yearbook*, it now has ten churches, four evangelistic meeting places, a membership of almost 2,500, and 31 pastors (two-thirds of whom are women).

The Bible is the standard of faith for this church, which uses the old literary translation with which the founder began. The primary concern of this group is to practice Christianity according to the Bible and the power of the Holy Spirit. Baptism of the spirit, speaking in tongues, healing, are all features this group shares in common with other Pentecostal churches. The church observes baptism and the Lord's Supper, as well as Christian memorial services for the dead according to the traditional Japanese calendar and family custom.

JAPAN ECCLESIA OF CHRIST 日本キリスト召団

FOUNDER: Koike Tatsuo 小池辰雄
YEAR ORGANIZED: 1940

Koike Tatsuo was born in 1904 and educated at Tokyo Imperial University. He became attracted to Christianity as a young man as a result of attending the

Bible lectures of Uchimura Kanzō, the well-known founder of the Nonchurch movement. After his conversion, he attended a Nonchurch Bible study group led by Takeshi Fujii, one of Uchimura's disciples, for a period of five years (1925–1930). In 1940 Koike established his own independent Bible study group based on the Nonchurch tradition. Over the next several decades, Koike's circle of influence widened and he eventually organized 12 groups around the country.

Although rooted in the Nonchurch movement, Koike became very critical of Uchimura and the "narrow intellectualism" of his disciples. He argued that both transplanted churches and Nonchurch Christianity were too conceptual in orientation. What people need is *life*, not just abstract *teaching*. This interpretation of Christianity was deeply influenced by Koike's experience of spirit baptism in 1950, while participating in a special evangelistic meeting with Teshima Ikurō, the charismatic founder of the Original Gospel movement.

In 1979, after 50 years of academic life, Koike retired from his position as professor of German Literature at the University of Tokyo. He devoted the remainder of his life to evangelistic work and died in 1996 with no clear successor.

PRIMARY SOURCE

小池辰雄著作集 (全十巻) [The collected works of Koike Tatsuo, 10 volumes]. Tokyo: The Koike Tatsuo Publications Committee 小池辰雄著作刊行会, 1988.

THE SPIRIT OF JESUS CHURCH イエスの御霊教会

FOUNDER: Murai Jun 村井 純
YEAR ORGANIZED: 1941
TREATMENT: Chapter 6

PRIMARY SOURCES

Murai Jun 村井純. 聖書神学: 根本教義 [Biblical theology: Basic doctrines]. Tokyo: Iesu no Mitama Kyōdan, 1957.

———. 基督教案内 [A guide to Christianity]. Tokyo: Iesu no Mitama Kyōkai Honbu, n.d.

SECONDARY SOURCES

Anzai Shin 安斎 伸. イエスの御霊教会 [The Spirit of Jesus Church] in Sakurai Tokutarō 桜井徳太郎 ed. 民俗宗教と社会 [Folk religion and society], vol. 5. Tokyo: Kōbunsha, 1980, 268–79.

————. 南島におけるキリスト教の受容 [The acceptance of Christianity in the southern islands]. Tokyo: Daiichi Shobō, 1984.

Mullins, Mark R. "Japanese Pentecostalism and the World of the Dead: A Study of Cultural Adaptation in Iesu no Mitama Kyōkai." *Japanese Journal of Religious Studies*, 17/4 (1990), 353–74.

THE HOLY ECCLESIA OF JESUS 聖イエス会

FOUNDER: Ōtsuki Takeji 大槻武二
YEAR ORGANIZED: 1946
TREATMENT: Chapter 6

PRIMARY SOURCES

Ōtsuki Takeji 大槻 武. 言泉集 [The collected works of Ōtsuki Takeji]. Kyoto: Logos Publishing Company, 17 volumes, 1976–1997.
Over the past 20 years 17 volumes of Ōtsuki's writings have appeared under his pen-name Gensen. One last volume is scheduled to be published in the near future.

————. 聖地賛歌 [Meditations on the Holy Land]. Kyoto: Sei Iesu Kai Logos Sha, 1993.

Ōtsuki Fudeko 大槻筆子. エルサレムをめざして [Aiming for Jerusalem]. Kyoto: Logos Publishing, 1993.
This is a history of the Holy Ecclesia of Jesus from its founding in 1946 until 1967, written by the founder's wife.

————. リベカ抄 [Selections from Rebecca]. Kyoto: Logos Publishing, 1993.
Parts 1 and 2 of this volume are selections from Ōtsuki Fudeko's essays, talks given to the Mariya Kai women's group, and notes from her diaries. Part 3 consists of selections written about her by close associates.

Satō Toshio 佐藤捷雄, ed. リバイバルの軌跡 [The tracks of revival]. Kyoto: Logos Publishing, 1996.
A volume prepared in 1996 to commemorate the fiftieth anniversary of the Holy Ecclesia of Jesus. It provides a historical overview of the life of Father Ōtsuki until the establishment of the Holy Ecclesia of Jesus in 1946, drawing on Ōtsuki's writings and interview materials.

MISCELLANEOUS CHURCH PUBLICATIONS

あかしびと [Witnesses].
A magazine published for members of the Holy Ecclesia of Jesus and not usually distributed to outsiders.

ぶどう樹 [The grapevine].
A short (4–6 pages) monthly publication used for evangelism and religious educa-tion. Approximately 80,000 copies are distributed through the 100 churches nation-wide.

ぶどう樹: 伝道用ダイジェスト版 [The grapevine: a compilation for evangelistic use]. Kyoto: Logos Publishing Company, 1991.
A concise introduction to the beliefs and practices of the Holy Ecclesia of Jesus based on articles published from the monthly news.

言 [Logos].
A journal published by Logos Theological Seminary.

みことばに仕える: 聖書教理入門講座1, 聖書論. [Serving the word: An introduction to Biblical doctrine, vol. 1, Doctrine of Holy Scripture]. Kyoto: Logos Publish-ing Company, 1974.
A textbook used for training ministers and evangelists at Logos Theological Semi-nary.

みことばに仕える: 聖書教理入門講座2, 神論, 人間論 [vol. 2, Doctrine of God, doc-trine of man]. Kyoto: Logos Publishing Company, 1974.
A textbook used for training ministers and evangelists at Logos Theological Semi-nary.

SANCTIFYING CHRIST CHURCH 聖成基督教団

FOUNDER: Konmoto Kaoru 紺本 薫
YEAR ORGANIZED: 1948

Konmoto Kaoru was born in 1914 and converted to Christianity at the age of seventeen as a result of attending a small home Bible study meeting. He went on to attend the Shioya Seisho Gakusha, a Bible school with roots in the early missionary work of Barclay Baxton (1860–1946), a low-church Anglican, who served as a missionary in Kōbe and Matsue, 1890–1891. He began independent evangelistic work in the early postwar period by holding services on the street, tent revival meetings, and services in the homes of early converts. Kōbe was the center of these evangelistic efforts and became the church headquarters. In 1952, Konmoto organized a Bible school (東洋聖書神学院) to train evangelists within the Kōbe church. Thirty individuals have prepared for ministry in the *juku*-style Bible school. Over the past fifty years, Konmoto and his disciples have organized eleven congregations.

Konmoto's primary concern has been to establish independent and self-supporting churches faithful to the apostolic tradition. While Japanese churches can learn from the experience of foreign churches and missionaries, they should not seek to copy them. Unlike some of the other indigenous Christian movements, Konmoto's writings and messages are essentially Biblical expositions and contain little or no reference to Asian religious traditions. Special emphasis is placed on the biblical teachings regarding spirit baptism and sanctification.The church observes the sacraments of baptism and the Lord's Supper and has developed memorial services in response to the Japanese concern to show special care and respect for the deceased. The founder is nearly ninety years old and preparing to designate one of his disciples to assume his position as head of the church (総理).

PRIMARY SOURCES

Konmoto Kaoru 紺本 薫, ed. 聖成基督教団創立四十周年記念誌 [A collection in commemoration of the fortieth anniversary of the founding of the Sanctifying Christ Church]. Kōbe: Seisei Kirisuto Kyōdan Honbu, 1987.
This volume contains a brief history of the church, photographs, and a collection of testimonials by various members and pastors.

———. 静なる細かき声 [A still small voice]. Kōbe: Seisei Kirisuto Kyōdan Honbu, 1988.
A collection the founder's writings that includes Bible study outlines, curriculum used for theological education used in Bible school, and several original hymns.

ORIGINAL GOSPEL (TABERNACLE) 原始福音 (幕屋)

FOUNDER: Teshima Ikurō 手島郁郎
YEAR ORGANIZED: 1948
TREATMENT: Chapter 6

PRIMARY SOURCES

Teshima Ikurō 手島郁郎. 原始福音信仰序説 [An introduction to the Original Gospel faith]. Tokyo: Kirisuto Seisho Juku, 1969.
———. 日本民族と原始福音 [The Japanese people and the Original Gospel]. Tokyo: Kirisuto Seisho Juku (Makuya Bible Seminary), 1984.
This is a collection of Teshima's writings published by his wife eleven years after his death.
———. 聖霊の愛 [The love of the Holy Spirit]. Tokyo: The Makuya Bible Seminary, 1950. The English version was published as *The Love of the Holy Spirit,* trans. Umemoto Aiko. Tokyo: The Makuya Bible Seminary, 1991.

————. *An Introduction to the Original Gospel Faith*. Tokyo: Makuya Bible Seminary, 1970.
In addition to Teshima's writings, this volume includes an essay by Dr. Otto Piper, Professor Emeritus of Princeton Theological Seminary, which suggests that Makuya is an indigenous Christian movement that represents a significant "third force" in Japanese Protestantism.

Makuya and Israel: In Memory of Abraham I. Teshima. Tokyo: Makuya Bible Seminary, 1976.
A collection of photographs and accounts of Teshima's involvements with Israel and Zionism. Also included are several reflections by Israelis, which include words of appreciation for Teshima's support of Israel. Includes photos of Teshima and 400 Makuya pilgrims in Israel for the 25th anniversary celebration of Israel's independence.

Magazine: 生命之光 [Light of life], published monthly.

SECONDARY SOURCES

Baba Toshihiko 馬場俊彦. "Problems of Charismatic Religion: The Case of the Original Gospel Movement," 名城大学人文紀要 [Meijō University Journal of Humanities] 5 (1967), 1–32.
A description and critique of the Original Gospel movement by a former member and editor of the Makuya magazine Light of Life, *who is currently Professor of Philosophy at Meijō University in Nagoya.*

————. ほんとうの自分: 上 [One's true self, vol. 1]. Aichi: Chūbu Nihon Kyōiku Bunka Kai, 1994; see especially 122–40, 174–76.

Caldarola, Carlo. "The Makuya Christian Movement." *Japanese Religions* 7/4 (1972), 18–34.

————. *Christianity: The Japanese Way*. Leiden: E. J. Brill, 1979. 192–208.

Miyazaki Akira 宮崎 彰. 原始福音研究 [A study of the Original Gospel]. Tokyo: Nihon Kirisuto Kyōdan, Senkyō Kenkyūjo, 1965.

Mori Satoshi 森 諭. 原始福音: 神の幕屋とは [The Original Gospel: What is God's Tabernacle (movement)]. Tokyo: New Life Publishing, 1986 (first published in 1965).
This is the fourth booklet by a conservative evangelical author in a series on modern heresies (現代異端シリーズ), which also includes Mormons, Jehovah's Witnesses, and the Unification Church.

Yoshimura Kiichirō 吉村騏一郎. わが師手島郁郎 [My teacher, Teshima Ikurō]. Tokyo: Kirisuto Seisho Juku, 1990.
A biography of Teshima by one of his close disciples.

LIFE-GIVING CHRIST 活かすキリスト

FOUNDER: Imahashi Atsushi 今橋 淳
YEAR ORGANIZED: 1966

This movement is essentially an independent version of the Original Gospel movement. Following a one-year period of study in Israel as a Makuya member, Imahashi returned to Japan in 1964 and began his ministry as an evangelist under the direction of Teshima Ikurō. A serious disagreement with Teshima forced him out of the Original Gospel movement and he began his own independent ministry in 1966. The Life-Giving Christ movement today consists of seven small ecclesia (house churches) under the direction of Imahashi.

PRIMARY SOURCES

Imahashi Atsushi 今橋 淳. 回心記 [A record of my conversion]. Tokyo: Kirisuto Shinbunsha, 1991.

―――. ヨハネ福音書講義 [Lectures on the Gospel of John]. Tokyo: Kirisuto Shinbunsha, 1976.

―――. ヨハネ黙示録講義 [Lectures on the Revelation of John]. Tokyo: Kirisuto Shinbunsha, 1981.

―――. 創世記講義 [Lectures on Genesis]. Tokyo: Kirisuto Shinbunsha, 1989.

Magazine: 活かすキリスト [Life-giving Christ], published monthly since 1966.

OKINAWA CHRISTIAN GOSPEL 沖縄キリスト教福音

FOUNDER: Nakahara Masao 仲原正夫
YEAR ORGANIZED: 1977

The founder of the Okinawa Christian Gospel, Nakahara Masao, was born in the town of Itoman on the main island of Okinawa in 1948. His father died when he was still a young child and he grew up in rather difficult circumstances. Following high school he moved to Kyoto and enrolled in a professional school in order to obtain credentials as a radiologist. It was while he was in Kyoto that he began to attend services at a Plymouth Brethren church. Within three months he converted to the Christian faith and received baptism. Nakahara returned to Okinawa to work as a radiologist in a local hospital. In 1977 an experience of divine healing and revelation from God led him to resign from his position as an X-ray technician to devote the remainder of his life to evangelistic work. His independent Christian fellowship grew rapidly and in less than twenty years had six branch churches, two mission outreach centers, and a membership of approximately 1,500. The movement also maintains several residences (brother-houses for men and sister-houses for women) to care for individuals who are troubled by various spiritual and psychological problems. This is a charismatic movement in which the practices of speaking in tongues, prophecy, healing, and exorcism play a central role.

SECONDARY SOURCES

Ikegami Yoshimasa 池上良正. 悪霊と聖霊の舞台: 沖縄の民衆キリスト教に見る救済世界 [A stage for demons and the Holy Spirit: The world of salvation as seen in popular Okinawan Christianity]. Tokyo: Dōbutsusha, 1991.

―――. "Okinawan Shamanism and Charismatic Christianity," *The Japan Christian Review* 59 (1993), 69–78.

Notes

References to works listed in the General Bibliography at the conclusion of this volume (pages 261–65) appear in the notes in abbreviated form, and Japanese titles listed there are given here in their English translation only.

Chapter 1: Christianity as World Religion and Vernacular Movement

[1] Hexham and Poewe, *New Religions as Global Cultures*, 41, 43.

[2] Robert W. Hefner, "The Rationality of Conversion," in Robert W. Hefner, ed., *Conversion to Christianity*, 5.

[3] Walls, *The Missionary Movement in Christian History*, 7.

[4] "Introductory Essay: on 'Native Christianity'," in Wendy James and Douglas H. Johnson, eds., *Vernacular Christianity*, 12, emphasis added.

[5] Wilbert R. Shenk, "Toward a Global Church History," *International Bulletin of Missionary Research* 20/2 (1996), 50.

[6] "Converting Buddhism to Christianity, Christianity to Buddhism," *Japanese Religions*, 22/2 (1997), 112.

[7] *The Diffusion of Religions*, 13.

[8] This is the definition provided by Morioka Kiyomi in "A Conceptual Examination of the Indigenization of Foreign-Born Religions," 52. Morioka makes a basic distinction between "acculturation" and "indigenization," explaining that in studies of acculturation the central focus or concern is to what extent the native culture has changed under the influence of a foreign religion; studies of indigenization, on the other hand, are primarily concerned with the nature and degree of change in the foreign-born religion through contact with native religion and culture.

[9] An important elaboration of this point may be found in Sanneh, *Translating the Message*.

[10] *Tradition Old and New* (Exetor: The Paternoster Press, 1970), 17–18.

[11] André Drooger, "Syncretism: The Problem of Definition, the Definition of the Problem," in Jerald D. Gort, Hendrik M. Vroom, Rein Fernhout, and Anton Wessels, eds., *Dialogue and Syncretism: An Interdisciplinary Approach* (Grand Rapids: Eerdmans, 1989), 16.

[12] Maruyama Masao, *Studies in the Intellectual History of Tokugawa Japan*, trans. Mikiso Hane (Tokyo: University of Tokyo Press, 1974), 331.

[13] See his now classic text, *The Sacred Canopy: Elements of a Sociological Theory of Religion* (Garden City: Anchor Books, 1969).

[14] This term I have borrowed from Winston Davis's *Japanese Religion and Society*, 31.

15 See, for example, 渡部照宏 Watanabe Shōkō, 日本の仏教 [Japanese Buddhism], (Tokyo: Iwanami Shoten, 1958), 102–32; and Morioka, "A Conceptual Examination of the Indigenization of Foreign-Born Religions," 55. Some of the difficulties involved in the transplantation of Japanese Buddhism to individualistic North America are closely related to the fact that it is tied to this cult of the dead; see my earlier study, "The Organizational Dilemmas of Ethnic Churches: A Case Study of Japanese Buddhism in Canada," *Sociological Analysis* 49/3 (1988), 226.

16 For a concise introduction and statistics on representative major New Religions in Japan, see Shimazono's "New Religious Movements," in Mullins et al., *Religion and Society in Modern Japan*, 221–30. For more details and an extensive bibliography, see *Dictionary of New Religions,* edited by Inoue Nobutaka.

17 Jan Swyngedouw, "The Christian Churches and Heretical Movements," in Kumazawa and Swain, eds., *Christianity in Japan, 1971–1990*, 184; emphasis added.

18 For an important examination of indigenization within the United Church of Christ in Japan (Nihon Kirisuto Kyōdan), the largest Protestant denomination in Japan, see David Reid, *New Wine.*

19 Robert J. Smith, "Something Old, Something New," 722.

20 Regarding the earlier case of transplantation from China, Albert M. Craig explains that "the eighth and ninth centuries were the time of Sinification, when Japan was deeply influenced by Chinese culture and institutions.... Then, as the embassies to China came to an end, Japan entered a period of digestion or indigenization, when the borrowed institutions were simplified and reshaped to fit Japanese society and its needs." See his "Introduction" to Albert M. Craig, ed., *Japan: A Comparative View* (Princeton: Princeton University Press, 1978), 6–7.

Chapter 2: The Social Sources of Christianity in Japan

1 This present exercise finds parallels in the classic work of H. Richard Niebuhr, *The Social Sources of Denominationalism* (1929). Over half a century ago, Niebuhr identified transplanted immigrant churches from Europe and new forms of American sectarianism as the primary social sources of denominational subcultures in the United States. One of Niebuhr's central concerns was with the "Americanization" of the immigrant churches, similar to the process we refer to as indigenization in this study. Although the development of indigenous movements in Japan certainly resembles some forms of sectarianism in America, it should be noted that the character and orientation of transplanted "mission churches" differs considerably from that of the "immigrant churches" in the United States. The aim of the mission churches has been to transmit a universal truth, not to preserve the language and culture of the old country. In the very act of translation, mission churches were transformed and inevitably began to differ from their sponsoring mother churches in the home country. As this study will show, however, many missionaries were unable to distinguish their religious message from their cultural baggage in a manner that could satisfy some Japanese leaders.

2 See P. F. Saeki, *The Nestorian Documents and Relics in China* (Tokyo: Maruzen, 1951), for a discussion of Nestorian relics in Japan from the tomb of the envoys from Kublai Khan who were executed in 1280 and from the tomb of others who died during the Mongolian invasion of 1281 (444–47).

3 For helpful studies of this initial period of missionary expansion, see Charles Ralph Boxer, *The Christian Century in Japan, 1549–1650* (Berkeley: University of California Press, 1951); Joseph Jennes, *A History of the Catholic Church in Japan from Its Beginnings to the Early Meiji Era, 1549–1873* (Tokyo: Oriens Institute for Religious Research, 1973, rev. ed.); Neil S. Fujita, *Japan's Encounter with Christianity: The Catholic Mission in Pre-Modern Japan* (New York: Paulist Press, 1991); and Andrew C. Ross, *A Vision Betrayed: The Jesuits in Japan and China, 1542–1742* (Maryknoll, New York: Orbis Books, 1994).

4 The literature on this indigenous *kakure kirishitan* tradition is vast. For helpful resources in English, see Ann M. Harrington, *Japan's Hidden Christians* (Chicago: Loyola University Press, 1993) and the chapters by Stephen Turnbull and Christal Whelan in Breen and Williams, *Japan and Christianity*.

5 In his *Studies in the History of the Christian Churches in the Meiji Period*, Ōhama Tetsuya notes that not everything was harmonious during the so-called period of cooperation. He recalls the dismay of Dr. Hepburn when Jonathan Goble and his wife, the first Baptist missionary couple to Japan, refused to remain in the Sunday worship service and participate in the sacrament of communion with other Protestant missionaries. This was one small incident pointing to the "sectarianism" and "denominationalism" that would characterize the Protestant missionary movement in subsequent years (11).

6 In this review of the earliest cooperative mission efforts and the shift to a denominational orientation, I have relied on Morioka Kiyomi, *Japan's Modern Society and Christianity*, 65–86; and Ōhama, *Studies in the History of the Christian Churches*, 10–12.

7 For a standard treatment of the role of the three "bands" in the development of Protestant Christianity in Japan, see Kuyama Yasushi, *Modern Japan and Christianity*, 43–54.

8 Murata Shirō argues that "the fact that the Covenant group at Sapporo had no knowledge of or instruction in the real nature of the church is not a little responsible for the subsequent development of Uchimura's movement." See his "The Character of the Protestant Church in Japan," *The Japan Christian Quarterly* 25/3 (1959), 204–5. For a similar observation, see Ōhama, *Studies in the History of the Christian Churches*, 33.

9 Watanabe Zenta, "The Lack of Cultural Consciousness and Power in the Church of Japan," *Japan Christian Quarterly* 25/1 (1959), 48–49.

10 キリスト教年鑑 [Christian yearbook] (Tokyo: Kirisuto Shinbunsha, 1981), 446–47.

11 This is found in Cary's summary of the Second Conference of Protestant Missionaries in his *A History of Christianity in Japan*, vol. 2, 166.

12 Although Protestant missions pioneered in the field of education, particularly for girls and women, the government subsequently stepped in and began to dominate this area. William K. Bunce explains:

> From the time of the opening of the first school for girls in Japan in 1870 to the time when government schools for women were being promoted around 1900, the history of education for women in Japan is almost identical with the history of the Christian schools for girls. In 1905, Christian high schools for girls represented 70 percent of the total number of girls' schools. However, by 1930, government education for women had advanced to the point where the Christian schools totaled less than 5 percent.

Religions in Japan: Buddhism, Shinto, Christianity (Tokyo: Charles E. Tuttle, 1955), 158.

13 This information was originally reported in Cyril H. Powles, *Victorian Missionaries in Meiji Japan, The Shiba Sect: 1873–1900* (Toronto: University of Toronto, York University Centre on Modern East Asia, 1987), appendix 4, 162. It was brought to my attention in Helen Hardacre's review of Notto R. Thelle's *Buddhism and Christianity in Japan* in the *Journal of Japanese Studies* 15/1 (1989), 316–20.

14 This is not to deny the significant contribution of Protestant mission work to Japan's modernization, particularly in the fields of education and social welfare. However, in the view of Ernest E. Best, because Protestant Christianity "failed to influence in any essential way those who held positions of decisive authority within the power structure of the nation, its influence was never determinative for the society as a whole." *Christian Faith and Cultural Crisis: The Japanese Case* (Leiden: E. J. Brill, 1966), 173.

15 キリスト教年鑑 [Christian yearbook] (Tokyo: Kirisuto Shinbunsha, 1976), 472–73. See Ikado Fujio, *Religion in a Secular Society*, 292–97, for a discussion of the link between Protestantism and the white-collar class.

16 I have borrowed this expression from Helen Hardacre's *Shinto and the State: 1868–1988* (Princeton: Princeton University Press, 1989).

17 Ebisawa Akira, the Executive Secretary of the National Christian Council of Japan, expressed this civil religious theology quite clearly in a 1939 article commemorating the second anniversary of the war with China:

> The policy of extending even to the continent our family principle which finds its center in an Imperial House so that all may bathe in its holy benevolence—this policy, can we not see?—is none other than the concrete realization on earth of the spiritual family principle of Christianity, which looks up to God as the Father of mankind and regards all men as brethren. This is the Christian conception of the kingdom of God. The basis of the Japanese spirit also consists in this; and thus, wonderful to relate, it is one with Christianity. Nay, this must indeed be the Great Way of Heaven and Earth.

Quoted in Darley Downs, *Effects of Wartime Pressures on Churches and Missions in Japan* (New York: Union Theological Seminary, Master of Sacred Theology Thesis, 1946), 32–35, from the *National Christian Council Bulletin*, 186, 1939.

18 For another example of this pattern of accommodation, see my recent case study of a Christian school during this same period, "The Struggle for Christian Higher Education in Japan: A Case-Study of Meiji Gakuin University," in Gerard Dekker, Donald Luidens, and Rodger Rice, eds., *Rethinking Secularization: Reformed Encounters with Modernity* (New York: University Press of America, 1997).

[19] Not all Christian groups gave in to the demands of the state. For a more detailed treatment of this period and an analysis of the Christian churches and sects that resisted these nationalistic pressures, see my "Ideology and Utopianism in Wartime Japan: An Essay on the Subversiveness of Christian Eschatology," *Japanese Journal of Religious Studies* 21/2–3 (1994).

[20] *New Wine*, 80.

[21] *Modern Japan and Shinto Nationalism: A Study of Present-Day Trends in Japanese Religions* (New York: Paragon, 1963), 95. Reflecting on the Protestant movement in Japan, Taiwan, and Korea between 1865 and 1945, A. Hamish Ion rather critically suggests:

> Missionaries, even after more than 70 years of Christian work in Japan, had failed to instill courage into Japanese Christians. In sharp contrast to the Japanese, the steadfastness of Korean and Taiwanese Christians in the face of persecution reveals no lack of courage.... The Japanese Christian movement failed to resist the demands of the Japanese government for complete state control over the movement. Despite the long exposure to Christian ideals and values, indigenous cultural values and national concerns remained paramount in determining the reactions of Japanese Christians.

The Cross and the Rising Sun, vol. 2, *The British Protestant Missionary Movement in Japan, Korea, and Taiwan, 1865–1945* (Waterloo, Ontario: Wilfrid Laurier University Press, 1993), 5–6.

[22] *World Christian Encyclopedia* (New York: Oxford University Press, 1982), 423.

[23] My suspicion is that the higher percentage indicated by survey research is probably related to the influence of certain well-known Japanese Christian writers (such as Endō Shūsaku, Sono Ayako, and Miura Ayako) and the numerous Christian educational institutions throughout Japan. For example, when compared with the number of private schools associated with other major religious organizations in Japan, the disproportionate role of Christians in this field is striking. By the early 1960s, for example, the number of Christian schools exceeded the number of Buddhist-and Shinto-related institutions combined. While there were 652 Buddhist-related schools (10 universities, 1 junior college, 77 high schools, 68 junior high schools, 1 elementary school, 410 kindergartens, and 85 "other"), and only 92 Shinto-related schools (2 universities, 1 junior college, 5 high schools, 6 junior high schools, 1 elementary school, 45 kindergartens, and 32 "other"), there were 840 Christian-related educational institutions (22 universities, 47 junior colleges, 106 high schools, 116 junior high schools, 33 elementary schools, 445 kindergartens, and 71 "other").The miscellaneous institutions in the "other" category include specialized schools for religious education and training (theological schools or seminaries in the case of Christian-related schools). Reported in 日本におけるキリスト教学校 教育の現状 [The current state of education in Christian schools in Japan] (Tokyo: Education Association of Christian Schools, 1961), 133.

[24] Inazō Nitobe, *The Intercourse between the United States and Japan: A Historical Sketch*, in 新渡戸稲造全集 [Collected works of Nitobe Inazō] (Tokyo: Kyōbunkan, 1970), vol. 13, 468.

[25] Inazō Nitobe, *The Intercourse between the United States and Japan,* 470. Sociologist Anzai Shin similarly suggests:

> The Church has forgotten to distinguish, even in its own western terms, the essential from the non-essential. It took many centuries for western Christianity to fashion a

beautiful square peg, and she has been trying to drive it into a round hole in Japan; the peg will not fit.

Cited in Caldarola, *Christianity: The Japanese Way*, 13.

26 See Inoue et al., *Dictionary of New Religions*. This indispensable volume contains over a thousand pages of information on new religions in Japan. This volume contains basic information on over three hundred religious movements and brief histories of over four hundred founders and leaders in Japanese religious movements (including basic information on several of the founders and movements mentioned in this book).

27 See Shimazono, *Salvation Religions in Contemporary Society*, 72.

28 In his helpful discussion of the use of typologies for comparative analysis in the study of Japanese religion, Winston Davis notes that "a good bridge is one that helps us to move forward, beyond the familiar. Once it has been crossed, we may leave it behind and be on our way" (*Japanese Religion and Society,* 15). For an alternative approach focusing on religious thought and Japanese intellectual history, readers are referred to the well-known work of Takeda Kiyoko, *Indigenization and Apostasy*. Takeda identifies the following five patterns of indigenization in Japanese Christianity: compromise (埋没型 *maibotsugata*), isolation (孤立型 *koritsugata*), apostasy (背教型 *haikyōgata*), confrontation (対決型 *taiketsugata*), and grafting (接木型 *tsugikigata*).

29 *Sociology Reinterpreted*, 4.

30 See Nishiyama Shigeru, "Youth, Deprivation, and New Religions: A Sociological Perspective," *The Japan Christian Quarterly* 57/1 (1991), 10.

31 Here I am drawing on rather standard distinctions made by sociologists in their revisions of the church-sect typology. See, for example, Roland Robertson, *The Sociological Interpretation of Religion* (New York: Schocken, 1970), 120–28, and Meredith McGuire, *Religion: The Social Context* (Belmont, California: Wadsworth Publishing Co., 1981), 110–13. The self-definition or self-understanding of a religious group is important not only for church-sect theorizing but also for analyzing indigenization, and this has been taken into account in this typology.

32 This typological framework was developed as a critical response to Morioka Kiyomi's fourfold typology of indigenization, which appeared in his "A Conceptual Examination of the Indigenization of Foreign-Born Religions," 52–57. In developing this alternative framework I am indebted to Ikegami Yoshimasa, Tsukuba University, who read my earlier critique of Morioka and made several helpful suggestions. Drawing upon church-sect theory, Morioka suggested that the nature of indigenization can be analyzed in terms of the following coaxial framework (see figure 6). One axis has to do with the relationship between the foreign-born religion and the receiving society. Is it sectarian in orientation and critical of the values and behavior of the larger society or is it essentially affirmative (church-like) in its orientation? Is the foreign-born religion in tension with the larger society or in a state of harmonious coexistence? The second axis has to do with the nature and degree of change in the imported religion. Here the question is whether in the process of cultural adaptation changes have occurred only in external form (nonessential aspects) or have reached to the core of the reli-

Relationship with Society	Degree of Change	
	Change in Form	Change in Essentials
Negative-Rejecting (Sect-like)	A Isolation	C Clandestinization
Affirmative-Accepting (Church-like)	B Indigenization	D Submergence

Figure 6. Typology of Indigenization (Morioka, 1972)

gion. A combination of these two axes leads to four possible types: isolation, indigenization, clandestinization, and submergence.

The utility of church-sect theory for sociological research has been questioned, particularly the approaches taken by Troeltsch and Niebuhr, because definitions of organizational types have been based upon the notion of "theological compromise" with the world (see Alan W. Eister, "H. Richard Niebuhr and the Paradox of Religious Organization: A Radical Critique," in Charles Y. Glock and Phillip E. Hammond, eds., *Beyond the Classics? Essays in the Scientific Study of Religion* (New York: Harper and Row, 1973). Morioka was unable to avoid this problem in his attempt to develop this fourfold typology of indigenization. In analyzing the nature and degree of change in the imported religion, Morioka's approach required that one determine whether in the process of cultural adaptation changes had occurred only in external form (nonessential aspects) or have reached to the core (essentials) of the religion. Without denying that this is a legitimate area of theological and missiological concern, it does not provide a helpful basis for comparative sociological research. Theologians and churches have considerable difficulty in determining the "core" of the faith and "boundaries" that delimit acceptable doctrine and practice. A typology that requires such a distinction is problematic. In terms of Morioka's framework, for example, the Spirit of Jesus Church would not be regarded as an "authentic" example of indigenization because it has dropped some "essentials" and still exists in tension with the larger society (placing it in the "clandestinization" category). Similarly, established churches would consider this group as heretical because of its rejection of trinitarian formulations of the Christian faith. The approach I am advocating here is to examine all groups that define themselves as Christian, then document what they do with the Christian faith when free of the control of Western churches, rather than exclude them prematurely on the basis of theological criteria. I should point out that several years after the 1972 article appeared, Morioka published *Japan's Modern Society and Christianity*, in which he stressed the importance of understanding the participants' view of reality in making sense of indigenization (279). He notes, for example, that the attitude of the believer towards what might be regarded as heretical practices is important. The Christian interpretation accorded certain practices is what distinguishes the "submergence-type" from the "indigenized-type." This observation, however, was not integrated into his typology.

33 I have used the denominational category in order to emphasize the self-understanding of these groups, even though they lack the characteristics normally associated with a denomination in the West (i.e., central bureaucracy, complex organizational structure, and formal system for ministerial training and ordination).

34 内村鑑三全集 [Complete works of Uchimura Kanzō] (Tokyo: Iwanami Shoten, 1981–1984) vol. 18, 256 (1911); emphasis in original.

35 These comments are from a sermon on the Lord's Supper by founder Murai Jun at the Naikai Spirit of Jesus Church on 20 August 1962. A transcribed manuscript of the taped sermon was made available to me. Field research and interviews with various pastors have shown me that Murai effectively transmitted his sectarian stance to his followers.

36 *Modern Japan and Shinto Nationalism*, 95; emphasis added.

Chapter 3: Charisma, Minor Founders, and Indigenous Movements

1 *Jesus: A New Vision* (San Francisco: Harper Collins, 1987), 225–26.

2 For a detailed study of the New Testament texts that deal with the charismatic nature of Jesus' religious experience and the early Christian movement, see James D. G. Dunn, *Jesus and the Spirit: A Study of the Religious and Charismatic Experience of Jesus and the First Christians as Reflected in the New Testament* (London: SCM Press, 1975). For a more recent treatment of spirit belief in the New Testament and the role of Jesus as an exorcist and healer see Stevan L. Davies, *Jesus the Healer: Possession, Trance, and the Origins of Christianity* (New York: Continuum, 1995).

3 Morton T. Kelsey observes, for example, that in the third century "the order of exorcists soon grew so large that one bishop in Rome complained that they outnumbered the priests." *Healing and Christianity: In Ancient Thought and Modern Times* (San Francisco: Harper & Row, 1973), 153.

4 See D. B. Barrett, "Global Statistics," in Stanley M. Burgess and Gary B. McGee, eds., *Dictionary of Pentecostal and Charismatic Movements* (Grand Rapids: Zondervan, 1988), 810–30.

5 Earhart's approach in *Gedatsu-kai and Religion in Contemporary Japan* was based on dissatisfaction with the sociological explanations that attributed the birth of New Religions primarily to social crisis and anomie. Following a critique of Western reductionistic accounts of New Religions, Earhart develops a model that draws attention to prior religious influences and the innovations brought about by founders. This framework provides a helpful corrective to approaches that ignore religious elements and attribute the emergence of New Religions to social dislocation or some form of deprivation. For another important discussion of the inadequacies of the "crisis approach" to New Religions, see Hardacre's *Lay Buddhism in Modern Japan*, 30–34.

6 Powles, "Foreign Missionaries and Japanese Culture in the Late Nineteenth Century," 17–18.

7 Powles points out, for example, that more tolerant or accommodating attitudes toward Japanese religion and culture were to be found in the Russian Orthodox and Anglican missionary traditions ("Foreign Missionaries and Japanese Culture in the Late Nineteenth Century," 14–28).

8 Joseph M. Kitagawa, "The Contemporary Religious Situation in Japan," *Japanese Religions* 2/2–3 (1961), 40–41.

9 内村鑑三全集 [Complete works of Uchimura Kanzō] (Tokyo: Iwanami Shoten, 1981–1984)(hereafter CWUK), vol. 1, 159 (1886).

10 CWUK, vol. 29, 476–47 (1925–1926).

11 The Japanese terms Teshima uses here are *gaikaku* (外殻, shell or crust) and *naijitsu* (内実, inner reality, true condition). See 手島郁郎 Teshima Ikurō, 日本民族と原始福音 [The Japanese people and the original gospel] (Tokyo: Kirisuto Seisho Juku, 1984), 34–37. This book is based on a collection of articles published years earlier in the movement's magazine 生命之光 [Light of life].

12 CWUK, vol. 22, 233 (1915–1916).

13 松村介石 Matsumura Kaiseki, 信仰五十年 [Fifty years in the faith] was first published in 1926. The headquarters of The Way (Tokyo: Dōkai Honbu) published a revised edition in 1989 to coincide with the fifty-year memorial service of his death.

14 Information on Kawai Shinsui's life may be found in the study by 大塚栄三 Ōtsuka Eisan, 郡是の川合信水先生 [Kawai Shinsui Sensei at Gunze] (Tokyo: Iwanami Shoten, 1931), and Kawai's own record, *My Spiritual Experiences,* trans. by Yoshinobu Kawai (Tokyo: Christ Heart Church, 1970).

15 See Marius Jansen, ed., *Changing Japanese Attitudes toward Modernization* (Princeton: Princeton University Press, 1965), 5.

16 Jansen also makes the interesting observation that the revival of Confucianism in reaction to the West in the late Meiji period no longer symbolized Chinese tradition, but the best of native tradition:

> The very enthusiasm of the Westernization mood provoked misgivings about the degree to which it was necessary to learn "the ways of Chou" and provided an opening for a return of Confucianists, who now appeared as defenders of the Japanese, and not the Chinese, tradition. Their spokesmen were numerous, but the common element was to be found in warnings that the native tradition ought not to be jettisoned so uncritically.

Changing Japanese Attitudes toward Modernization, 70.

17 Notto Thelle helpfully reminds us that this indigenous impulse "was not merely a result of anti-Western reaction, but sprang out of a deep concern for Christian propagation." *Buddhism and Christianity in Japan*, 174.

18 Earhart, *Gedatsu-kai and Religion in Contemporary Japan,* 236.

19 While these are the three major sources, Shimazono points out that elements of Shinto, *mikkyō, kakure nembutsu*, Christianity, and spiritualism, have also been incorporated into various new religions (*Salvation Religions in Contemporary Society*, 55ff).

20 Admittedly, this distinction is often difficult to make due to the eclectic nature of religious belief and practice. Nevertheless, the category of "folk religion" is widely accepted in the world of Japanese religious scholarship. See for example, Hori, *Folk Religion in Japan*; 孝本貢 Kōmoto Mitsugu, 現代都市の民俗信仰 [Folk religion in the modern city], in Ōmura Eishō and Nishiyama Shigeru, eds., *The Religion of People Today*; Miyake Hitoshi, "Folk Religion," in Noriyoshi Tamaru and David Reid, eds., *Religion in Japanese Culture*. In chapter seven, I consider in some detail the manner in which indigenous Christian groups have addressed folk religious concerns and the ancestor cult. For a discussion of the problematic nature of this distinction and an alternative conceptualization of religion in Japan in terms of "common religion," see the forthcoming book by Ian Reader and George J. Tanabe, Jr., *Practically Religious: Worldly Benefits and the Common Religion of Japan* (Honolulu: University of Hawai'i Press).

21 The Holy Ecclesia of Jesus, one of the few exceptions, does expect members to confess the Apostles' Creed.

22 The experiential orientation of missionaries from the Assemblies of God and Holiness church traditions is undeniable. For the first half century of Protestant mission work in Japan, however, there were no representatives from these Western church traditions.

23 Although Dunn's primary concern in this work is to identity the diverse streams within early Christianity, he does not deny that there are common or unifying elements across these traditions. See *Unity and Diversity in the New Testament: An Inquiry into the Character of Earliest Christianity* (London: SCM Press, 1990), 373–74; emphasis added.

24 Earhart, *Gedatsu-kai and Religion in Contemporary Japan,* 236.

25 Joachim Wach, *Sociology of Religion* (Chicago: University of Chicago Press, 1944), 133. Thomas F. O'Dea argued similarly:

> From the unusual religious experiences of unusual people the founded religions emerge, translating and transforming the insights of founders into institutional structures. Thus there arise the formed and formulated entities of belief-systems, systems of ritual and liturgy, and organization. It is important therefore especially in the study of the founded religions to begin with a phenomenological analysis of the religious experience as such, for out of it emerge the chief dimensions of religious institutions as well as their chief functional problems.

"Five Dilemmas in the Institutionalization of Religion," *Journal for the Scientific Study of Religion* 1/1 (1961), 31. This concern has been raised again more recently in a number of areas. In the sociology of religion, for example, see Rodney Stark, "Normal Revelations: A Rational Model of 'Mystical Experiences'," in David G. Bromley, ed., *Religion and the Social Order: New Developments in Theory and Research* (Greenwich: JAI Press, 1991). This concern has also appeared in the study of the New Testament and early Christianity. Larry W. Hurtado, for example, suggests:

> Especially in the study of new religious movements and the development of religious innovations, such as early Christianity, greater attention should be given to the *creative role of the religious experiences of founders and founding groups....* History, both ancient and more recent, affords us many examples of new religious movements often arising as an innovative reinterpretation of an established religious tradition, an innovation

flowing from an altered hermeneutical perspective provided by potent religious experiences of influential members and/or groups in the new movement.

One God, One Lord: Early Christian Devotion and Ancient Judaism (Philadelphia: Fortress Press, 1988), 126–27; emphasis added. Stevan L. Davies similarly argues that religious experience (pneumatology) preceded doctrine (Christology) in the early Christian movement. See his *Jesus the Healer: Possession, Trance, and the Origins of Christianity* (New York: Continuum, 1995).

[26] See Max Weber, *The Sociology of Religion*, trans. Ephraim Fischoff (Boston: Beacon Press, 1963), 46.

[27] Werner Stark, *The Sociology of Religion: A Study of Christendom* (New York: Fordham University Press, 1970), 4:84.

[28] Anthony J. Blasi, *Making Charisma: The Social Construction of Paul's Public Image* (New Brunswick, New Jersey: Transaction Publishers, 1991), 14–15.

[29] Fujii Masao, "Founder Worship in Kamakura Buddhism," in George A. DeVos and Takao Sofue, eds., *Religion and the Family in East Asia* (Berkeley: University of California Press, 1984), 156.

[30] Hoshino Eiki, "A Pillar of Japanese Buddhism: Founder Belief," *Journal of Oriental Studies* 26 (1987), 80. For an interesting discussion of the shift from "institutional charisma" to "personal charisma" in Japanese Buddhism, see 森 竜吉 Mori Ryūkichi, 日本仏教とカリスマ: 親鸞・道元・日蓮 [Japanese Buddhism and charisma: Shinran, Dōgen, Nichiren] in 佐々木宏幹 Sasaki Kōkan, 宮田 登 Miyata Noboru, 山折哲雄 Yamaori Tetsuo, eds. カリスマ [Charisma] (Tokyo: Shunjūsha, 1995), 32–43.

[31] For a more detailed treatment, see 島薗 進 Shimazono Susumu, 教祖と宗教的指導者崇拝の研究課題 [Studies on the veneration of founders and religious leaders] in 教祖とその周辺 [Founders and their surroundings], edited by the Shūkyō Shakaigaku Kenkyūkai (Tokyo: Yūyama, 1987), 23–26.

[32] Summarizing the Weberian perspective on charisma, Robin Theobald notes:

Charismatic authority involves a relationship between a group of followers or disciples and a leader to whom they attribute extraordinary qualities. The leader has a mission or message which in some way harmonizes with the basic needs, hopes, desires, ambitions or fears of his followers. However, during the early stages of charismatic upsurge leader and message are inseparable as the prime orientation of the followers is to the *person* of the leader himself.

"The Role of Charisma in the Development of Social Movements," *Archives de Sciences Sociales des Religions* 49/1 (1980), 85.

[33] 川合信水 Kawai Shinsui, ガラテヤ書玄義 [The mysteries of Galatians] (Fujiyoshida: Kirisuto Shinshū Kyōdan Jimukyoku Shuppanbu, 1965). This volume is based on lectures Kawai gave at the Gunze Silk Factory during 1928 and 1929.

[34] Kawai Shinsui, *My Spiritual Experiences,* trans. by Yoshinobu Kawai (Tokyo: Christ Heart Church, 1970), 12. In this spiritual autobiography, Kawai records numerous revelatory experiences throughout his life at Mt. Fuji and elsewhere.

35 In his study of Ellen G. White and Seventh-day Adventism cited above, Robin Theobald makes a similar observation:

> Although it is true that Mrs. White did not produce her own "Bible," in reality it seems to be the case that her writings are treated on a par with the Bible. In sermons and in Bible study meetings passages from the Bible and Mrs. White's interpretation of them are often mingled in a manner which makes them virtually indistinguishable.

"The Role of Charisma in the Development of Social Movements," 98.

36 Nakamura Hajime, *The Ways of Thinking of Eastern Peoples: India, China, Tibet, Japan*, ed. by Philip P. Wiener (Honolulu: East-West Center Press, 1964), 454; emphasis added.

37 Minor founders in Japanese movements are prime examples of what Irving Hexham and Karla Poewe have recently referred to as "iconic leadership," particularly important in various African independent churches and other new religious movements (see *New Religions as Global Cultures,* 55).

38 CWUK, vol. 25, 592 (1920); emphasis added. Some years earlier, Uchimura wrote about the importance of direct religious experience as follows:

> They call us mystics because we do not walk with them, and work like them; because we trust in the invisible Spirit, and *not* in visible institutions, organizations, "Christian movements," and those things. Mystics? Yes, we rather like the name. Was not Luther a mystic, and Paul the greatest of all mystics? "And it shall come to pass in the last days, saith God, I will pour out my Spirit upon all flesh; and your sons and daughters shall prophesy, and your young men shall see visions, and your old men shall dream dreams"; i e., they shall all be mystics. Why then should we not attempt to be mystics ourselves, and be unlike unmystical, practical, political, world-serving modern Christians?

CWUK, vol. 20, 274 (1914).

39 For a helpful discussion of Uchimura's "charisma" and emphasis on "returning to the original Scriptures," see 中村勝己 Nakamura Katsumi, 近代文化の構造：近代文化とキリスト教 [The structure of modern culture: Modern culture and Christianity] (Tokyo: Chikuma Shobō, 1972), 301–2.

40 Teshima Ikurō, the founder of the Original Gospel movement, left the Nonchurch movement because it lacked the power of the Holy Spirit and miracles of New Testament Christianity. Although the movement initially represented a return to Biblical Christianity, Teshima thought that it had stopped short and become another conceptual or intellectual expression like the Western churches. What is missing in both established churches and Mukyōkai is the living Christ and power of the Holy Spirit. See 手島郁郎 Teshima Ikurō, 原始福音信仰序説 [An introduction to the Original Gospel faith] (Tokyo: Kirisuto Seisho Juku, 1969), 112. Koike Tatsuo, the founder of Japan Ecclesia of Christ, similarly explains that he entered the Christian faith through the Nonchurch movement but became an outsider because of his experience of the baptism of the Spirit and recognition of charismatic gifts. See his 無の神学 [A theology of nothingness], vol. 3 in 小池辰雄著作集 [The collected works of Koike Tatsuo] (Tokyo: Nihon Kirisuto Shōdan, 1982), 200.

41 See Kawai, *My Spiritual Experiences,* 4, 22; and 川合信水先生の論語講話 [Kawai Shinsui's lectures on the *Analects* of Confucius], ed. by E. Yasui (Tokyo: Kirisuto Shin Shūdan

Shuppanbu, 1970). Kawai is not alone in his development of a "fulfillment" theology in the Japanese context. Teshima Ikurō provides a similar interpretation of Asian religions and various Buddhist saints. In fact, Part II of a volume of his collected writings is entitled "the Old Testament of Japan" and explores the teachings and experiences of various religious leaders (such as Kōbō Daishi, Hōnen, Nichiren, and Hakuin) who have shaped the Japanese religious tradition (Teshima, *The Japanese People and the Original Gospel,* 55). Teshima finds in these Asian traditions numerous experiences, teachings, and practices that can be usefully incorporated in the development of a Japanese Christian spirituality.

[42] See one of the early issues of Dōkai's magazine 道 [The way] 7 (November 1908).

[43] See 松村介石 Matsumura Kaiseki, ed., 道会詩集第一集 [A first collection of Dōkai poems] (Tokyo: Dōkai Jimusho, 1929, first ed.).

[44] 道会バイブル [The Dōkai bible] (Tokyo: Dōkai Jimusho, 1928).

[45] See 松村吉助 Matsumura Kichisuke, 暗夜を憂うること勿れ：言志四録抄書 [Lament not the dark night: Selections from *Genshi shiroku*] (Tokyo: Dōkai Jimusho, 1949). This is essentially a commentary on *Genshi shiroku*, the work of Satō Issai 佐藤一斎 (1772–1859).

[46] This viewpoint is expressed in a number of Teshima Ikurō's writings. For one example, see *The Japanese People and the Original Gospel*, 51–52.

[47] In the case of the Okinawa Christian Gospel movement, exorcism receives a particular emphasis. See the helpful study by Ikegami, *A Stage for Demons and the Holy Spirit*, 78–105.

Chapter 4: The Fountainhead of Japanese Christianity Revisited

[1] *Complete Works of Uchimura Kanzō*, vol. 30, 192 (1926–1927); hereafter referred to as CWUK, with volume number, page, and original year of publication. Emphasis added.

[2] F. F. Bruce, *Tradition Old and New* (Exetor: Paternoster Press, 1970), 15.

[3] 今井館図書資料センター蔵書目録 [An inventory of Imai Hall Book and Resource Center holdings] (Tokyo: Imai Kan Seisho Kōdo Kyōyūkai, 1990).

[4] Mukyōkai leader Yanaihara Tadao, for example, emphasizes this point in his preface to Emil Brunner's 日本の無教会運動 [The Nonchurch movement in Japan] (Tokyo: Kishinsha, 1959), an article translated by Yanaihara Tadao and Takahashi Saburō from the German original "Die Christliche Nicht-Kirche-Bewegung in Japan," *Evagelische Theologie* 4, 1959. See also Emil Brunner, "A Unique Mission in Japan: The Mukyōkai ('Non-Church') Movement in Japan," in Walter Leibrecht, ed., *Religion and Culture: Essays in Honor of Paul Tillich* (London: SCM Press, 1959). In an effort to alleviate some of the tension between Mukyōkai and the established churches, Brunner in 1954 even addressed the General Assembly of the United Church of Christ in Japan, the largest Protestant denomination, and appealed for mutual respect and recognition. Brunner insisted that "both believe in Jesus Christ, the Son of God, as our only Savior. The Body of Christ is not limited to the Church. The Mukyōkai people are right in saying, 'If ecclesia is translated by "church," then there is "salvation outside the church".' The Lord of the Church is free to use other means than those of the institutional church to draw people to Himself and make them disciples. But the spirit of Christ

also does use the churches and their sacraments for His work and purpose." Emil Brunner, "Ecclesia and Evangelism," *Japan Christian Quarterly* 21 (April 1955), 154–55.

5 Caldarola, *Christianity: The Japanese Way*, vii.

6 "The World and Japan in Young Uchimura Kanzō's Work," *KBS Bulletin on Japanese Culture*, No. 115 (August–September) 1972, 1–28. Ohara Shin makes a similar observation, writing that "it is ironic that Uchimura and his friends in Sapporo, usually called the 'Sapporo Band,' were in the 1870s and 1880s among the most Americanized people in Japan. Most of their schooling was in English, and their correspondence, except with their parents, was all written in English. Yet it was from this group that a man like Uchimura could emerge to call for a Christian faith adapted to Japan without any formal institutions"(see his essay, "The Thought of Uchimura Kanzō and Its Relevance to Contemporary American Religion," in Ray A. Moore, ed., *Culture and Religion in Japanese-American Relations: Essays on Uchimura Kanzō, 1861–1930* (Ann Arbor: Center for Japanese Studies, The University of Michigan, 1981), 116.

7 Although Uchimura did not have a direct relationship with Clark, he nevertheless felt indebted to him and expressed a deep appreciation and respect for his witness to the Christian faith. See Uchimura's tribute, "The Missionary Work of William S. Clark, Ph.D., LL.D., Ex-President of Amherst Agricultural College" (originally published in *The Christian Union*, April 22, 1886; see CWUK, vol. 1, 136–41 (1877–1892). The full text of the "Covenant of Believers in Jesus" is also recorded in this article.

8 CWUK, vol. 3, 117 (1894–1896).

9 CWUK, vol. 29, 429–30 (1925–1926).

10 CWUK, vol. 3, 131 (1894–1896).

11 On the relationship between Mukyōkai and Quakerism, see 佐藤全弘 Satō Zenkō, 無教会伝導とクエーカー [Nonchurch evangelism and Quakers], in 田村光三 Tamura Kōsan, ed., 1985 年無教会夏期懇話会記録 [Proceedings of the 1985 Nonchurch summer colloquium] (Tokyo: Mukyōkai Kaki Konwakai Jimukyoku, 1986), 27–35.

12 CWUK, vol. 31, 132 (1928).

13 Paul Peachey, "Mukyōkai-Shugi: A Modern Attempt to Complete the Reformation," *The Mennonite Quarterly Review* 35 (Jan. 1961), 71.

14 See Hiroshi Miura, *The Life and Thought of Kanzo Uchimura, 1861–1930* (Grand Rapids: Eerdmans, 1996), 43–49, regarding Uchimura's changing views on Japan's military involvements in Asia and his eventual conversion to pacifism.

15 Regarding Uchimura's involvement in the "Second Coming of Christ" movement, see 小原 信 Ohara Shin, 内村鑑三の生涯 [The life of Uchimura Kanzō] (Tokyo: PHP, 1992), 328–29.

16 Uchimura writes that this doctrine was "very unpopular" among Japanese churches and notes that he was "attacked and adversely criticized" by such well-known Christian leaders as Rev. Danjō Ebina (Congregationalist), Dr. T. Sugiura (Episcopalian), Rev. K. Shiraishi (Methodist), Rev. T. Tominaga (Presbyterian), and Rev. S. Uchigasaki (Unitarian). Uchimura

records, for example, that "Rev. Danjō Ebina, the leader of Congregational Churches in Japan, characterizes belief in the Second Coming of Christ as 'destructive to national existence, unreasonable, unscientific, unbiblical and unchristian'" (CWUK, vol. 24, 486 [1918–1919]).

17 This expression is borrowed from Kwame Bediako's *Christianity in Africa: The Renewal of a Non-Western Religion* (Edinburgh: Edinburgh University Press/Orbis Books, 1995), 75–87.

18 CWUK, vol. 29, 425 (1925–1926).

19 CWUK, vol. 29, 456 (1925–1926); emphasis added.

20 CWUK, vol. 3, 10 (1894–1896).

21 CWUK, vol. 22, 161 (1915–1916). A decade later, Uchimura similarly wrote: "As far as Japan is concerned, there are many things in Bushidō and Buddhism which come very close to Christianity; and by judicious use of these, preaching Christianity is made very much easier. There is no need of presenting Christianity as a strange religion to my countrymen." CWUK, vol. 29, 454 (1925–1926).

22 CWUK, vol. 25, 362 (1920).

23 See Uchimura's discussion of this ideal in his chapter on "Nakae Tōjū: A Village Teacher," CWUK, vol. 3, 249–67 (1894–1896). The samurai background and Confucian orientation of Uchimura and many other Japanese Christians in Meiji Japan has been noted in a number of studies. Sumiya Mikio, for example, points out that many of the early Japanese Christians came from the samurai class and had a strong background in Confucianism. Of the first eleven members of the Yokohama Band (*Kōkai,* 公会) two were Buddhist priests, one was a doctor, and the rest were samurai (*shizoku,* 士族). He notes that their Neo-Confucian education served as a preparation for their conversion to Christianity as well as influenced their subsequent interpretation of the faith (*Christianity and the Formation of Modern Japan*, 15, 26–28). In addition to the importance of the Confucian background, Kudō Eiichi draws attention to the downward mobility of many from the samurai class during this period as a significant factor in their conversion to Christianity (*Studies in the Economic History of Japanese Christian Society*, 37–44).

24 One of the problems associated with this group occurred when Uchimura proposed that the Apostles' Creed be used as the confession of faith that each member of the Brotherhood be required to sign. This proposal generated a critical reaction, with Uchimura being accused of taking a "backward step" into Western ecclesiasticism. Regarding these early organizational efforts, see William H. H. Norman, "Kanzo Uchimura: Founder of the Nonchurch Movement," *Contemporary Religions in Japan* 5/1 (1964), 34–44.

25 The contrast between ordained clergy in Christian denominations and charismatic leadership in Mukyōkai is elaborated by 中村勝己 Nakamura Katsumi, 近代文化の構造: 近代文化とキリスト教 [The structure of modern culture: Modern culture and Christianity] (Tokyo: Chikuma Shobō, 1972), 302–3.

26 Ohara Shin, "The Thought of Uchimura Kanzō and Its Relevance to Contemporary American Religion," in Ray A. Moore, *Culture and Religion in Japanese-American Relations*, 126.

231

27 "Mukyōkai: Churchless Christians in Japan," *Japan Christian Quarterly* 52/3 (1986), 172.

28 Regarding Uchimura's conservative Confucian orientation with regard to women, see Ohara, *The Life of Uchimura Kanzō*, 15–18, 47, 112. According to Ohara, Uchimura's Confucian understanding of the place of women was a source of conflict with the churches and mission schools. His first wife, Asada Take, with whom he had such difficulty, was educated at Dōshisha in Kyoto and Kyōritsu Jogakkō in Yokohama. As an intellectual fluent in English, she was a new type of woman and rather distant from Uchimura's Confucian ideal.

29 Caldarola, *Christianity: The Japanese Way*, 90–93. In a 1926 essay Uchimura explained that Christianity involved both "other power" and "self-power" (CWUK, vol. 29, 249–53, 1925–1926). When compared with the views of Matsumura Kaiseki and Kawai Shinsui, the focus of the following chapter, it will become clear that faith and dependence on "other power" is the dominant emphasis in Uchimura's interpretation.

30 CWUK, vol. 29, 521 (1925–1926).

31 At the first memorial following Uchimura's death in 1930, for example, 藤井 武 Fujii Takeshi gave a lecture entitled 預言者としての内村先生 [Uchimura as prophet], in which he identified Uchimura with the Hebrew prophets and emphasized that he was the most "anti-priest" type of person he had ever known. See 内村鑑三先生記念キリスト教講演集 [A collection of Uchimura Kanzō memorial lectures on Christianity] (Tokyo: Kirisutokyō Yakan Kōza Shuppanbu, 1972), 222–25.

32 See, for example, I Timothy 3 , 5, and Titus, and I Peter 5. For helpful discussion of early institutionalization reflected in the New Testament canon, see Raymond E. Brown, *The Churches the Apostles Left Behind* (London: Geoffrey Chapman, 1984), 31–46, and James D. G. Dunn's *Unity and Diversity in the New Testament: An Inquiry into the Character of Earliest Christianity* (London: SCM Press, 1990 edition; originally published in 1977), 344, 359–66.

Chapter 5: Christianity as a Path of Self-Cultivation

1 For a concise overview of Matsumura's life and work see 大内三郎 Ōuchi Saburō, 松村介石研究序説 [An introduction to research on Matsumura Kaiseki], 東北大学日本文化研究所研究報告 12 (1976), 1–18. Brief discussion of the "three muras of the Christian world" (基督教界の三村論) may be found in 秋山繁雄 Akiyama Shigeo, 明治人物拾遺物語：キリスト教の一系譜 [Stories of Meiji figures: One lineage of Christianity] (Tokyo: Shinkyō Shuppansha, 1982), 155. This sometimes appears as the "four muras," with the addition of 田村直臣 Tamura Naomi. See, for example, 鈴木糊久 Suzuki Norihisa, 明治宗教思潮の研究 [Studies of trends in Meiji religious thought] (Tokyo: University of Tokyo Press, 1979), 130. Tamura was another important Protestant pastor and leader, associated with the founding and editing of the magazine 六合雑誌 [The universe] and widely known for his controversial book in English, *The Japanese Bride* (Harper and Brothers, 1893), which described various marriage customs and the generally low status of women in Japanese society.

2 See 近代文学研究叢書, vol. 45 [The library of modern literature] (Tokyo: Shōwa Joshi Daigaku Kindai Bungaku Kenkyūshitsu, 1977), 209–68.

3 References to Matsumura's wider influence on new religious movements may be found in Inoue et al., *Dictionary of New Religions*, 853, 896.

4 大内三郎 Ōuchi Saburō, 松村介石: 内村鑑三との関連において [Matsumura Kaiseki: His relationship to Uchimura Kanzō], 内村鑑三研究 8 (1977), 70–71.

5 This is recounted in Matsumura's 信仰五十年 [Fifty years in the faith] (Tokyo: Dōkai Jimusho, 1929, 1989 reprint edition), 34–35. Elsewhere he mentions many other problems, so this particular crisis was probably just the "last straw" for Matsumura.

6 For a helpful discussion of the impact of Western science and the theory of evolution on Japanese Protestant leaders in Meiji Japan, including Matsumura Kaiseki, see Helen Ballhatchet, "The Religion of the West versus the Science of the West: The Evolution Controversy in Late Nineteenth Century Japan," in Breen and Williams, eds., *Japan and Christianity*, 107–21.

7 A concise introduction to Kanamori's views and the debate surrounding the New Theology in Japan may be found in Akio Dohi's, "The First Generation: Christian Leaders in the First Period," in Yasuo Furuya, ed. and trans., *A History of Japanese Theology*, 21–34. Dohi summarized Kanamori's basic position as follows: "Although there are various religions in Japan, a religion of truth and life will triumph. However, one religion or denomination cannot monopolize the truth of religion. So far as Christianity is concerned, the Bible's miracle stories, the prohibition of smoking and drinking, the imported denominational disputes from foreign countries, and the ritualization of Christianity are stumbling blocks for Japanese people" (22).

8 Matsumura uses the term *kaikakuteki kirisutokyō* (改革的キリスト教 reformational Christianity) to refer to his new endeavor in 諸教の批判 [A critique of religions] (Tokyo: Dōkai Jimusho, 1929), 64. This is, of course, in stark contrast to what the mission churches meant by "reformed," i.e., a recovery of "Biblical" Christianity.

9 In the following synopsis I have relied heavily on the following works: Matsumura's religious autobiography, *Fifty Years in the Faith*; an extensive review of articles in the magazine 道 [The way], published since 1908; 道会栞 [Dōkai guidebook] (Tokyo: Dōkai Jimusho, 1917), a small pamphlet (36 pages) that gives a basic summary of the four central beliefs of The Way, the oath made by its members, and prayers and songs (四綱領の歌) ; the 道会問答 [Questions and answers about The Way] (Tokyo: Dōkai Jimusho, 1919); 新宗教 [New religion] (Dōkai Jimusho), 1925; and 道会の信仰 [The Dōkai faith] (Tokyo: Tōhō Shoin), 1934.

10 *The Way* 7 (November 1908).

11 Suzuki, *Studies of Trends in Meiji Religious Thought*, 137.

12 Matsumura, *A Critique of Religions*, 61–66.

13 Matsumura, *A Critique of Religions*, 57–67.

14 Matsumura explains that the remarkable aspects of Jesus are his utter dependence on God the Father and his submission of all to the will of God. But it is a fact that Jesus was only a young man of thirty years, and in terms of knowledge, personality, insight, was not yet fully developed. He also did not have the knowledge of evolution and other facts, that have been

discovered in our time. He also showed signs of weakness in his prayer in Gethsemane, asking the Father to take "this cup from him." His "remuneration morality" (報酬道徳) is greatly inferior to that of Confucius or Mencius (paraphrased from *A Critique of Religions*, 12). Matsumura's Christology from below also assumed a total discontinuity between the life and teachings of Jesus and the subsequent interpretations of Christianity by the Apostle Paul. Commenting on the Lord's Prayer recorded in Matthew's Gospel, he points out that the practice of praying in the name of Christ, which is common among Christians today, did not begin with Jesus or his direct disciples. This began later with Paul after he elaborated the atonement theory of Christ's vicarious death on the cross. See Matsumura, ed., 道会バイブル [The Dōkai bible] (Tokyo: Dōkai Jimusho, 1928), 25.

15 See chapter three (48–51) for a brief discussion of Matsumura's open-ended canon and critical edition of the Bible.

16 There have been numerous printings of this booklet. I am using the postwar edition (Tokyo: Dōkai Shuppanbu, 1977).

17 Matsumura claims that the faith of The Way can be distinguished from traditional Christianity because it combines faith in the Other-Power of God with human effort and self-discipline; see *New Religion*, 82, 354–55.

18 The Christian theology of atonement, Matsumura argues, is something the Apostle Paul elaborated and cannot be found in the original teaching of Jesus. In this parable, no sacrificial death is required (see Matsumura, *The Dōkai Bible*, 75).

19 For helpful background on Yōmeigaku in the Tokugawa period and its influence on many Protestant leaders in the Meiji period, see 山下龍二 Yamashita Ryūji, 儒教の宗教的性格: 日本 [The religious character of Confucianism in Japan], in 日本宗教辞典 [Dictionary of Japanese religion] (Tokyo: Kōbundō, 1994 abridged version,) 499–500; Jan Van Bremen, "Neo-Confucianism in Japan: Heritage and Vista," *Senri Ethnological Studies* 29 (1990) 75–86; and Sumiya, *Christianity and the Formation of Modern Japan*, 26–28.

20 See *The Faith of The Way*, 32.

21 *Dōkai Guidebook*.

22 These ritual adaptations and guidelines for corporate and individual worship are described in *The Faith of The Way*, 14–23.

23 This appears in an article by Matsumura Kichisuke in *The Way*, 567–74 (1959), 7.

24 For details regarding these publications see the bibliographical guide to Kawai's works in the appendix.

25 Kawai's mentor, 押川方義 Oshikawa Masayoshi, was an important Christian figure during the Meiji period. Oshikawa (1851–1928) was the third son of a samurai family in Matsuyama. At the age of nineteen he went to Tokyo to study and eventually entered Yokohama Eigakkō run by Ballagh and Brown. Under their influence he professed the Christian faith and was baptized by Ballagh in 1872. With these missionaries and other early Japanese Christians he helped organize the first church in Yokohama. Following nine years of evangelistic work in Niigata, he moved to Sendai to assist W. E. Hoy in the establishment of Sendai The-

ological School (仙台神学校), which later became Tōhoku Gakuin. He left Tōhoku Gakuin in 1901 to become involved in politics, but was not very successful. The collection of correspondence (1026 letters) between Kawai and Oshikawa from 1893 to 1929 reveals their extremely close relationship (see 川合道雄 Kawai Michio, ed., 押川方義川合信水両先生往復書翰集 [Collected Correspondence between Oshikawa Masayoshi and Kawai Shinsui], Tokyo: Kirisuto Shin Shūdan, 1981). For more detailed information on the relationship between Kawai and Oshikawa, see 川合道雄 Kawai Michio, 武士の成ったキリスト者: 押川方義 [The samurai who became a Christian: Oshikawa Masayoshi] (Tokyo: Kindai Bungeisha, 1991).

26 See chapter three (38–39) for additional biographical details and discussion of Kawai's break with the mission churches.

27 Here I am quoting from *My Spiritual Experiences*, trans. Kawai Yoshinobu (Tokyo: Christ Heart Church, 1970), 13, the English translation of Kawai's 神の誠と吾が体験 [The sincerity of God and my experiences] (Tokyo: Kirisuto Shin Shūdan Shuppanbu, 1956).

28 *My Spiritual Experiences*, 14.

29 *My Spiritual Experiences*, 15.

30 Kawai Shinsui, 完全訓講話 [Lectures on the perfect teaching] (Tokyo: Kirisuto Shin Shūdan Shuppanbu, 1977), 1. This volume is based on lectures Kawai gave at Gunze Silk Company between 1925 and 1932, while he was director of education.

31 *My Spiritual Experiences*, 22–23; emphasis added. Kawai's communion with the spirit world was apparently not limited to his encounter with Confucius. According to one informant, Kawai was also involved in communication with other spirits through the medium (*reinōsha* 霊能者) Furuya Toyoko. Kawai recognized the spiritual power of Furuya and on a number of occasions had her bring back various spirits, including that of his son (who had died in the war), his mentor Oshikawa, as well as the spirits of the great Buddhist saint Dōgen. This informant also stated that Kawai regarded Dōgen as his protective spirit (守護神).

32 The Japanese expression here 一切の宗教の真善美を集めて, appears repeatedly in various publications of Christ Heart Church.

33 In his lectures on Galatians, Kawai points out that people often misunderstand him and think he teaches that all religions are the same because he so often quotes from Buddhist and Confucian sources. While they are not the same, Kawai maintains that they do share a great deal in common (共通の所) and this provides a good foundation for discussions of Christianity in the Japanese context. He makes this point in ガラテヤ書玄義 [The mysteries of Galatians] (Fujiyoshida: Kirisuto Shin Shūdan Jimukyoku Shuppanbu, 1965), 21–22. This volume is based on lectures Kawai gave during morning worship services at Gunze (1928–1929).

34 In addition to Kawai Shinsui's writings, in this section I am particularly indebted to helpful discussions and interviews with Kawai Hideo, the founder's grandson and current head of Christ Heart Church.

35 Kawai, *Lectures on the Perfect Teaching*, 232.

36 Kawai, *Lectures on the Perfect Teaching*, 108 and 222.

37 Here, Kawai's interpretation departs from the Protestant tradition and more closely resembles the Catholic teaching regarding purgatory.

38 The Japanese term here is 完全信仰. This is how he defines his teaching in the small booklet 信者心得 [Rules for believers] (Fujiyoshida: Kirisuto Shinshū Kyōdan Jimukyoku Shuppanbu,1940). The same expression reappears in many of his lectures and writings.

39 In a lecture on the "Sermon on the Mount" (19 March 1961) Kawai explained that he could not accept the recent German theology that rejected the divinity of Christ and that he continued to follow the incarnational theology (i.e., "the Word became flesh") found in the Gospel of John. This lecture was republished in the church's magazine 基督の心 [The mind of Christ] 191 (1993), 10–11.

40 This appears in an explanatory note in his *A Eulogy on Jesus Christ,* trans. Kawai Yoshinobu (Tokyo: Christ Heart Church, 1961), 68–69.

41 安井英二 Yasui Eiji, ed., 山月川合信水先生御教話覚書 [A memorandum of talks by Sangetsu Kawai Shinsui] (Tokyo: Kirisuto Shin Shūdan Shuppanbu, 1969), 154. This is a collection of lectures, sermons, and talks given by Kawai at various locations from 1940 to 1962.

42 The *locus classicus* for this model of discipleship in the New Testament is Luke 6:40: "A disciple is not above the teacher, but everyone who is fully qualified will be like the teacher."

43 While the Pure Land tradition has a negative connotation for Kawai, it is interesting to recall here that this was the Japanese Buddhist tradition for which Uchimura Kanzō had such high regard (see chapter four, 64–66).

44 See Yasui, *A Memorandum of Talks by Sangetsu Kawai Shinsui*, 198.

45 In the introduction to 耶蘇基督讃 [A eulogy on Jesus Christ] (Tokyo: Kobundo, 1927), for example, Kawai recounts how moved he was by a letter written by Francis Xavier to one of his disciples, prior to his departure for mission work in Japan in the sixteenth century. In this letter Xavier instructed his disciple to continue ascetic practices and to meditate every morning on the life of Christ. Kawai explains that he wrote *A Eulogy on Jesus Christ* so that Japanese Christians could pursue a similar path of discipline.

46 The English translation of the creed appears in Kawai's *My Spiritual Experiences*, 30; emphasis added.

47 This is referred to as his 開宗宣言 [Inaugural proclamation] and recorded in *A Eulogy on Jesus Christ* (1927), 23, 236–38.

48 Kawai claims that it is the first time in the history of Christianity that this kind of composition on the life of Christ has been attempted. He notes, however, that his work resembles a similar text on Aśvagoṣa's life of Buddha, *Buddhacarita*, though the latter is much longer and reads more like a biography (see the introduction to the 1927 version, 9).

49 The following synopsis is based on a more detailed discussion of the meaning of these vows found in Kawai's lecture, 主の祈りと七大誓願 [The Lord's prayer and the seven great vows], given on 3 April 1960, and reprinted in *The Mind of Christ* 174 (1990), 1–14. The earliest version of the Vows was published in 1939 and was entitled the "Six Great Vows"

(六大誓願). It did not include the fifth vow of the final version published in 1951, which is recognized as a part of the official church canon today.

50 The original Buddhist vows may be given as: (1) I vow to save boundless numbers of sentient beings; (2) I vow to extinguish innumerable evil passions; (3) I vow to study all the inexhaustible Buddhist teachings; and (4) I vow to attain the supreme Buddha way. Cited from Hisao Inagaki, *A Dictionary of Japanese Buddhist Terms* (Kyoto: Nagata Bunshōdō, 1992), 522.

51 Kawai also claims that the Seven Great Vows and Prayers supersede even the Lord's Prayer recorded in the New Testament. This is because, unlike the Lord's Prayer, the Vows include the additional commitment to love and respect God's Son.

52 This is an adaptation of the first of the four vows of the Buddha (see note 50 above), to save boundless numbers of sentient beings. Kawai explains that he added the word 万物, the whole universe, to this vow in order to incorporate the Apostle Paul's teaching that all of creation groans and waits for the appearance of the children of God (Romans 8:19–21). Kawai explains that this vow includes the intention to work for the salvation of all sentient beings, but at the same time to seek to preserve and cultivate all created things, such as trees, plants, water, and mountains.

53 The following summary draws on Kawai Shinsui's writings as well as sermons, lectures, interviews, and instruction by Kawai Hideo, the grandson of the founder and current head of Christ Heart Church.

54 At a training session during the annual retreat several years ago, Kawai Hideo distributed a handout with the founder's teaching regarding meditation (御教訓瞑想) and provided the following instructions:

At the initial stage of meditation it is best to close one's eyes, since external things easily lead to distraction. After some practice, one should be able to meditate with one's eyes open without being distracted. As the focus (題目) for one's meditation, one should concentrate on offering one's self as a "living sacrifice to God." Keeping the proper posture is very important. One should not be "thinking with the mind" (頭で考えず) or "feeling with the heart" (胸で感ぜず), but concentrate or think with the guts or stomach (腹で思う). One is not using "reason" (道理) to think about being a "living sacrifice"; you simply are a living sacrifice. If one is sitting in meditation on a chair, consider the chair to be the altar and one's body the offering to God. Through this process one will become quiet and pure. In time this will lead to the experience of union with God. One should not be preoccupied with achieving this experience of *satori*, for God will give it to you when the time is right; that is, when you have prepared an appropriate place, that is, a heart of sincerity and good faith. (Author's fieldnotes)

55 See his lecture, "My Spiritual Experiences," given in Sendai on 1 October 1961, and recently republished in the Christ Heart Church magazine *The Mind of Christ* 191 (1995), 24.

56 Kawai, *Lectures on the Perfect Teaching*, 100.

57 Takahashi's own account of her pilgrimage was published after her death as 嗚呼神恩無量 [Calling on the immeasurable goodness of God] (Tokyo: Christ Heart Church, 1952).

In a lengthy postscript (341–460), Kawai Shinsui explains that the way of Christ includes feminine beauty and virtue (女性美), which Takahashi fully expressed in her life of faith.

58 My guess is that the ritual places so much emphasis on Other-Power that its observance would distract members from the primary task of self-cultivation.

59 *Kyōkenjutsu* training began as a part of the educational program for both men and women at Gunze Silk Factory. It was carried over into Christ Heart Church as another helpful discipline for training and exercising the body. Kawai's brother was primarily responsible for this aspect of the movement, and he taught his own particular type of *kyōkenjutsu*, known as *Hidashiki kyōkenjutsu* 肥田式強健術, using his adopted name. It is not nearly as common today, but instruction for men is still provided at the annual retreat and training program.

60 The *Shingaku* movement was founded by Ishida Baigan (1685–1744) and mobilized into a nationwide movement by his disciple and successor, Teshima Tōan (1718–1786). For helpful resources on this movement, see Robert Bellah's well-known study, *Tokugawa Religion: The Values of Pre-Industrial Japan* (Boston: Beacon Press, 1970), and the more recent study by Janine Anderson Sawada, *Confucian Values and Popular Zen: Sekimon Shingaku in Eighteenth-Century Japan* (Honolulu: University of Hawai'i Press, 1993).

61 See Shimazono, *Salvation Religions in Contemporary Society*, 55–76, and Hardacre, *Kurozumikyō and the New Religions of Japan*, 16–31.

Chapter 6: Japanese Versions of Apostolic Christianity

1 Ikado Fujio's analysis of the education levels and social status of Protestant church members has shown that this stereotype is not without foundation; see his *Religion in a Secular Society*, esp. 292ff.

2 Tetsunao Yamamori, *Church Growth in Japan*, 53.

3 Ariga Tetsutarō, "From Confucius to Christ: A Feature of Early Protestantism in Japan," *Japanese Religions* 2/2–3 (1961), 11.

4 *Christianity: The Japanese Way*, 208.

5 吉山 宏 Yoshiyama Hiroshi, ed., 御霊に導かれて: 創立三十年 [Led by the Spirit: A history of the first thirty years] (Tokyo: Japan Assemblies of God, 1979), 23.

6 This is mentioned in Murai Jun's sermon on the Lord's Supper preached at Nakai Spirit of Jesus Church on 20 August 1962.

7 In his study of Pentecostal movements in China, Daniel H. Bays notes that a 1919 doctrinal statement of the True Jesus Church defined its beliefs, practices, and membership requirements as follows:

    1. receive full immersion face-down baptism;
    2. seek the baptism of the Holy Spirit, with speaking in tongues as evidence;
    3. keep Saturday as the Sabbath for worship;
    4. seek the power of healing and of exorcising demons;
    5. in communion break the bread, not cut it;
    6. implement the sacrament of foot-washing among church members;

7. have ordination by the laying on of hands;

8. have no time limit for Sabbath worship;

9. all have the right to speak during services;

10. all be permitted to pray aloud during services;

11. seek revelation of the Holy Spirit in choosing overseers (*jiandu*, "bishops"), elders (*zhanglao*), and deacons (*zhishi*);

12. if evangelists, not receive a set salary;

13. devote their heart, spirit, and livelihood to the Lord, and give at least 10 percent of their income.

In a subsequent statement, the True Jesus Church also instructed other churches to purify themselves by teaching the unitary and undivided (*shu'i wu'er*) "true God" and to "baptize only in the name of Jesus," rather than persisting in teaching the man-made doctrine of the Trinity (*sanwei iti*). Murai's adoption of several of these doctrines and practices led to his separation from the Japan Bible Church upon his return to Japan. Cited from Daniel H. Bays, "Indigenous Protestant Churches in China, 1900–1937: A Pentecostal Case Study," in Steven Kaplan, ed., *Indigenous Responses to Western Christianity* (New York: New York University Press, 1995), 134–35. For additional background on the True Jesus Church, see Murray A. Rubinstein, *The Protestant Community on Modern Taiwan: Mission, Seminary, and Church* (New York: M. E. Sharpe, 1991).

8 For one treatment of the "Jesus-only" unitarianism within North American Pentecostalism, see Thomas A. Robinson, "The Conservative Nature of Dissent in Early Pentecostalism: A Study of Charles F. Parham, the Founder of the Pentecostal Movement," in Malcolm R. Greenshields and Thomas A. Robinson, eds., *Orthodoxy and Heresy in Religious Movements: Discipline and Dissent* (Lewiston: Edwin Mellen Press, 1992), 134–61.

9 Bays, "Indigenous Protestant Churches in China, 1900–1937: A Pentecostal Case Study," 137–38.

10 C. Norman Kraus, "Dispensationalism," in Mark A. Noll and Nathan O. Hatch, eds., *Eerdmans Handbook to Christianity* (Grand Rapids: Eerdmans, 1983), 327–30.

11 J. D. Douglas, ed., *The New International Dictionary of the Christian Church* (Grand Rapids: Zondervan Corporation, 1974), 103.

12 While adult converts are usually baptized immediately, the church does practice infant baptism for the children of members. This practice probably reflects Murai's own early background in the Methodist Church. Unlike other churches, however, there is no special education for confirmation of faith later in life. It is simply expected that children will eventually receive spirit baptism and speak in tongues as they grow up in the church.

13 In their forthcoming book, *Practically Religious: Worldly Benefits and the Common Religion of Japan* (Honolulu: University of Hawai'i Press), Ian Reader and George J. Tanabe, Jr., suggest that one of the reasons that the Christian churches have failed to make much headway in Japanese society is their failure to take seriously the "common religion of Japan." The Spirit of Jesus Church is clearly one exception to this general pattern. I am indebted to Ian Reader for sharing portions of this manuscript with me prior to publication.

14 The Spirit of Jesus hymnbook, 霊讃歌 [Spirit hymns], also reflects this concern for healing and various miracles (see hymns 18 and 28).

15 Here I am indebted to Anzai Shin's informative analysis of the Spirit of Jesus Church in Okinawa in his *The Acceptance of Christianity in the Southern Islands*, 1984, 125–26.

16 One pastor reminded me in an interview that it was Judas, the "treasurer," who caused Jesus so much trouble. In other words, it is best not to entrust laity with heavy responsibility in financial matters.

17 The influence of Jewish tradition is also apparent in other areas of the Spirit of Jesus Church. For example, this church observes the Sabbath as the primary day of worship (although they still hold meetings on Sunday). Also, "unleavened bread" must be prepared for the sacrament of the Lord's Supper.

18 See his イエス之御霊教会: 沖縄伝道の諸相 [The Spirit of Jesus Church: Aspects of evangelism in Okinawa], in Wakimoto Tsuneya 脇本平也, ed., 宗教と歴史 [Religion and history] (Tokyo: Yamamoto Shoten, 1977), 42.

19 Yamamori, *Church Growth in Japan*, 118–19; I have also relied on Yamamori for a synopsis of Holiness Church growth (especially 116–22). Apparently, Nakada's interpretation of various passages in the Bible "included the idea that the Japanese people were probably a part of one of the Ten Lost Tribes of Israel. Thus at the Second Coming of Christ the Japanese, too, would enter into the same blessings promised to the Israelites with the restoration of their nation." See John Jennings Merwin, "The Oriental Missionary Society Holiness Church in Japan, 1901–1983" (Pasadena: Doctor of Missiology Thesis, School of World Mission, Fuller Theological Seminary, 1983), 379.

20 This is recorded in the volume of Ōtsuki's recollections, リバイバルの軌跡 [The tracks of revival], edited by Satō Toshio 佐藤捷雄 (Kyoto: Sei Iesu Kai Logos Sha, 1996), 66–67.

21 In the following account, I am drawing on several interviews with Father Ōtsuki, selections from his 言泉集 *Gensenshū* (a seventeen-volume collection of his writings, sermons, and lectures) and various church publications.

22 Ōtsuki, for example, refers to Isaiah's vision of God in the temple: "And I said: 'Woe is me! I am lost, for I am a man of unclean lips, and I live among a people of unclean lips; yet *my eyes have seen the King*, the Lord of hosts!' Then one of the seraphs flew to me, holding a live coal that had been taken from the altar with a pair of tongs. The seraph touched my mouth with it and said: 'Now that this has touched your lips, your guilt has departed and your sin is blotted out'" (Isaiah 6:5–7). Another passage he found expressive of his own experience is recorded in Ezekiel: "...the heavens were opened, and I saw visions of God" (1:1). "So I opened my mouth, and he gave me the scroll to eat. He said to me, Mortal, eat this scroll that I give you and fill your stomach with it. Then I ate it; and in my mouth it was as sweet as honey" (3:2–3). For more details, see his account in *The Tracks of Revival*, 109–13.

23 変わって新しい人となる [To change and become a new person], *Logos* 138 (1996), 27.

24 While the founder frequently presents additional revelations from God, some guidelines are observed in order to prevent the movement from falling into heresy. Both clergy and laity who claim to have received a special revelation from God must present it for considera-

tion to the leadership of the church (教授会) and receive approval from the bishop before speaking about it in public. This may be found in 聖イエス会教規 [Regulations of the Holy Ecclesia of Jesus] (Kyoto: Holy Ecclesia of Jesus, 1996), 5.

25 Holy Ecclesia of Jesus publications suggest that the Apostle Thomas spread "authentic" Christianity (i.e., "calling on the name") to the East and may have influenced the development of a new form of Buddhism in China, the Amida faith, which eventually became a popular form of Buddhism in Japan. See, for example, ぶどう樹: 伝道用ダイジェスト版 [The grapevine: a compilation for evangelistic use] (Kyoto: Logos Publishing Company, 1991), 105.

26 The basic expression used to refer to this conversion and life-transforming experience is 御名による神との出会い, encountering God through his holy name. This is the central teaching of this movement and elaborated in the founder's writings and numerous church publications. See, for example, one of the texts used for theological education, みことばに仕える: 聖書教理入門講座1, 聖書論 [Serving the word: An introduction to Biblical doctrine, vol. 1, Doctrine of Holy Scripture] (Kyoto: Logos Publishing, 1974), 5–11; *The Grapevine*, 78–108.

27 For background on the early development of *nembutsu* in Japan, see Hori Ichiro, *Folk Religion in Japan*, 73–74, and chapter three.

28 Ōtsuki grew up in this religious atmosphere and recalls that on the occasion of his mother's untimely death his father sat quietly beside her chanting *Namu Amida Butsu* (see *The Tracks of Revival*, 49).

29 William J. Jackson, "Name-Devotion in Indian Religions and Kaveri Delta Namasiddhanta," *Journal for the Study of Religions* 7/2 (1994), 33, 42; emphasis added.

30 For a concise statement on the centrality of healing to the mission of the church, see 山根元一 Yamane Motoichi, イエスの名による完全な救いと癒し [Complete salvation and healing in the name of Jesus], *Logos* 138 (1996), 1–5. It should be noted that the Holy Ecclesia of Jesus distances itself from Pentecostal movements and does not recognize speaking in tongues as a valid manifestation of spirit baptism.

31 During the Tokugawa period, the *kakure kirishitan* ("hidden Christians") resorted to concealing Christian symbols in statues of Buddha in order surreptitiously to continue practicing the foreign religion proscribed by the authorities. As Neil S. Fujita explains: "engravings of the Madonna with the baby Jesus were modified to look like a representation of Kannon (the embodiment of Buddha's mercy) holding a child. The sign of the cross was often concealed at the back of a Buddha's statue." *Japan's Encounter with Christianity: The Catholic Mission in Pre-Modern Japan* (New York: Paulist Press, 1991), 238. It was one of these statues that was apparently discovered at the site of this healing spring.

32 A testimonial by one member who followed these methods and experienced healing is recorded in the church paper, *The Grapevine* 453 (11 November 1993). In addition to the testimonial, this issue also provides a brief description of the miraculous spring and compares it to a similar manifestation in the nineteenth century in Lourdes, France.

33 Ōtsuki writes that he abandoned his mistaken and warped view of the Roman Catholic tradition after reading the diary of Ignatius of Loyola, whom he came to regard as a great spiritual leader. This led him to reconsider many aspects of the Catholic tradition that have been

disregarded by most Protestants, including the saints and mystics as models for Christian spirituality and the important role of Mary in salvation history. Ōtsuki's new appreciation of Roman Catholic spirituality is expressed most clearly in his recent collection of meditations 聖地賛歌 [Meditations on the Holy Land] (Kyoto: Sei Iesu Kai Logos Sha, 1993).

34 While all followers are encouraged to prepare a written confession, it is not something that is rigorously checked before individuals are allowed to participate in the communion service. Individual pastors submit their written confessions to the *shiboku* (司牧, bishop or president of the Holy Ecclesia of Jesus).

35 While Father Ōtsuki is still living and recognized as the spiritual guide of the movement, he no longer holds an official position in the church. His son, Ōtsuki Masaru, now holds the highest office of *shiboku* (see note 34 above). Ordained clergy are responsible for the selection of the bishop at the general meeting. At this meeting twenty-four ministers are also elected to serve as representatives on the church council. This council then selects five ministers to serve as elders, who are responsible for ministerial assignments for the entire church. The bishop, nevertheless, continues to exercise considerable authority. Clergy are expected to receive the bishop's approval before distributing any publications that have not already received the church's endorsement. Likewise, the bishop's prior approval is required for all special events sponsored by the ministers of local churches, such as films or guest speakers invited from outside the church.

Ordained leaders are referred to as clergy (聖職者 *seishokusha*) and divided into pastors (牧師 *bokushi*, men) and teachers (正教師 *seikyōshi*, women), all of whom are graduates of Logos Theological Seminary. Each May the church holds a three-day seminar for members seriously considering entering the ministry. The minimum requirements for applying to the program for ministerial preparation are the experience of the indwelling Christ, a clear sense of God's call to ministry, and graduation from either a university or junior college. As many as 100 attend this seminar each year to explore the possibility of training for the ministry and between twenty and thirty apply for admission. Of that number, only ten candidates are selected for admission to the four-year study program at Logos Theological Seminary.

36 This teaching is based on the following New Testament passage: "And all of us, with unveiled faces, seeing the glory of the Lord as though reflected in a mirror, are being transformed into the same image from one degree of glory to another; for this comes from the Lord, the Spirit" (2 Cor 3:18). It is by the indwelling of the Spirit and practice of spiritual disciplines that we can be remade in the image (icon) of God. In recent years, Ōtsuki has borrowed from the Greek Orthodox tradition to refer to this process as divinization (神化) and the Christification of the self (自己のキリスト化). In sum, the goal of the Christian life is sainthood.

37 Compared with other Protestant churches, the Holy Ecclesia of Jesus places far greater emphasis on the notion that the ordained clergy are a special priesthood set apart from the laity for religious work. To symbolize this distinctive identity, the church requires religious leaders to wear special clothing designed by Father Ōtsuki. For those who satisfactorily complete the first year of training at Logos there is a special service for putting on the religious garments for the first time.

38 It is interesting to note that religious diffusion over kinship ties is prominent at the leadership level within this movement just as in the Spirit of Jesus Church. The percentage of

ordained clergy from the Matsuda and Ōtsuka families is particularly striking. One evangelist informed me, for example, that following her parents' conversion to the Holy Ecclesia of Jesus, five of their seven children received the call to ministry, attended Logos Theological Seminary, and entered full-time Christian ministry. Ten of her cousins have also been trained and ordained as clergy.

39 Regarding Nakada's views, David G. Goodman and Masanori Miyazawa explain that he "believed the Holiness Church had a unique role to play in the realization of Japan's divine mission. 'If we love our nation and fellow-countrymen,' he preached, 'we should pray ever more earnestly for the Jews.' The Holiness Church had been praying fervently for the salvation of the Jews and had been making monthly contributions on their behalf, and Nakada was convinced God would take notice of these devotions." *Jews in the Japanese Mind: The History and Uses of a Cultural Stereotype* (New York: The Free Press, 1995), 55.

40 These revelations are recorded in 聖なる道 [The holy way], *Gensenshū* vol. 2, 335, and *The Tracks of Revival*, 123.

41 Ōtsuki sees the debate that has gone on among Christians and Jews for nearly two thousand years over the identity of the Messiah as futile. At this time it is more important to simply pray for the coming of the Messiah. His identity will be clear enough to all people at his coming. Although the Holy Ecclesia of Jesus does attempt to evangelize the Jews, Ōtsuki teaches that the movement will somehow have a role to play in fulfilling the prophecy regarding the 144,000 people of Israel who will be marked by God's seal (Rev 7:2).

42 All of these efforts represent Ōtsuki's concern to follow the example of the Apostle Paul, who sought to be "all things to all men" and "give no offense to Jews or Greeks" (1 Cor 9:20–21, 10:32–33). Out of respect to the Jews, therefore, Ōtsuki wears a yarmulke when receiving Jewish visitors and makes a point not to wear a clerical collar, which for many symbolizes centuries of persecution by the established church. In recent years Father Ōtsuki rarely appears without the yarmulke (even when receiving a "gentile" visitor like myself).

43 A report of this concert tour is contained in the church magazine あかしびと [The witness] 75 (1996), 16–31.

44 For another brief description of these activities, see Ben-Ami Shillony, *The Jews and the Japanese: The Successful Outsiders* (Tokyo: Charles E. Tuttle, 1991), 212–13.

45 Part of the inspiration for establishing this center came from the moving encounter the director had with the father of Anne Frank in Europe some twenty-five years ago. In their conversations, Otto Frank challenged Rev. Ōtsuka Makoto not just to feel sorry for the death of his daughter and many others but to do something on behalf of peace.

46 Reported in *The Japan Times*, 19 June 1995, 2.

47 Interview notes, 22 May 1996, Rev. Ōtsuka Makoto; and ガイドブック: ホロコスト記念館 [Guidebook: The Holocaust Memorial Hall] (Kyoto: Logos Publishing, 1995).

48 The week before Pentecost, for example, Holy Ecclesia of Jesus churches hold prayer meetings every night to ask God to pour out his spirit on themselves and on Jerusalem, chanting "Come Holy Spirit, Come to Jerusalem, O Holy Spirit."

49 聖イエス会讃美歌 [The Holy Ecclesia of Jesus hymnbook] (Kyoto: Sei Iesu Kai Logos Publishing, 1990).

50 Even the Japanese garden at Logos Theological Seminary was designed by the founder in the shape of the Holy Land, with streams and ponds representing the Jordan river and the Sea of Galilee—one more way of reminding the movement of its spiritual roots and final goal.

51 In 1982 the church published 楽しい家庭のシャバット [A joyful household sabbath] (Kyoto: Sei Iesu Kai Logos Sha, 1982), a short booklet and cassette that provided simple guidelines for observing family worship in the home, including instructions on lighting the candles, singing songs in Hebrew and Japanese, words for the blessing of children, blessing and thanksgiving to the wife, and prayers before and after dinner. The introduction explains that this tradition has held together the Jewish people for 3,500 years and points out that Jesus Christ was also raised in this tradition. Readers are assured that following this ritual of family worship will help preserve peace and harmony in their own family in a society characterized by widespread divorce and family conflict. I should point out that observances related to the Jewish calendar and traditions are more likely to be observed by members in the Kansai area, who have more frequent contact with Jewish guests visiting the headquarters in Kyoto. The students enrolled in Logos Theological Seminary observe the sabbath ritual and dinner each Friday evening and look forward to this weekly celebration. One of my most unusual experiences as a field researcher was to participate in this Japanese version of sabbath in the secluded seminary in the mountains outside of Kyoto with Japanese seminarians singing and praying in Hebrew.

52 See his *Meditations on the Holy Land*. This collection of meditations is based on Ōtsuki's three pilgrimages. It is divided into sections on the Holy Land, Europe, and Greece and Asia Minor, reflecting his special interest in Israel as well as his concern to recover the valuable insights and examples of Roman Catholic and Orthodox spirituality as seen in the lives of the mystics and saints.

53 A *furoshiki* 風呂敷 is a multipurpose cloth, typically between eighteen and twenty-four inches square, used to wrap up and carry items in lieu of a bag. As the Chinese characters suggest, the term was originally used to refer to a cloth used to gather up one's personal effects at a public bath. The prefix *ō-* in this case means "large."

54 Two other movements based on Nonchurch Christianity are the *Nihon Kirisuto Shōdan* (Japan Ecclesia of Christ), founded by Koike Tatsuo in 1940, and *Ikasu Kirisuto* (Life-Giving Christ), founded by Imahashi Atsushi in 1966. Imahashi was a part of the Original Gospel movement but was forced to leave following a serious disagreement with Teshima.

55 For resources in English, see the sociological study by Carlo Caldarola, "The Makuya Christian Movement," *Japanese Religions* 7/4 (1972), 18–34; and chapter 7 of his *Christianity: The Japanese Way*, 192–208; 馬場俊彦 Baba Toshihiko, "Problems of Charismatic Religion: The Case of the Original Gospel Movement," 名城大学人文紀 5 (1967), 1–32, which is a critical analysis of Teshima and his movement by a professor of philosophy who was once a close disciple of Teshima and editor of the magazine 生命之光 [Light of life]. The movement has also published two of Teshima's works in English: *The Love of the Holy Spirit* (Tokyo: The Makuya Bible Seminary, 1991), a translation of his first book 聖霊の愛, originally published

in 1950; and *An Introduction to the Original Gospel Faith* (Tokyo: Makuya Bible Seminary, 1970). This volume includes an essay by Otto Piper, Professor Emeritus of Princeton Theological Seminary, who suggests that the Original Gospel is an indigenous Christian movement that represents a significant "third force" in Japanese Protestantism. *Makuya and Israel: In Memory of Abraham I. Teshima* (Tokyo: Makuya Bible Seminary, 1976), is a memorial collection of photographs and accounts of Teshima's involvements with Israel and Zionism published several years after his death.

56 Teshima Ikurō, *An Introduction to the Original Gospel Faith* (Tokyo: Light of Life Press, 1970), 45.

57 手島郁郎 Teshima Ikurō, 日本民族と原始福音 [The Japanese people and the original gospel] (Tokyo: Kirisuto Seisho Juku, 1984), 190.

58 Teshima, *The Japanese People and the Original Gospel*, 20–24.

59 These magazines are so important for Nonchurch groups that Ohara Shin refers to this movement as a "paper-Church":

> Uchimura and his close followers who became *sensei* in the Sunday lectures usually published their own small monthly magazines, which were sent directly to each participant's home. Mukyokai can therefore be called a "paper-Church" in the sense that the magazines keep alive the relationship between a *sensei* and followers. The members dislike sacraments, but they value the magazines and books and are eager to receive their teacher's periodic publications.

See his essay, "The Thought of Uchimura Kanzō and Its Relevance to Contemporary American Religion," in Ray A. Moore, ed., *Culture and Religion in Japanese-American Relations: Essays on Uchimura Kanzō, 1861–1930* (Ann Arbor: Center for Japanese Studies, The University of Michigan, 1981), 125.

60 Teshima's biographer and close disciple, 吉村騎一郎 Yoshimura Kiichirō, stresses that this "Makuya Pentecost" marks the starting point of the Original Gospel as an independent movement; see his わが師手島郁郎 [My teacher, Teshima Ikurō] (Tokyo: Kirisuto Seisho Juku, 1990), 184.

61 Quoted in 無教会史 3, 第三期: 結集の時代 [Mukyōkai history, vol. 3, The third period: Age of concentration], edited by the Mukyōkai Historical Association (Tokyo: Shinkyō Shuppansha, 1995), 158.

62 See 高橋三郎 Takahashi Saburō, 無教会精神の探究 [In search of the spirit of Mukyōkai] (Tokyo: Shinkyō Shuppansha, 1970), 197.

63 On this trip he made contact with Pentecostal leaders in the United States, among them Oral Roberts, and was impressed to discover that the apostolic faith was still alive in the West.

64 Two of Teshima's sons, in fact, completed degrees at the Hebrew University of Jerusalem before proceeding to the United States for doctoral studies. One completed his doctorate under Abraham Heschel at the Jewish Theological Seminary in New York. Another went on to complete doctoral studies in Hebrew Literature and Jewish hermeneutics at Harvard University.

65 In Japanese this practice is referred to as 無銭徒歩伝道 *musentoho dendō*. Testimonies regarding the spiritual benefits of these "evangelistic walks" appear from time to time in the Original Gospel magazine *Light of Life*.

66 See Isaiah Teshima, "Abraham Teshima's Makuya and Pinchas Peli," *Jewish Spectator* 54/4 (1990), 57–60, an article by the founder's son that provides helpful insight into the Zionistic orientation of the movement.

67 For a description of various Original Gospel activities in relation to Israel see *Light of Life* 512 (1994), and Caldarola, *Christianity: The Japanese Way*, 203–4.

68 See the 幕屋聖歌集 [Makuya hymnbook] (Tokyo: The Committee for the Makuya Hymnbook, 1992).

69 Teshima, *The Japanese People and the Original Gospel*, 27.

70 Teshima, *The Love of the Holy Spirit*, 13.

71 The Japanese phrase he uses here is 人間らしい人間. See Teshima, *The Japanese People and the Original Gospel*, 31–32.

72 Teshima,*The Japanese People and the Original Gospel*, 55.

73 This explanation was provided by Dr. Yūrō Jacob Teshima, the founder's second son; the same development is also noted by Yoshimura Kiichirō, *My Teacher, Teshima Ikurō*, 298.

74 This point has also been widely recognized by scholars outside of Teshima's circle. See, for example, Goodman and Miyazawa, *Jews in the Japanese Mind*, 40–46, and Doron B. Cohen, "Uchimura Kanzō on Jews and Zionism," *Japan Christian Review* 1 (1992), 111–20.

75 For some examples, see *Light of Life* 521 (1995) and 538 (1997).

76 手島千代 Teshima Chiyo, ああ、日本! 紀元節に寄せて [Oh Japan! On the occasion of founding day] *Light of Life* 537 (1997), 13–17.

77 See 長原 眞 Nagahara Shin, アイデンタティの確立 [The establishment of identity], *Light of Life* 533 (1996), 40–45.

Chapter 7: Japanese Christians and the World of the Dead

1 Hori, *Folk Religion in Japan*, 18.

2 Miyake Hitoshi, "Folk Religion," in Tamaru and Reid, eds., *Religion in Japanese Culture*, 80.

3 Morioka Kiyomi, "Ancestor Worship in Contemporary Japan: Continuity and Change," in George A. DeVos and Takao Sofue, eds., *Religion and Family in East Asia* (Los Angeles: University of California Press, 1984), 201.

4 Robert J. Smith, *Ancestor Worship in Contemporary Japan* (Stanford: Stanford University Press, 1974), 44.

5 Hoshino Eiki and Takeda Dōshō, "*Mizuko Kuyō* and Abortion in Contemporary Japan," in Mullins, Shimazono, and Swanson, eds., *Religion and Society in Modern Japan*, 174–75.

6 For treatment of changes in the ancestral cult, see Smith, *Ancestor Worship in Contemporary Japan*, 220–26; Morioka, "Ancestor Worship in Contemporary Japan," 206; Hardacre, *Lay Buddhism in Contemporary Japan,* 101–3; 孝本 貢 Kōmoto Mitsugu, 現代都市の民俗信仰 [Folk religion in the modern city], in Ōmura and Nishiyama, eds., *The Religion of People Today*, 49; 71–74.

7 *The Religious Consciousness of the Japanese*. For a helpful review of the NHK survey results in English, see Swyngedouw, "The Quiet Reversal," 4–13.

8 A more recent review of various opinion polls on Japanese religious beliefs also found that ancestral concerns and spirit beliefs remain strong. Fleur Wöss concluded that "belief in continuing family ties beyond death is still one of the pillars of Japanese religious sentiment.... The majority believe that the *reikon* separates itself from the dead body and becomes a benevolent ancestor, provided that the proper rituals are conducted by family members." Furthermore, he found that spirit belief was particularly high among young people: "Three-quarters of teenagers believe in the existence of *yūrei*—spirits, the same percentage in the curse of malevolent spirits in general." "When Blossoms Fall, Japanese Attitudes towards Death and the Otherworld: Opinion Polls 1953–1987," in Roger Goodman and Kirsten Refsing, eds., *Ideology and Practice in Modern Japan* (London: Routledge, 1992), 94–95.

9 For this line of argument see Shimazono Susumu, "Spirit-belief in New Religious Movements and Popular Culture: The Case of Japan's New Religions," *The Journal of Oriental Philosophy* 26/1 (1987); Kōmoto, "Folk Religion in the Modern City," and 井上順孝 Inoue Nobutaka, 情報化時代の民俗宗教 [Folk religion in the information age], in 日本の民俗宗教 [Japan's folk religion] (Tokyo: Niwano Foundation, Research Forum, 1992).

10 Hardacre, *Lay Buddhism in Contemporary Japan* (chapter four) and *Kurozumikyō and the New Religions of Japan*, 151, 173–76; Earhart, *Gedatsu-Kai and Religion in Contemporary Japan*, 172–90; Winston Davis, *Dōjō: Magic and Exorcism in Modern Japan*, 41–46; and Ian Reader, "The Rise of a Japanese 'New New Religion': Themes in the Development of Agonshū," *Japanese Journal of Religious Studies* 15/4 (1988), 238–40.

11 Hardacre, *Lay Buddhism in Contemporary Japan,* 106.

12 See Hoshino Eiki and Takeda Dōshō, "*Mizuko Kuyō* and Abortion in Contemporary Japan," in Mullins et al., *Religion and Society in Modern Japan*, 171–90, and Richard Fox Young, "Abortion, Grief and Consolation: Prolegomena to a Christian Response to *Mizuko Kuyō*," *Japan Christian Quarterly* 55/1 (1989).

13 黒田みのる Kuroda Minoru, 霊を売る女 [The woman who sells souls] (Tokyo: Tōen Shobō, 1990).

14 See, for example, 中牧弘允 Nakamaki Hirochika, 宗教に何がおきているか [What is happening in religion?] (Tokyo: Heibonsha, 1990); and David C. Lewis, "Religious Rites in a Japanese Factory," in Mullins et al., *Religion and Society in Modern Japan*, 157–70.

15 Dickson Kazuo Yagi, "Protestant Perspectives on Ancestor Worship in Japanese Buddhism: The Funeral and the Buddhist Altar," *Japanese Religions* 15/1 (1988), 30.

16 Morioka, *Japan's Modern Society and Christianity,* 101–12; 142–43.

17 Reid, *New Wine,* 108–9. In this section I am drawing on Reid's helpful explanation of linear and cyclical rites for the dead, especially 103–7.

18 One Uchimura scholar, for example, notes that the well-known disciple of Uchimura, Yanaihara Tadao, visited his teacher shortly after the death of his father to inquire about the fate of those who died without encountering Christ in this life. Uchimura candidly replied that this was something for which he had no answer (see Ohara, *The Life of Uchimura Kanzō,* 257).

19 Anzai gives considerable attention to the negative approach of the Spirit of Jesus Church in his book, *The Acceptance of Christianity in the Southern Islands.* The Okinawa Christian Gospel movement takes a similarly hard line regarding the traditional ancestral cult (see Ikegami, *A Stage for Demons and the Holy Spirit,* 66–67).

20 ぶどう樹 [The grapevine] (Kyoto: Logos Publishing Company, 1991), 148.

21 生命之光 [Light of life] 500 (1993), 136–43.

22 Written in the church bulletin, for example, as 召天一周年, 二周年 (i.e., first- or second-year memorial since being "called to heaven").

23 The founder of the Sanctifying Christ Church (聖成基督教団), for example, has written hymns commemorating the first anniversary of the death of his father and the tenth anniversary of the death of his mother, as well as a special hymn commemorating the tenth-year anniversary since the church built a crypt at a cemetery in Kōbe.

24 Berentsen, *Grave and Gospel,* 196–98.

25 See Reid, *New Wine*; Nishiyama, "Indigenization and Transformation of Christianity in a Japanese Community"; Doerner, "Comparative Analysis of Life after Death in Folk Shinto and Christianity"; and Luttio, "The Passage of Death in the Japanese Context."

26 See *Jesus: A New Vision* (San Francisco: Harper Collins, 1987), 225–26.

27 杉田好太郎 Sugita Kōtarō, 栄光の福音後篇 [The glorious gospel, part 2] (Aso, Kyūshū: Eikō no Fukuin Kirisuto Kyōkai Shuppanbu, 1961), 53–55.

28 This is also recorded in 今橋 淳 Imahashi Atsushi's account of his conversion in 回心記 [A record of my conversion] (Tokyo: Kirisuto Shinbunsha, 1991), 40.

29 村井純 Murai Jun, 聖書の神学: 根本教義 [Biblical theology: Basic doctrines] (Tokyo: Iesu no Mitama Kyōkai, 1957), 32–33.

30 A similar emphasis on the interdependence of the living and the dead and the practice of various baptisms for the dead may be seen in the Mormon Church. In addition to First Corinthians 15:29, Mormons point to Hebrews 11:40 to support their interpretation that our predecessors depend on us for their complete salvation ("His [God's] purpose was that only in company with us would they be made perfect"). Likewise, Mormons recognize the reality of the unseen spirit world and receive communication from the departed. For an overview of Mormon teaching in relation to African beliefs regarding the dead and the spirit world, see Dennis L. Thomson, "African Religion and Mormon Doctrine: Comparisons and Commonalities," in Thomas D. Blakely, Walter E. A. Van Beek and Dennis L. Thomson, eds., *Religion in Africa: Experiences and Expressions* (London: James Currey, 1994), 89–99.

31 This is a collection of 166 hymns all said to have been received from heaven by Tsu-ruhara Tama, a woman who was active in the early years of this church. Since these hymns were given in a revelation directly from God, no changes are permitted. One sociologist has commented upon the "indigenous" character of this hymnbook and suggested that these songs do not have the melodies and rhythms of Western hymns, but are more like Japanese folk songs; see Anzai,"The Spirit of Jesus Church," 277–88. A young Japanese woman to whom I showed this hymn was similarly impressed. She was immediately struck by the Buddhist influence upon the lyrics and the Japanese-sounding melody.

32 This, along with records of those "baptized vicariously," resembles the practice of Reiyūkai members in keeping a death register, or *Book of the Past* (過去帳); see Hardacre, *Lay Buddhism in Contemporary Japan*, 65–66.

33 Hori, *Folk Religion in Japan*, 72–73.

34 For additional background on "bad death," malevolent spirits (*onryō* 怨霊), spirit pacification (*chinkon* 鎮魂), and the development of "vengeful spirit cults" (*goryō shinkō* 御霊信仰) in Japanese religion, see Klaus Antoni's "Yasukuni-Jinja and Folk Religion," in Mullins et al., *Religion and Society in Modern Japan*, 121–32, and Kuroda Toshio, "The World of Spirit Pacification: Issues of State and Religion," trans. Allan Grapard, *Japanese Journal of Religious Studies* 23/3–4 (1996), 321–51.

35 *Light of Life* (1993), 138–39.

36 *The Protestant Ethic and the Spirit of Capitalism* (New York: Charles Scribner's Sons, 1958), 104–5.

37 For a helpful recent discussion and comparison of the Protestant and Roman Catholic views of death and the "geography" of the other world, see Tony Walter's *The Eclipse of Eternity: A Sociology of the Afterlife* (London: Macmillan Press, 1996), 17–18. While Protestants have traditionally taught that individuals go directly to either heaven or hell at the moment of death, the Roman Catholic tradition, with its "threefold eternal geography of Heaven-Purgatory-Hell," recognizes an intermediate state of the dead and "multidirectional traffic" between this world and the unseen world.

Chapter 8: Comparative Patterns of Growth and Decline

1 Dean M. Kelley, *Why Conservative Churches Are Growing* (New York: Harper and Row, 1972).

2 Dean R. Hoge and David A. Roozen, *Understanding Church Growth and Decline: 1950–1978* (New York: The Pilgrim Press, 1979).

3 Wade Clark Roof and William McKinney, *American Mainline Religion: Its Changing Shape and Future* (New Brunswick: Rutgers University Press, 1987).

4 For a more detailed discussion and analysis of postwar patterns of growth and decline, see 戒能信生 Kainō Nobuo, 教勢から見た日本キリスト教団の五十年 [Looking at fifty years of the United Church of Christ from the point of view of numerical strength], in 日本キリスト教団五十年史の諸問題 [Problems in the fifty-year history of the United Church

of Christ in Japan], edited by 雨宮栄一 Amemiya Eiichi and 森岡 巌 Morioka Gen (Tokyo: Shinkyō Shuppansha. 1992), 109–33; 熊澤義宣 Kumazawa Yoshinobu, 戦後五十年の日本伝導 [Fifty years of evangelism in postwar Japan], in キリスト教年鑑 1995 [Christian yearbook, 1995] (Tokyo: Kirisuto Shinbunsha, 1995), 45–49; and Thomas Hastings and Mark R. Mullins, "Denominational Renewal or Fragmentation? An Exploratory Study of Reformed/Evangelical Movements within the United Church of Christ in Japan," *Japan Christian Review* 64, 1998.

5 David R. Heise, "Prefatory Findings in the Sociology of Missions," 49.

6 Hayashi Minoru, "Learning from the Japanese New Religions" (Pasadena: Doctor of Missiology thesis, Fuller Theological Seminary, 1988), 14.

7 Uchimura, *Complete Works of Uchimura Kanzō*, vol. 31, 380 (1928). For other details regarding the early development of the Nonchurch movement, I have relied on William H. Norman, "Kanzo Uchimura: Founder of the Non-Church Movement," *Contemporary Religions in Japan* 5/1 (1964), 34–44; John F. Howes, "The Non-Church Christian Movement in Japan," *The Transactions of the Asiatic Society of Japan*, Third Series 5 (1957), 119–37; and Caldarola, *Christianity: The Japanese Way*.

8 Howes, "The Non-Church Christian Movement in Japan," 124.

9 高橋三郎 Takahashi Saburō, 無教会精神の探求 [In search of the spirit of the Nonchurch movement] (Tokyo: Shinkyō Shuppansha, 1970), 176–78, 197. The groups associated with the Original Gospel movement were excluded from this number since Takahashi regards Teshima's pentecostal version of Nonchurch Christianity as an aberration.

10 Caldarola, *Christianity: The Japanese Way*.

11 Since many individuals subscribe to more than one Nonchurch publication, membership estimates in the past have been too high. One insider suggested that a more accurate (though rough) estimate of Nonchurch participants could be made by multiplying the three or four hundred groups by ten. There are undoubtedly many more who could be regarded as *kakure mukyōkai*, individuals who follow Uchimura's understanding of Christianity but do not participate in meetings. Over the years, the *Christian Yearbook* (キリスト教年鑑) has offered the following estimates for Nonchurch membership: 30,000–50,000 (1958), 15,000 (1966), 1,500 (1970), and 1,414 (1976).

12 For the most recent information on Nonchurch Christianity I am indebted to the staff of Imai Hall for introducing me to various records and reports, especially the published proceedings of the national meetings held since 1987 (see the appendix for details regarding these publications). 高木謙次 Takagi Kenji, in particular, was kind to respond to my many inquiries regarding membership. See his article for a helpful overview of the Nonchurch movement today: 平信徒運動としての無教会 [Nonchurch Christianity as a lay movement], 福音と宣教 [Gospel and mission], 49 (March 1994), 25–29.

13 日本教会名簿 [Japan church membership list] (Tokyo: Nihon Kyōkai, 1911); 道会名簿 [List of members of The Way] (Tokyo: Dōkai Headquarters, 1936).

14 Reported in the *Christian Yearbook* (1970).

[15] This number was reported in the introduction to the English version of *A Eulogy on Jesus Christ,* trans. Yoshinobu Kawai (Tokyo: Christ Heart Church, 1961).

[16] Iglehart, *A Century of Protestant Christianity in Japan,* 339. Although outsiders tend to classify this church as "Protestant," this is a designation that the Spirit of Jesus Church representatives reject. They maintain that this church is neither Catholic nor Protestant, but a recovery of the authentic "primitive" church. While outsiders may refer to this church as "Protestant," most add that it is a heretical group because of its practice of baptism of the dead and its rejection of the doctrine of the trinity.

[17] See, for example, Anzai, "The Spirit of Jesus Church," 277–88.

[18] Comparison with membership in another new religious movement might be helpful here. In a study of Sūkyō Mahikari, for example, Winston Davis estimates "that although as many as one million amulets have probably been distributed to new members, the de facto membership probably numbers about 100,000 to 200,000 or even less" (*Dōjō,* 7).

[19] My observations here are supported by Anzai's study of the Spirit of Jesus Church in Okinawa. He also found that the figures for baptism were very high, but less than ten percent of those reported as baptized members actually attended services; see his *The Acceptance of Christianity in the Southern Islands,* 119. It might also be helpful to recognize here that Japanese religiosity and understanding of membership are quite different from some Western notions. As a rule, Japanese do not commit themselves to one particular religious organization; rather, they participate in the annual festivals and rituals of both Shinto shrines and Buddhist temples throughout the year. Regular weekly attendance at religious meetings is the exception rather than the norm in Japan. While this church strongly discourages participation in Buddhist and Shinto rituals, their understanding of membership seems similarly undemanding. From my limited observation, there is little pressure placed on members to attend meetings. As long as one has received "water" and "spirit" baptism, other obligations are viewed rather lightly. Hence, the small number of regular attendants does not seem to bother leaders. Members can attend for services and rituals that seem important to them through the year and life cycle just as other Japanese visit Shinto shrines and Buddhist temples for special events or rituals.

[20] Caldarola included a chapter on the Original Gospel movement in his book, *Christianity: The Japanese Way.* About the time Caldarola was conducting his study, the 1976 *Christian Yearbook* reported that the Original Gospel had 200 groups and 50,000 members. The discrepancy between Caldarola's figures and that of the yearbook indicate how difficult it is to obtain accurate statistics on these groups.

[21] The 10,000 figure may be too high, but it is not unreasonable in light of participation rates in various meetings. In 1992, 7,000 members attended the annual meeting, and 1,600 members participated in the pilgrimage to Israel two years ago. Approximately 500 members usually attend the annual three-day study meeting for leaders of the house-meetings.

[22] For membership and attendance figures I have relied on church reports made available to me by the head of the Evangelism Division of the Holy Ecclesia of Jesus.

[23] Hugh Trevor, *Japan's Postwar Protestant Churches* (Tokyo: Mimeographed, 1994), 28.

24 Two other indigenous movements show similar patterns of growth and decline. The Glorious Gospel Christian Church, founded in 1936 by Sugita Kōtarō, grew to a membership of 3,929, with seven churches and fourteen centers for evangelism. The membership began to decline after the death of the founder's wife and in 1996 reported membership of only 1,130. The Christian Canaan Church, which was started by Taniguchi Toku with house meetings in 1940, grew in three decades to a membership of 2,797 with eight churches and six centers for evangelism. This church has also begun to show signs of decline, with a total of 2,483 members in 1995. These observations are based on interviews and reports in the *Christian Yearbook*.

25 Milton J. Yinger, *The Scientific Study of Religion* (Toronto: Collier-Macmillan, 1970), 112.

26 Stark, "How New Religions Succeed: A Theoretical Model," 16.

27 It should be noted that the founder of Christ Heart Church, Kawai Shinsui, made it clear from the beginning that he was not interested in attracting great numbers, but was concerned to train and cultivate the *few*. Perfection was the goal and self-cultivation was the means. As one of his followers explained: "Kawai Sensei always emphasized that self-cultivation was the number one concern." The emphasis on "perfection" and members' own sense of inadequate progress on the "path to perfection" discourages them from inviting others. Informants note that there are visitors from time to time, but they usually do not return to meetings. "The path is hard and requires considerable discipline," they explain, "and is not like so many New Religions that worship this-worldly benefits."

28 Reginald W. Bibby and Merlin Brinkerhoff, "The Circulation of the Saints: A Study of People Who Join Conservative Churches," *Journal for the Scientific Study of Religion* 12 (1973). Their study of churches in North America discovered that conservative churches tended to benefit from the "circulation of the saints" (i.e., switching from denomination to denomination) and that effective proselytizing of individuals outside of the Christian community was minimal. It would be interesting to know what percentage of the growth reported by evangelical churches in Japan is related to such denominational switching. As noted above, leaders of the Original Gospel Movement estimate that roughly fifty percent of their members come from other Christian churches.

29 Stark, "How New Religions Succeed," 13.

30 This dilemma has been expressed most effectively by Endō Shūsaku in *Silence*, a historical novel dealing with this first period of Christian mission in Japan. In one passage the veteran missionary Ferreira, who apostasized under torture, explains to his former student and still zealous missionary Rodrigues the difficulty of transplanting Christianity in the Japanese cultural environment:

> The one thing I know is that our religion does not take root in this country.... This country is a swamp. In time you will come to see that for yourself. This country is a more terrible swamp than you can imagine. Whenever you plant a sapling in this swamp the roots begin to rot; the leaves grow yellow and wither. And we have planted the sapling of Christianity in this swamp. (237)

31 See Morioka's "A Conceptual Examination of the Indigenization of Foreign-Born Religions" and *Japan's Modern Society and Christianity*.

[32] Davis, *Japanese Religion and Society,* 31.

[33] As far as missionary efforts are concerned, it is interesting to note that more Protestant missionaries have been sent to Japan than Korea during the past century (see Grayson, *Early Buddhism and Christianity in Korea,* 138).

[34] Montgomery, "The Spread of Religions and Macrosocial Relations," 38–39. See also his earlier "Receptivity to an Outside Religion: Light from Interaction between Sociology and Missiology," *Missiology: An International Review* 14/3 (1986), 287–99.

[35] David Martin, *Tongues of Fire: The Explosion of Protestantism in Latin America* (Oxford: Basil Blackwell, 1990), 155–56.

[36] During the postwar period, Christian churches in Korea seem to have filled the role that new religions have in Japan. Apparently only five percent of the South Korean population belonged to a new religion in the early 1980s, while ten to twenty percent of the Japanese are members of one of the new religions (closer to the percentage of Christians in Korea). For the data on South Korea I have relied on Joseph B. Tamney, "Religion in Capitalist East Asia," in William H. Swatos, Jr., ed. *A Future For Religion? New Paradigms for Social Analysis* (Beverley Hills: A Sage Focus Edition, 1992), 62.

[37] Reported in the *MARC Newsletter* 95/1 (March 1995), 1.

[38] Information and current statistics regarding Yoido Full Gospel Church were gathered by the author on a field trip to Seoul in September 1989. Reported statistics should not be taken at face value. There are always inactive members and many "floating Christians" whose membership is reported by more than one church. Even with these qualifications, I would imagine that there are several hundred thousand members active in one of the programs of Yoido Church. Regarding membership composition, I am only aware of one sociological survey of the church conducted by Syn-Duk Choi in 1978 and reported in his "A comparative study of two new religious movements in the Republic of Korea: the Unification Church and the Full Gospel Central Church," in James Beckford, ed. *New Religious Movements and Rapid Social Change* (Beverley Hills: Sage Publications, 1986), 113–45. According to Choi's study, the majority of the Full Gospel Church members have less than a high school education and women outnumber men by more than two to one. He summed up the results of this survey with the following generalization: "The educational level, occupation and living conditions of the members of Full Gospel Church show that it is a church of the middle and lower classes." Choi's findings are based upon 300 responses (28 percent men and 72 percent women) to his questionnaire distributed in eight large parishes. For fuller treatment of Yoido Church see the work of Daniel J. Adams, "Reflections on an Indigenous Christian Movement: The Yoido Full Gospel Church," *Japan Christian Review* 57/1 (1991); Jae Bum Lee's "Pentecostal Type Distinctives and Korean Protestant Church Growth" (Ph.D. dissertation, School of World Mission, Fuller Theological Seminary, Pasadena, California, 1986), and Boo Woong Yoo's "Response to Korean Shamanism by the Pentecostal Church," *International Review of Mission* 75/297 (1986), and *Korean Pentecostalism: Its History and Theology* (New York: Peter Lang, 1988).

[39] See Paul Yonggi Cho's "Ministry Through Home Cell Groups," (with John W. Hurston) in Ro Bong-Rin and Marvin L. Nelson, eds., *Korean Church Growth Explosion* (Seoul:

Word of Life Press, 1983) for a discussion of the role of home cell groups in pastoral care and church growth.

40 Jae Bum Lee, "Pentecostal Type Distinctives and Korean Protestant Church Growth," 285.

41 See, for example, James Huntley Grayson's *Korea: A Religious History* (New York: Oxford University Press, 1989), 205; and David Kwang-Sun Suh's *The Korean Minjung in Christ* (Hong Kong: The Christian Conference of Asia, 1991), 114–16.

42 Byong-Suh Kim, "The Explosive Growth of the Korean Church Today: A Sociological Analysis," *International Review of Mission* 74/293 (1985), 70.

43 David Suh, *The Korean Minjung in Christ*, 116.

44 Quoted from the church pamphlet, *Yoido Full Gospel Church Doctrine and Creed* (n.d.).

45 Bong-Ho Son, "Some Dangers of Rapid Growth," in Ro Bong-Rin and Marvin L. Nelson, eds., *Korean Church Growth Explosion* (Seoul: Word of Life Press, 1983), 338.

46 James Huntley Grayson's *Korea: A Religious History* (New York: Oxford University Press, 1989: 205). Bong-Ho Son, extremely critical of Korean church life, goes so far as to say that "many give in order to receive more, based on the shamanistic practice of bribing the demons"; "Some Dangers of Rapid Growth," 339.

47 Kwang-il Kim, "Kut and the Treatment of Mental Disorder," in Chai-Shin Yu and R. Guisso, eds., *Shamanism: The Spirit World of Korea* (Berkeley: Asian Humanities Press, 1988), 133.

48 Yohan Lee, "An Analysis of the Christian Prayer Mountain Phenomenon in Korea" (Ph.D. dissertation, School of World Mission, Fuller Theological Seminary, Pasadena, California, 1985), 10.

49 Lee, "An Analysis of the Christian Prayer Mountain Phenomenon in Korea," 51.

50 Paul Yonggi Cho, *More Than Numbers* (Waco, Texas: Word Books, 1984), 102–3.

51 The growth of the Tokyo Full Gospel Church and its branch churches is described in a book by the senior pastor, Kang Hun Rhee, 日本一千万救霊は可能だ [The salvation of ten million Japanese souls is possible] (Tokyo: Division of Mission of the Tokyo Full Gospel Church, 1989). The growth of Full Gospel churches in Japan over the past decade is undoubtedly related to the fact that these ethnic churches provide a home away from home for many Korean immigrants working in Japan. The degree of success in incorporating Japanese into these ethnic organizations varies from church to church. In most Full Gospel Churches the Japanese membership is below 20 percent (many spouses of interethnic marriages). I have been informed, however, that there are some exceptions. The church in Fukuoka (southern Japan), for example, is dominantly Japanese. What is clear, in any case, is that these churches are making an effort to transcend ethnic boundaries. This is hardly the only factor related to their growth. Following the model of Yoido Church in Seoul, all of these churches have organized multiple services on Sunday and scores of home cell groups. The Tokyo Church, for example, has six worship services on Sunday. Two are conducted in Japanese and four in Korean (with simultaneous interpretation provided for three of these).

[52] For an overview of this social context, see my essay "Japan's New Age and Neo-New Religions: Sociological Interpretations," in James R. Lewis and J. Gordon Melton, eds., *Perspectives on the New Age* (Albany, New York: State University of New York, 1992), 232–46.

[53] Hori, *Folk Religion in Japan,* 14.

[54] I borrowed this term from Kenneth J. Dale's *Circle of Harmony: A Case Study of Popular Japanese Buddhism* (Tokyo: Seibunsha, 1975), 157.

[55] Davis, *Dōjō,* 302.

[56] Hayashi Minoru, "Learning from the Japanese New Religions" (Pasadena: Doctor of Missiology thesis, Fuller Theological Seminary, 1988), 14.

[57] Paul Yonggi Cho, *More Than Numbers,* 119.

[58] Daniel J. Adams, "Reflections on an Indigenous Christian Movement: The Yoido Full Gospel Church," *The Japan Christian Quarterly* 57/1 (1991), 43.

Chapter 9: The Broader Context of Japanese Christianity

[1] Jean Danielou, *A History of Early Christian Doctrines before the Council of Nicaea,* vol. 2: *Gospel Message and Hellenistic Culture.* Translated by J. A. Baker (Philadelphia: Westminster Press, 1973), 33.

[2] See 宮崎 彰 Miyazaki Akira, 原始福音研究 [A study of the Original Gospel] (Tokyo: Nihon Kirisuto Kyōdan Senkyō Kenkyūjo, 1965), 62. To my knowledge, this represents the only effort by one of the established churches to study an indigenous movement in Japan. In addition to elaborating the "pluralistic" perspective on Japanese culture and providing some basic information on the Original Gospel movement, the author suggests that the success of indigenous movements is related in part to the failures and deficiencies of the established churches.

[3] There are some exceptions to this generalization. Christ Heart Church, for example, does observe baptism as a rite of initiation. Also, some groups related to the Nonchurch tradition may observe baptisms on an occasional basis, but these have not become institutionalized requirements.

[4] On the gender issue, the Holy Ecclesia of Jesus should be placed in an intermediate position on a continuum between the Confucian male-dominated approach of the Nonchurch movement on the one end and the egalitarian pentecostal Spirit of Jesus Church on the other. Women called to ministry in the Holy Ecclesia of Jesus are recognized as "gifted" and receive theological education. Following graduation from Logos Theological Seminary, however, they can only be ordained as teachers (*seikyōshi* 正教師) or evangelists. Only ordained men (牧師 *bokushi*) are allowed to officiate at the Lord's Supper and perform the benediction at the end of worship services. If women marry after completion of this seminary training, they are expected to devote themselves fully to housework and to the care and education of their children. Of course, they are expected to play a supportive role in their husband's pastoral work and church activities. While this church gives men priority in the hierarchy of religious authority, it is widely recognized that many women are some of the most successful evange-

lists. They often begin evangelistic activities in difficult new areas, and after establishing a church of fifty to one hundred members, they move on to begin a new work and pass on the job of pastoral care to one of the ordained men. This is, of course, a typical pattern in many Christian churches and mission organizations.

5 These observations are based on the lecture by 奥田暁子 Okuda Akiko, 無教会と女性解放 [The Nonchurch movement and women's liberation] and some of the discussion that followed her lecture (fieldnotes, 17 May 1996, Imai Hall, Tokyo). The lecture I attended attracted 17 women and one other man. If this is typical of the events sponsored by the women's group, it is going to take a long time to transform the male constituency that has dominated the movement to date. In addition to these special lectures and discussion meetings, the Women's Planning Group has also been publishing a series of booklets that address the concerns of women within the Nonchurch movement. In the introduction to booklet no. 6, the editor notes that lectures by men tend to focus on abstract principles and are quite distinct from everyday life, whereas talks by women tend to draw on personal experiences and relate the Bible to the difficulties encountered at the workplace, the home, and in the fields of education and social welfare. The booklet series is available from Imai Hall (今井館双書 nos. 1–6). Some examples from the series are: 無教会における教育と伝道 (1) [Education and evangelism in the Nonchurch movement], and 女の視点で語る (6) [Speaking from a woman's point of view]. For a more accessible English volume by a Japanese feminist from the Nonchurch tradition, see Hisako Kinukawa's *Women and Jesus in Mark: A Japanese Feminist Perspective* (Maryknoll: Orbis Books), 1994.

6 For historical background and discussion of leadership succession and transmission of religious authority in Japanese Buddhist sects, see Michael Solomon, "Kinship and the Transmission of Religious Charisma: The Case of Honganji," *Journal of Asian Studies*, 33/3 (1974), 403–13; and Fujii Masao, "Founder Worship in Kamakura Buddhism," in George A. DeVos and Takao Sofue, eds., *Religion and the Family in East Asia* (Berkeley: University of California Press, 1986), 155–67. For a helpful analysis of this pattern of leadership succession in Japanese New Religions unrelated to the Christian tradition, see Inoue Nobutaka, *Deciphering New Religions*, 150–57.

7 Leadership succession in the Original Gospel, a movement based on Nonchurch principles, is a bit more complicated. Following the death of Teshima in 1973, the movement has continued under the joint leadership of the teachers based primarily in Tokyo, but also in Kumamoto (Kyūshū), where the movement began. Carlo Caldarola observed that Mrs. Teshima is recognized as the most powerful figure in the movement, since "she is regarded as the living memory of Teshima and his personality and charisma are perceived to be still operative in the movement through her" (*Christianity: The Japanese Way*, 198). He went on to speculate that Teshima's son, Jacob, who was at the time completing doctoral studies in Jewish studies in the United States, would eventually return to Japan "to take up the mantle of leadership." As it turns out, however, Jacob was unable to accept the direction the Original Gospel had taken since his father's death and left the movement to establish the Gilboa Institute of the Humanities, where he is currently active as an independent scholar of Biblical and Judaic Studies. There is now some speculation that Issac Teshima, the founder's son by his second marriage, who recently completed doctoral studies at Harvard in Hebrew Bible and

Jewish hermeneutics, may return to take an active leadership role in the movement. In interviews, however, he indicated that academic work would most likely be his primary calling.

8 Even in the rather individualistic North American context, for example, Billy Graham's son was appointed as his successor in the Billy Graham Association and Jimmy Swaggart's son appears to be waiting in the wings to assume leadership of the evangelistic television ministry if it survives the scandals associated with his father's ministry.

9 The proceedings of these annual meetings have been published each year since 1988 as 無教会キリスト教全国集会記録 [The proceedings of the Nonchurch Christianity national meeting] (Tokyo: The Office of the Nonchurch Christianity National Meeting), and are available from the Imai Hall in Tokyo. These are probably the most useful publications for understanding the situation of the Nonchurch movement today.

10 This was reflected in the composition of those who attended the first nationwide meeting: the majority of participants was over age 50, with 68 percent of the participants in the 50–80 age bracket; only twelve percent of the participants were age 30 or younger; see 第 1 回 (1987) 無教会キリスト教全国集会記録 [The proceedings of the first Nonchurch Christianity national meeting] (Tokyo: The Office of the Nonchurch Christianity National Meeting, 1988), 79.

11 Here I am drawing on 第 2 回 (1988) 無教会キリスト教全国集会記録 [The proceedings of the second Nonchurch Christianity national meeting] (Tokyo: The Office of the Nonchurch Christianity National Meeting, 1989) 64; and 第 3 回 (1989) 無教会キリスト教全国 集会記録 [The proceedings of the third Nonchurch Christianity national meeting] (1990), 4.

12 As it turns out, some of the applicants were interested non-Christians, so the classes not only educate members but also represent an opportunity for reaching new people.

13 Caldarola, *Christianity: The Japanese Way*, 75–76.

14 第 6 回 (1992) 無教会キリスト教全国集会記録 [The proceedings of the sixth Nonchurch Christianity national meeting] (1993), 62.

15 This style of leadership is often referred to as the *takotsubo* (octopus-pot) type, since the vertical relationship between teacher and disciple is strong, but horizontal relationships between members tend to be weak. This is particularly the case with the larger Bible study groups in the city, but less so in rural areas where the groups tend to be small and family-like; see *Proceedings of the Third Nonchurch Christianity National Meeting*, 39.

16 Some members also mention the difficulty of finding their own burial site at a Buddhist temple graveyard or elsewhere since Nonchurch groups do not maintain their own properties; see *Proceedings of the Third Nonchurch Christianity National Meeting*, 47, 53.

17 This observation was initially made with reference to the African independent churches, but it is equally true for these Japanese movements; see Joel Kailing, "Inside, Outside, Upside Down: In Relationship with African Independent Churches," *International Review of Mission* 77 (January 1988), 40. The personal reflections of Harold Turner, who spent a large part of his career researching the African Independent churches, provides a helpful illustration of how these movements are in process: "As one in the high Reformed tradition of sound doctrine and decency and order in worship it would have been nonsense to

suggest that I might actually enjoy dancing in African independent churches with a very uncertain Christology. And now the church where I did most of my dancing is a member of the WCC." "A Global Phenomenon," in Allan R. Brockway and J. Paul Rajashekar, eds., *New Religious Movements and the Churches*, 14.

18 See their "Introductory Essay: on 'Native Christianity'," in Wendy James and Douglas H. Johnson, eds., *Vernacular Christianity*, 5.

19 *The Religious Consciousness of the Japanese*. This survey was carried out in November 1981 with interviews conducted in 300 locations in rural and urban settings across Japan. A total of 3,600 individuals over age 16 were interviewed. Out of this number there were 2,692 (74.8 percent) usable (valid) interviews. Of the total sample, 44.7 percent (1,203) were male and 55.3 (1,489) were female.

20 "The Quiet Reversal: A Few Notes on the NHK Survey of Japanese Religiosity," *Japan Missionary Bulletin* 39/1 (1985), 5–6 .

21 Here I am drawing on Jan Swyngedouw's discussion of the division of labor in Japanese religion and the new ritual contribution of Christianity. See his *The Structure of Harmony and Apportionment*.

22 The two surveys mentioned were conducted by Sanwa Bank and the Bridal Market Research Institute. For more details see BB 白書 [Bib Bridal white paper] 7 (Tokyo, 1993).

23 For brief discussions of this legend see John Koedyker, "Another Jesus," *Japan Christian Quarterly* 52/3 (Summer 1986), 167–69, and キリスト渡来伝説と日本の宗教風土 [The legend of Christ's visit and the religious climate of Japan] in the popular volume coauthored by 瓜生中 Uriu Naka and 渋谷伸博 Shibuya Nobuhiro , 日本宗教のすべて [All about Japanese religion] (Tokyo: Nihon Bungeisha, 1997), 214–15.

24 Legends of this kind are not limited to Japan. In India, for example, there is a similar tradition that claims Jesus did not die on the cross in Jerusalem but lived another forty years in Northwest India before his death and burial in the area. This example is mentioned briefly in Diana L. Eck, *Encountering God: A Spiritual Journey from Bozeman to Banaras* (Boston: Beacon Press, 1993), 113–14; and from a believer's standpoint in Fida Hassnain and Dahan Levi, *The Fifth Gospel* (Srinagar: Dastgir, 1988).

25 For a more detailed treatment, see the following studies by Richard Young, "The 'Christ' of the Japanese New Religions" and "The Little-Lad Deity and the Dragon Princess." Young has shown how the "Christ" (whether related to the Jesus of the gospel or not) has been revered and integrated into indigenous belief systems, but often for reasons of personal self-aggrandizement and to promote or legitimize aspirations toward a specious universality. In the latter study, he analyzes how Fujita Himiko incorporates Jesus, along with other deities and saints, into the mythology of Megami no Umi (女神ノ海, Ocean of the Goddess).

26 See his キリスト言 [Proclamation as Christ] (1991), and part 2 of the same work (1992). For additional information on Asahara and Aum Shinrikyō, see Ian Reader, *A Poisonous Cocktail? Aum Shinrikyō's Path to Violence* (Copenhagen: Nordic Institute for Asian Studies, 1996); Shimazono Susumu, "In the Wake of Aum: The Formation and Transformation of a Universe of Belief," *Japanese Journal of Religious Studies* 22/3–4 (1995), 381–415; and my essays "Aum

Shinrikyō as an Apocalyptic Movement," in Thomas Robbins and Susan J. Palmer, eds., *Millennium, Messiahs, and Mayhem* (New York: Routledge, 1997), 313–24, and "The Political and Legal Response to Aum-Related Violence in Japan," *Japan Christian Review* 63 (1997), 37–46.

[27] An English translation of Ōkawa's work on Christ was published as *The Spiritual Guidance of Jesus Christ: Speaking on the Resurrection of Love and the Spirit of the New Age* (Tokyo: IRH Press, 1991).

[28] It is perhaps for this reason that Jaroslav Pelikan, in his illuminating cultural history, refers to Jesus Christ as "the Man Who Belongs to the World." *Jesus through the Centuries: His Place in the History of Culture* (New York: Harper and Row, 1987), 220–21. Richard Young, who has examined the place of Jesus in a number of Japanese New Religions, similarly writes that "Jesus Christ belongs to the public domain. Like it or not, his is a name that can neither be registered, trademarked, or copyrighted..." ("The 'Christ' of the Japanese New Religions," 117).

[29] Rodney Stark, "Modernization, Secularization, and Mormon Success," in Thomas Robbins and Dick Anthony, eds., *In Gods We Trust: New Patterns of Religious Pluralism in America* (New Brunswick: Transaction Publishers, 1990), 201.

[30] Peter L. Berger, *The Sacred Canopy: Elements of a Sociological Theory of Religion* (Garden City, New York: Doubleday, 1967), 171.

[31] Herbert Passin, "Modernization and the Japanese Intellectual," in Marius B. Jansen, ed. *Changing Japanese Attitudes toward Modernization* (Princeton: Princeton University Press, 1965), 482–83; emphasis added.

[32] This point has been helpfully elaborated by Munakata Iwao in his essay, "The Ambivalent Effects of Modernization on the Traditional Folk Religion of Japan," 99–126.

[33] Peter L. Berger, *A Far Glory: The Quest for Faith in an Age of Credulity* (New York: Anchor Books, 1992), 28, 32; see also "Epistemological Modesty: An Interview with Peter Berger," *The Christian Century* 114 (29 October 1997), 974. This revised view finds substantial support in David B. Barrett's most recent statistical update, which reports that there are "over 15,000 distinct, separate, and different religions and religious movements. Two or three entirely new non-Christian religions are begun on earth every day." See his "Annual Statistical Table on Global Mission: 1997," *International Bulletin of Missionary Research* 21/1 (January 1997), 24. My guess is that Barrett's total figure is too small, since several hundred New Religions have been documented in Japan alone.

[34] Irving Hexham and Karla Poewe, "Charismatic Churches in South Africa: A Critique of Criticisms and Problems of Bias," in Poewe, ed., *Charismatic Christianity as a Global Culture*, 60.

[35] "Transformations of Christianity: Some General Observations," in George R. Saunders, ed., *Culture and Christianity*, 181.

[36] For some representative works treating indigenous concerns with kinship, spirits, exorcism, healing, and ancestors in various regions of the world, see Harold W. Turner, *Religious Innovation in Africa: Collected Essays on New Religious Movements* (Boston: G. K. Hall and Co., 1979); Gerhardus C. Oosthuizen, *The Healer-Prophet in Afro-Christian Churches* (Leiden: E. J. Brill, 1992); Alan Hunter and Kim-Kwong Chan, *Protestantism in Contemporary*

China (Cambridge University Press, 1993); and Steven Kaplan, ed., *Indigenous Responses to Western Christianity* (New York: New York University Press, 1995).

37 David B. Barrett, ed. *World Christian Encyclopedia: A Comparative Survey on Religions in the Modern World, A.D. 1900–2000* (New York: Oxford University Press, 1982), 9.

38 Andrew F. Walls, *The Missionary Movement in Christian History*, 9–10.

39 In an important international and cross-cultural study of charismatic and pentecostal movements, for example, Irving Hexham and Karla Poewe discovered that these new forms of Christianity were developing simultaneously in various local contexts and mutually influencing each other through international networks, associations, and modern technology. "It is this international perspective," Hexham and Poewe conclude, "that brought home the lesson that North American and European churches are as deeply affected by African, Asian, and Latin American churches as vice versa." See "Charismatic Churches in South Africa," 66.

40 Donald W. Dayton, "Yet Another Layer of the Onion: Or Opening the Ecumenical Door to Let the Riff-raff In," *The Ecumenical Review* 40/1 (1988), 87–110.

41 "Global Religion(s): Hope or Hoax of the 20th Century?," *Harvard University Center for the Study of World Religions News* 3/2 (1966), 1–3.

General Bibliography

Abe Yoshiya. "From Prohibition to Toleration: Japanese Government Views Regarding Christianity." *Japanese Journal of Religious Studies* 5/2–3 (1978), 107–38.

Anzai Shin 安斎 伸. イエス之御霊教会 [The Spirit of Jesus Church]. In 桜井徳太郎 Sakurai Tokutarō, ed., 民俗宗教と社会 [Folk religion and society]. Tokyo: Kōbunsha, 1980, 268–79.

———. 南島におけるキリスト教の受容 [The acceptance of Christianity in the southern islands]. Tokyo: Daiichi Shobō, 1984.

Berentsen, J. M. *Grave and Gospel*. Leiden: E. J. Brill, 1985.

Berger, Peter and Hansfried Kellner. *Sociology Reinterpreted: An Essay on Method and Vocation*. Garden City, New York: Anchor Books, 1981.

Breen, John and Mark Williams, eds. *Japan and Christianity: Impacts and Responses*. London: Macmillan Press, 1995.

Brockway, Allan R. and J. Paul Rajashekar, eds. *New Religious Movements and the Churches*. Geneva: WCC Publications, 1987.

Caldarola, Carlo. *Christianity: The Japanese Way*. Leiden: E. J. Brill, 1979.

Cary, Otis. *A History of Christianity in Japan*. Tokyo: Charles E. Tuttle, 1976 (reprint of the 1909 two-volume edition).

Davis, Winston Bradley. *Dōjō: Magic and Exorcism in Modern Japan*. Stanford: Stanford University Press, 1980.

———. *Japanese Religion and Society: Paradigms of Structure and Change*. Albany: State University of New York Press, 1992.

Doerner, David L. "Comparative Analysis of Life after Death in Folk Shinto and Christianity." *Japanese Journal of Religious Studies* 4/2–3 (1977), 151–82.

Dohi Akio 土肥昭夫. 日本プロテスタント史 [A history of Protestant Christianity in Japan]. Tokyo: Shinkyō Shuppansha, 1980.

Dōshisha University Humanities Research Institute, ed. 日本プロテスタント緒教派史の研究 [Studies in Japanese Protestant denominational histories]. Tokyo: Kyōbunkan, 1997.

Drummond, Richard H. *A History of Christianity in Japan*. Grand Rapids: Eerdmans, 1971.

Earhart, H. Byron. *Gedatsu-Kai and Religion in Contemporary Japan*. Bloomington and Indianapolis: Indiana University Press, 1989.

Ebisawa Arimichi 海老沢有道, editor-in-chief. 日本キリスト教歴史大事典 [Historical dictionary of Christianity in Japan]. Tokyo: Kyōbunkan, 1988.

Endō Shūsaku. *Silence*. trans. William Johnston. Tokyo: Kodansha International, 1982.

Furuya, Yasuo, ed. and trans. *A History of Japanese Theology*. Grand Rapids: Eerdmans, 1997.

Grayson, James H. *Early Buddhism and Christianity in Korea: A Study in the Emplantation of Religion*. Leiden: E. J. Brill, 1985.

Hardacre, Helen. *Lay Buddhism in Contemporary Japan: Reiyūkai Kyōdan*, New Jersey: Princeton University Press, 1984.

———. *Kurozumikyō and the New Religions of Japan*. Princeton: Princeton University Press, 1986.

Hefner, Robert W., ed. *Conversion to Christianity: Historical and Anthropological Perspectives on the Great Transformation*. Berkeley: University of California Press, 1993.

Heise, David R. "Prefatory Findings in the Sociology of Missions." *Journal for the Scientific Study of Religion* 6/1 (1967) 49–76.

Hexham, Irving and Karla Poewe, *New Religions as Global Cultures: Making the Human Sacred*. Boulder, Colorado: Westview Press, 1997.

Hori Ichirō. *Folk Religion in Japan: Continuity and Change*. Joseph M. Kitagawa and Alan L. Miller, eds. Chicago: University of Chicago Press, 1968.

Howes, John F. "Japanese Christians and American Missionaries." In Marius B. Jansen, ed. *Changing Japanese Attitudes toward Modernization*. Princeton, New Jersey: Princeton University Press, 1965.

———. "Japanese Christianity and the State: From Jesuit Confrontation / Competition to Uchimura's Non-Institutional Movement / Protestantism." In Steven Kaplan, ed. *Indigenous Responses to Western Christianity*. New York: New York University Press, 1995.

Iglehart, Charles W. *A Century of Protestant Christianity in Japan*. Tokyo: Charles E. Tuttle, 1959.

Ikado Fujio 井門富二夫. 世俗社会と宗教 [Religion in a secular society]. Tokyo: Nihon Kirisuto Kyōdan Shuppankyoku, 1972.

Ikegami Yoshimasa 池上良正. 悪霊と聖霊の舞台: 沖縄の民衆キリスト教に見る救済世界 [A stage for demons and the Holy Spirit: The world of salvation as seen in popular Okinawan Christianity]. Tokyo: Dōbutsusha, 1991.

Inoue Nobutaka 井上順孝. 新宗教の解読 [Deciphering the new religions]. Tokyo: Chikuma Shobō, 1992.

Inoue Nobutaka 井上順孝, Kōmoto Mitsugu 孝本 貢, Tsushima Michihito 対馬路人, Nakamaki Hirochika 中牧弘允, and Nishiyama Shigeru 西山 茂, eds. 新宗教辞典 [Dictionary of New Religions]. Tokyo: Kōbundō, 1990.

James, Wendy and Douglas H. Johnson, eds. *Vernacular Christianity: Essays in the Social Anthropology of Religion Presented to Godfrey Lienhardt.* Oxford: JASO Occasional Papers No. 7, 1988.

Kishimoto, Hideo, ed. *Japanese Religion in the Meiji Era.* Trans. and adapted by John F. Howes. Tokyo: Ōbunsha, 1956.

Kudō Eiichi 工藤栄一. 日本キリスト教社会経済史研究: 明治初期を中心として [Studies in the economic history of Japanese Christian society: The early Meiji period]. Tokyo: Shinkyō Shuppansha, 1980.

Kumazawa Yoshinobu and David L. Swain, eds., *Christianity in Japan, 1971–1990.* Tokyo: Kyo Bun Kwan, 1991.

Kuyama Yasushi 久山 康, ed. 近代日本とキリスト教 (明治篇). [Modern Japan and Christianity: The Meiji period]. Tokyo: Sōbunsha, 1956

Lee, Robert. *Stranger in the Land: A Study of the Church in Japan.* London: Lutterworth Press, 1967.

Luttio, Mark D. "The Passage of Death in the Japanese Context: In Pursuit of an Inculturated Lutheran Funeral Rite." *The Japan Christian Review* 62 (1996), 18–29.

Montgomery, Robert L. "The Spread of Religions and Macrosocial Relations." *Sociological Analysis* 52 (1991), 37–53.

————. *The Diffusion of Religions: A Sociological Perspective.* New York: University Press of America, 1996.

Morioka Kiyomi 森岡清美. 外来宗教の土着化をめぐる概念的整理 [A conceptual examination of the indigenization of foreign-born religions]. 史潮 109 (1972), 52–77.

————. *Religion in Changing Japanese Society.* Tokyo: University of Tokyo Press, 1975.

————. 日本の近代社会とキリスト教 [Japan's modern society and Christianity]. Tokyo: Hyōronsha, 1976.

Mullins, Mark R. "Japan's New Age and Neo-New Religions: Sociological Interpretations." In James R. Lewis and J. Gordon Melton, eds. *Perspectives on the New Age.* Albany: State University of New York, 1992.

————. "Ideology and Utopianism in Wartime Japan: An Essay on the Subversiveness of Christian Eschatology." *Japanese Journal of Religious Studies* 21/2–3 (1994), 261–80.

Mullins, Mark R., Shimazono Susumu, and Paul Swanson, eds. *Religion and Society in Modern Japan.* Berkeley: Asian Humanities Press, 1993.

Mullins, Mark R. and Richard Fox Young, eds. *Perspectives on Christianity in Korea and Japan: The Gospel and Culture in East Asia.* Lewiston, New York: Edwin Mellen Press, 1995.

Munakata, Iwao. "The Ambivalent Effects of Modernization on Traditional Folk Religion." *Japanese Journal of Religious Studies* 3/2–3 (1976), 99–126.

Nishiyama Shigeru. "Indigenization and Transformation of Christianity in a Japanese Community." *Japanese Journal of Religious Studies* 12/1(1985), 17–61.

Ōhama Tetsuya 大濱徹也. 明治キリスト教会史の研究 [Studies in the history of Christian churches in the Meiji Period]. Tokyo: Yoshikawa Kōbunkan, 1979.

Ohara Shin 小原 信. 内村鑑三の生涯 [The life of Uchimura Kanzō]. Tokyo: PHP Kenkyūsho, 1992.

Ōmura Eishō 大村英照 and Nishiyama Shigeru 西山 茂, eds. 現代人の宗教 [The religion of people today]. Tokyo: Yūhikaku, 1988.

Pelikan, Jaroslav. *Jesus through the Centuries: His Place in the History of Culture*. New York: Harper and Row, 1985.

Phillips, James M. *From the Rising of the Sun: Christians and Society in Contemporary Japan*. Maryknoll, New York: Orbis Books, 1981.

Plath, David W. "Where the Family of God is the Family: The Role of the Dead in Japanese Households." *American Anthropologist* 66 (1964), 300–317.

Poewe, Karla, ed. *Charismatic Christianity as a Global Culture*. Columbia, South Carolina: University of South Carolina Press, 1994.

Powles, Cyril H. "Foreign Missionaries and Japanese Culture in the Late Nineteenth Century: Four Patterns of Approach." *The Northeast Journal of Theology* (September 1969), 14–28.

Reader, Ian. *Religion in Contemporary Japan*. London: Macmillan Press, 1991.

Reid, David. *New Wine: The Cultural Shaping of Japanese Christianity*. Berkeley: Asian Humanities Press, 1991.

Sakurai Tokutarō 桜井徳太郎, ed. 民俗宗教と社会 [Folk religion and society], vol. 5. Tokyo: Kōbunsha, 1980.

Saniel, Josefa M. "The Mobilization of Traditional Values in the Modernization of Japan." In Robert N. Bellah, ed. *Religion and Progress in Modern Asia*. New York: The Free Press, 1965.

Sanneh, Lamin. *Translating the Message: The Missionary Impact on Culture*. Maryknoll, New York: Orbis Books, 1989.

Saunders, George R., ed. *Culture and Christianity: The Dialectics of Transformation*. New York: Greenwood Press, 1988.

Shimazono Susumu 島薗 進. 現代救済宗教論 [Salvation religions in contemporary society]. Tokyo: Seikyūsha, 1992.

Smith, Robert J. "Something Old, Something New—Tradition and Culture in the Study of Japan." *The Journal of Asian Studies* 48/4 (1989), 715–23.

Stark, Rodney. "How New Religions Succeed: A Theoretical Model," in David G. Bromley and Phillip E. Hammond, eds. *The Future of Religious Movements*. Macon, Georgia: Mercer University Press, 1987.

Steward, Charles and Rosalind Shaw, eds. *Syncretism/Anti-Syncretism: The Politics of Religious Synthesis*. London: Routledge, 1994.

Sumiya Mikio 隅谷三喜男. 近代日本の形成とキリスト教 [Christianity and the formation of modern Japan]. Tokyo: Shinkyō Shuppansha, 1961.

Swyngedouw, Jan. 和と分の構造 [The structure of harmony and apportionment]. Tokyo: Nihon Kirisuto Kyōdan Shuppankyoku, 1981.

———. "The Quiet Reversal: A Few Notes on the NHK Survey of Japanese Religiosity." *Japan Missionary Bulletin* 39/1 (1985), 4–13.

Takeda Kiyoko 武田清子. 土着と背教 [Indigenization and apostasy]. Tokyo: Shinkyō Shuppansha, 1967.

Tamaru Noriyoshi and David Reid, eds. *Religion in Japanese Culture: Where Living Traditions Meet a Changing World*. Tokyo: Kodansha International, 1996.

Thelle, Notto R. *Buddhism and Christianity in Japan: From Conflict to Dialogue, 1854–1899*. Honolulu: University of Hawai'i Press, 1987.

Turner, Harold W. "New Religious Movements in Primal Societies." In John R. Hinnells, ed. *A Handbook of Living Religions*. London: Penguin Books, 1984.

Wallace, Anthony F. C. "Revitalization Movements." *American Anthropologist* 58 (1956), 264–81.

Walls, Andrew F. *The Missionary Movement in Christian History: Studies in the Transmission of Faith*. Maryknoll, New York: Orbis Books, 1996.

Yamamori, Tetsunao. *Church Growth in Japan: A Study in the Development of Eight Denominations, 1859–1939*. South Pasadena: William Carey Library, 1974.

Young, Richard Fox. "The Little-Lad Deity and the Dragon Princess: Jesus in a New World Renewal Movement," *Monumenta Nipponica* 44/1 (1989), 31–44.

———. "The 'Christ' of the Japanese New Religions," in Mark R. Mullins and Richard Fox Young, eds. *Perspectives on Christianity in Korea and Japan: The Gospel and Culture in East Asia*. Lewiston, New York: Edwin Mellen Press, 1995.

日本人の宗教意識 [The religious consciousness of the Japanese]. Tokyo: NHK, 1984.

Acknowledgments

The author and publisher wish to thank the following institutions and individuals for permission to reproduce the photographs and illustrations on the following pages of this volume:

pp. 56, 57, 65, 141 Courtesy of the International Christian University Library, Uchimura Kanzō Collection, Tokyo

pp. 74, 79, 80 Courtesy of The Way, Matsumura Kaiseki and Dōkai Archives, Tokyo

pp. 83–85, 90, 91 Courtesy of Christ Heart Church, Kawai Shinsui Archives, Fujiyoshida

p. 109 Courtesy of Rev. Hideo Nakamura, Holy Ecclesia of Jesus, Kyoto

pp. 119, 121, 124, 125 Courtesty of Mr. Yūrō Jacob Teshima, Gilboa Institute of Humanities, Fujisawa

p. 134 Courtesy of Tōen Shobō, Tokyo

p. 194 Courtesy of the Shingo Tourist Association, Shingo Village, Aomori Prefecture

[Photographs on **pp. 104, 113, 126, 142, 145, 146** are from the author's personal collection.]

The author would like to express appreciation to the following publishers and journals for permission to use and adapt previously published materials in this volume:

"The Situation of Christianity in Contemporary Japanese Society." *Japan Christian Quarterly* 55/2 (1989).

"Japanese Pentecostalism and the World of the Dead: A Study of Cultural Adaptation in Iesu no Mitama Kyōkai." *Japanese Journal of Religious Studies* 17/4 (1990).

"The Transplantation of Religion in Comparative Sociological Perspective." *Japanese Religions* 16/2 (1990).

"The Sociology of Church Growth: An Introduction to the Literature." *Japan Christian Quarterly* 56/1 (1990).

"Christianity as a New Religion: Charisma, Minor Founders, and Indigenous Movements." In Mark R. Mullins, Shimazono Susumu, and Paul Swanson, eds. *Religion and Society in Modern Japan*. Berkeley: Asian Humanities Press, 1993.

"The Social Forms of Japanese Christianity." In John Breen and Mark Williams, eds. *Japan and Christianity: Impacts and Responses*. London: Macmillan Press, 1995.

"The Empire Strikes Back: Korean Pentecostal Mission to Japan." *Japanese Religions* 17/1 (1992) and in Karla Poewe, ed. *Charismatic Christianity as a Global Culture*, University of South Carolina Press, 1994.

"Christianity Transplanted: Toward a Sociology of Success and Failure." In Mark R. Mullins and Richard Fox Young, eds. *Perspectives on Christianity in Korea and Japan*. Lewiston: Edwin Mellen Press, 1995.

Index

About the Author

Mark R. Mullins is professor of sociology of religion and Christian studies at Meiji Gakuin University, Japan. He is the author of *Religious Minorities in Canada* (1989), and coeditor of *Japanese New Religions Abroad* (1991), *Religion and Society in Modern Japan* (1993), and *Perspectives on Christianity in Korea and Japan* (1995).